FAMILY MATTERS

ALSO BY LANCE LEE

Poetry

ELEMENTAL NATURES (selected poetry, art, and prose)
Homecomings
Transformations
Seasons of Defiance
Human/Nature
Becoming Human
Wrestling With the Angel

Plays

Time's Up and other Plays
Time's Up
Fox, Hound & Huntress
    (in Vol. 10, Playwrights for Tomorrow)
Rasputin

Novels

Second Chances

Children's Books: Tales & Novels

The Tale Of Brian And The House Painter Mervyn
Orpheus Rising
    a Best Book of 2021, Indie (Kirkus Reviews)

Nonfiction

The Death and Life of Drama
    reflections on writing and human nature
On the Waterfront
    (essays: contributor)
A Poetics for Screenwriters
The Understructure of Writing for Film and Television
    (with Ben Brady)

FAMILY MATTERS—
dreams I couldn't share

and
how a dysfunctional family
became America's darling,
The Addams Family

by

Lance Lee

 BOOKS

Copyright © 2022 Lance Lee

All rights reserved. No part of this book may be used or reproduced by any means, graphic, electronic, or mechanical, including photocopying, recording, taping or by any information storage retrieval system without the written permission of the author except in the case of brief quotations embodied in critical articles and reviews.

Book, Cover, Logo Designs by Leopard Design Studio.
Portrait, jacket and text: John Robertson
Line Drawing: Ron Sandford
Photo: Lance Lee

ISBN 9798218025397 (hc)
ISBN 9798218025410 (sc)
ISBN 9798218025403 (e)

FAMILY MATTERS - may be ordered online and through all booksellers.

Reviews and Queries should be directed to: poetlee@earthlink.net

Web page: lanceleeauthor.com

 BOOKS

Printed by Ingram Lightning Source.

CONTENTS

FLASH FORWARD   3

Foreword   4
    Blueprints   6
One Evening in 1968   7

PART ONE: THE DREAM IN OPERATION   13

MY BIRTH, THEIR MARRIAGES   15

    Arrival   16
What I Believed   17
My Parents' Standard Versions   19
Revelations   23
The Real Story   31
Further Complications   37
    Letters   42

THE WHIRLWIND AND THE BEAUTY   43

    "Gar"   44
The Whirlwind   45
Dream Girl   52
First Flight   59
Return   67

AN EARTHLY PARADISE   71

    Poseur   72
Tales of Great Neck and Washington, 1942-1949   73
Memory Awakens, 1946   78
    Apples and Irises   81
Second Flight   83
    What I Remember   83
    What I Forgot   84
The Long Return   89
    The Wolf   94
The Earthly Paradise   96
    Night Solace/Mothers   101

MANHATTAN STORIES   103

Leaving Great Neck   104
Manhattan   106

42nd St. Drive	112
Machiavelli on Park Avenue	113
The Scurrilous Letter	113
A Struggle of Signs and Symbols	115
Aftermath	121
The Good Wife's Guide	124
The World According to "The Correct Thing"	126
Hairdresser	131
Master of the House	132
The Cat	137
MIDNIGHT IN MANHATTAN	139
War Games	140
Kidnapping	144
An Awkward Boy	146
Oscar	154
Linda, Memory, Destiny	155
Linda	155
Memory & Destiny	160
Waffles	163
Jonah in Manhattan	164
Shazzam	172
PART TWO: MAKING THE DREAMS	173
THE LEVY MYTH	175
Waldorf Astoria	176
Myth and Story	177
The Mouse	179
The Descent from Garchmarski	180
The Descent from Levy	185
The Potasch Addition	188
The Affair	193
Abner	194
A Trip to Philadelphia	196
Disowned	200
The Myth of a Golden Age	207
The Mustache	210
THE WILDS MYTH	211
Bananas	212
Where Do We Experience Experience?	213
The Woman Who Knows	215

Femme Fatale	216
Matron	222
A Welsh Lord	225
A Man Larger Than Life	226
Grandfather Daddy Wilds	233
Despite Clay Feet	236
Aftermath	240
Gown	242

PART THREE: SURVIVAL & REBELLION   243

SURVIVAL, WESTHAMPTON   245

A Dinner in Westhampton Village	246
One Spring Day in 1950	247
Police Chase	249
An Ocean House	250
Daluanda	254
Master Builder	257
Idylls	258
Unk & Jill	265
A Spring Day in 1958	269
On The Beach	271

REBELLION, WESTON PRELUDE   275

Washington vs. Weston	276
The Closet	282
Going to Extremes	283
King	289
Weston Idylls	290
An Old Barn in Weston	294
Weston Woods	295

REBELLION, WESTON OUTBREAK   297

The Lord's Prayer	298
Another Ending, A New Beginning	301
Jeanne	303
A Stolen Car	309
A Long Walk	310

DAWN IN BOSTON   313

Arrival and Arrival and....	314
Quantum Dreams and the Physics of Love	322

PART FOUR: FAILURE AND METAMORPHOSES 325

Debacle at NBC 326
The Chameleons 331
The Addams Family: An American Family 336
   Genesis 336
   Triumph 339
The Real Addams Family 344
Denouement 352
   Anniversary Card 354

APPENDIX 357

FAMILY MATTERS IN 28 POEMS OF FAMILY AND FRIENDS 359

   Turtle & Elephant 360
   Hawk Forever in Mid-dive 362
   Dreams 363
   Father & Son at 4 AM 365
   My Hunger for Meaning 367
   Sledding Time in Carl Schurz Park 368
   The Ghost 370
   Our Great Loneliness 372
   Late Spring 373
      1. What a Man Gives 373
      2. My Father's Song 377
      3. Father Death 379
      4. Haunting 381
      5. By Love's Doing 383
      6. Virgin Spring 385
      7. Late Spring 387
      8. Soft Weathers 389
      9. Peace 391
   Escape 392
   Kidnapped 394
   My Best Friend 395
   Hard Grace 397
   Live in the Lie of Love 398
   The Death of a Sparrow 399
   William James to a Friend in Trinity Church, Boston 401
   Reverend John Thomas 403
   My Father's Shade at Delphi at the World's Center Amid the Ruins
      Above the Olive-swaddled Valleys 405
   Poker-Faced 407
   Hauntings in Weston 408

THE SHOWS OF DAVID LEVY	409
Young & Rubicam Shows	410
NBC Shows	412
Independent Shows	414
NOTES AND BIBLIOGRAPHY	415

VISUAL ESSAYS: view at: lanceleeauthor.com/fmvisualessays.html *

1. Marriage & Birth
2. The Whirlwind
3. The Dream Girl
4. "The Correct Thing"
5. The Levy Family
6. The Wilds Family
7. Westhampton 1950-1958
8. Weston 1956-1967
9. Los Angeles And *The Addams Family* 1963-1971

These both illustrate and expand the persons and events in the text substantially, ranging from personal and professional photos, news clippings, etiquette columns, posters and images from the WWII Treasury Department to the signed-off first page of the first episode of the original The Addams Family television series of 1964-1966.

*ACKNOWLEDGEMENTS

My thanks to the Thornton family for the use of the photos and newsclips from my mother's years at Walter Thornton's Model Agency in the 1930s and 1940s. Thanks also to *The New York Daily News* for permission to use "The Correct Thing" columns mentioned in the chapter, Manhattan Stories, and reproduced in "The Correct Thing" Visual Essay online. *The Addams Family* photos are part of the inheritance of my father's intellectual rights and properties. All other photos or newsclips or other materials are either from the personal albums my grandmother, Alma Wilds, kept for my mother, Lucille Wilds (then Levy), from which she removed all labels and dates, or from those of my father David Levy, including the mementos he kept for himself from his years in the Radio Division in the Department of Treasury 1944-1946, and from War Bond Drives he helped before and after his wartime service while at Young & Rubicam.

DRAMATIS PERSONAE*

THE DESCENT FROM GARCHMARSKI, THEN LEVY & POTASCH

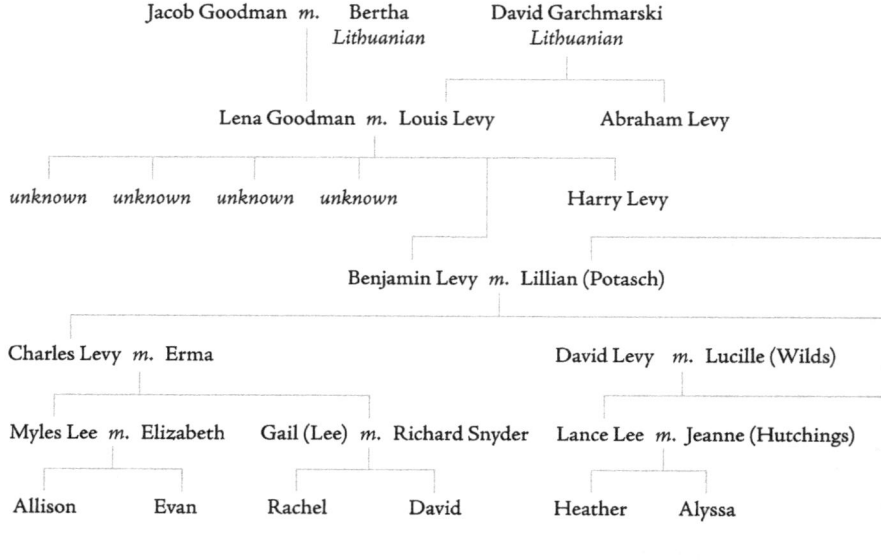

THE DESCENT FROM WILDS & AINSLEY

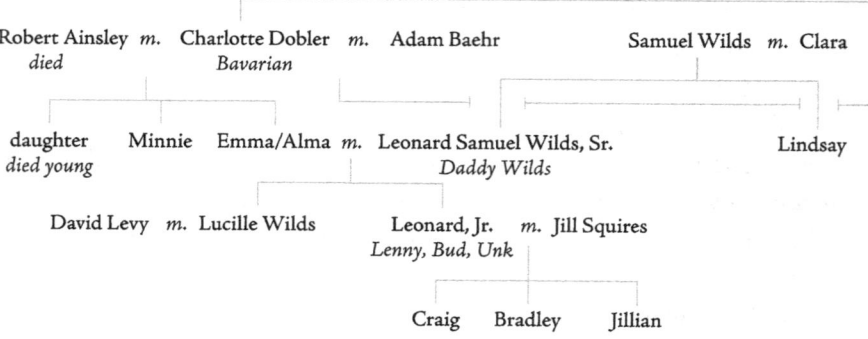

*Notes:

1. The Wilds family descends from Welsh baronets who left England in the Regency, settled in Jamaica, and then Florida.
2. Harold C von Wart - Charlotte's great grandfather.
3. Lord High Mayor, Nuremberg, 1890s; a Dobler cousin

DRAMATIS PERSONAE*

THE DESCENT FROM GARCHMARSKI, THEN LEVY & POTASCH

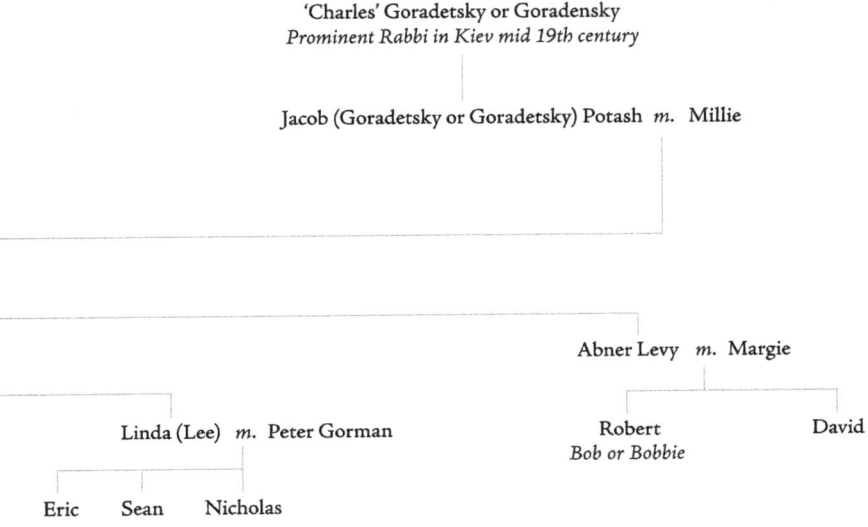

'Charles' Goradetsky or Goradensky
Prominent Rabbi in Kiev mid 19th century

Jacob (Goradetsky or Goradetsky) Potash *m.* Millie

Abner Levy *m.* Margie

Linda (Lee) *m.* Peter Gorman   Robert   David
                                          Bob or Bobbie

Eric   Sean   Nicholas

THE DESCENT FROM WILDS & AINSLEY

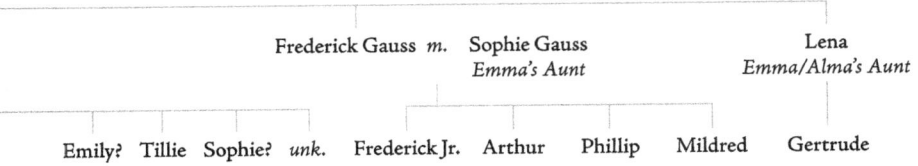

Frederick Gauss *m.* Sophie Gauss   Lena
                       Emma's Aunt   *Emma/Alma's Aunt*

Emily? Tillie Sophie? *unk.* Frederick Jr. Arthur Phillip Mildred   Gertrude

*Notes:
4. Emma (Alma) Wilds, referred to as Mother and Mothie, in text.
5. Samuel Wilds & Clara had four other children.

for Jeanne
and
Alyssa & Heather, Hansjorg
and
Milena & Thomas & Sam

Sports and gallantries, the stage, the arts, the antics of dancers,
The exuberant voices of music,
Have charm for children but lack nobility; it is bitter earnestness
That makes beauty; the mind knows, grown adult.

    Robinson Jeffers, "Boats in a Fog," *Roan Stallion*

FAMILY MATTERS

FLASH FORWARD

Foreword

This tale stretches over many generations and the way a set of myths conditioned my family and our varied inheritances of character and identity. A century after the tale began I finally broke away confused, traumatized, yet happily released into the inevitable struggle to define my own life. Myth may strike some as an odd term to use in a family history, a history familiar to many Americans involving immigrants and their descendants building lives together. But then, myth has two primary natures.

The first is of a Sacred Tale dealing with the origin of the world and life, with divine to merely mortal players intermingled as in our great inherited mythologies, or those of fantasy like J.R.R. Tolkien's *Lord Of The Rings*. But myth has a more mundane meaning relevant here, that of the innate daily way in which each of us participates in the largely unconscious story in which we feel our lives pass individually and in our group(s), and from which we gain our meaning and sense of identity. What we don't know we fill in—we are all products of genetics, nurture, social influence, and imagination. This down to earth working of myth also provides a bridge to understand how generational patterns of behavior are passed on and modified, or become so oppressive they finally spark rebellion. This story traces the formation of my family's movement through this pattern that climaxed with my parents and my ultimate break with them.

The family's early roots were certainly transcended by my father who began as a young Jew from a poor background who graduated first from the University of Pennsylvania and soon after its Wharton School of Economics in 1936 . But it was as a writer not a businessman that he broke into Young & Rubicam (Y&R) when the great advertising agencies were the creative engines for radio and, later, television content. They were not hospitable to Jews, yet my father soon became the director and producer of a hugely popular radio program, *We The People*. In WWII it reached 50% of American households. After the war he shone as an early pioneer in the development of television, reeling off famous shows, starting famous careers. He was an executive who transformed perennial second place NBC into the leading television network for a short time after he left Y&R in 1959. He was then one of the three most influential shapers of popular taste in the country. Thereafter as the creator of the first and still seminal television series, *The Addams Family*, he set that inverted yet oh so typical middle-class family careering into our culture.

He adored my mother, the former Lucille Wilds, one of the country's first supermodels, whose face was everywhere by the late 1930s. She was the Queen of the Models, her measurements public knowledge, the model's Miss America in 1939, the country's Dream Girl in 1940. She modeled for Truman's Cabinet in the mid-1940s, and was the scion of "The Correct Thing" that week in and out for decades advised Americans how to think and deport themselves socially in *The New York Daily News*. Once she was no longer the ultimate model she became the ultimate mother.

Culture, fame, identity, inheritance, religion, success: a WASP princess, a Jew climbing the cultural heights: theirs is a very American story.

Even more so is how my father's deeply dysfunctional family warped his and his brothers' youths, with parents who later fought tooth and nail to destroy their sons' marriages, perpetuating their damages into new generations, a history which, ironically, was metamorphosized by my father into *The Addams Family* and became one of America's favorite families in popular culture. His falsification of family life has found a permanent place in our collective psyche.

Blueprints

Recently I found the blueprints of the home in Great Neck, Long Island where I spent my first seven years with the exception of two in wartime Washington, D.C., 1944-46. I was transported back over fifty years in a flash: here was the house where Daddy Wilds, my larger than life maternal grandfather, died in my mother's arms from a heart attack a month before I was born, according to family myth. Here I was so frightened by Prokofiev's Peter and the Wolf that for years I ran across the living room to the stairs to the second floor, afraid a wolf lurked in the dark corner below the stairs as they reached the landing above. Here I had my first friends, first fights, first kiss from a girl at seven that flustered me then and which I still feel viscerally now. Here my father, Gar, and Uncle Bud, Unk, Mom's brother, when he came home from the war, contested for mastery until Bud's mother, Mothie, sold the house, and forced each to get their own apartment in New York.

I was called away and left the blueprints sitting on my desk. When I came back I was shocked at how badly they had faded from a short exposure daylight. Sadly I folded them away and stored them in a book of memorabilia. Moved by what unknown sense a few days later I retrieved them, wanting to look again even in their faded condition at the site of my beginning. I was surprised by the pristine blue of the background that had recovered in darkness.

Truth can't be taken for granted: it can be overexposed. It can require nurturing. Yet at other times it strikes with the force of revelation and we realize it was always there, only waiting for the right time. But there aren't any guarantees about there being a right time, are there? I imagine there are entire lives that pass by with the sense of something pending that never arrives.

I was lucky.

One Evening in 1968

Late one early summer day in 1968 my sister Linda, my wife Jeanne and I sit in the living room of my parents' Robin Drive house in the hills next to Beverly Hills in Los Angeles, California. We are stiff with tension. Decades of unhappiness in my parents' marriage have come to a head, and one of them doesn't know that yet....

As with most California days the sun is shining, now setting to the west. We can see the Pacific through the picture windows from our hillside perch above Beverly Hills. In the distance, fog hovers just off the long curve of the western shoreline south to Palos Verdes, whose hill arches like a whale's back. A TV plays in the corner beyond the windows as we idle nervously on the long arc of the couch Mom is forever recovering. Those in the know when they sit take care not to be pricked by one of the pins invariably left behind.

Gar comes home late, working on a successor to *The Addams Family*, his greatest success. He immediately goes into his study and gets on the phone, as he did in Weston, Connecticut and before that in Manhattan, and earlier in Great Neck, Long Island. Some time passes before he emerges, wanting to know where are Mom and his dinner. He is used to having that served to him on a tray in his study every night by her or her mother, always Alma to Gar. To Linda and me she is Mothie, Muddy in our childhood, while our mother is always Mom.

We explain Mom went to bed early, not feeling well; Mothie has gone to bed in the little room between the kitchen and garage. Jeanne and I and our two girls live in the studio apartment that was the garage while I wait to start teaching at the University of Southern California. We tell Gar something was left for him in the refrigerator. He frowns, fumbles in the kitchen, always terra incognito to him, passing the room where my mother is 'sleeping' as he goes back and forth down the long central hall. We stay put in the living room, except Jeanne, who has to take care of our daughters Alyssa, an infant, and Heather, just five....

He doesn't notice our tension. We are all practiced deceivers.

The evening drags on interminably, the TV images no more than static to us as we wait for the moment of discovery. At last we hear the study door open, and a few moments later the master bedroom door close at the far end of the hallway. Linda and I look at each other. We imagine our father neatly putting his clothes away as he undresses, downing a few of his endless pills, and going through his bathroom routine. Finally he sits on the edge of the bed, alone. We can see clearly, from Mom's description of his obsession, the moment before he turns off the light when he opens the cabinet beside him and pulls out his bankbooks for their nightly inspection.

At least tonight there was no family dinner, no strange conversation about gun practice with his cardiologist friend, Steve, no veiled threats like the one he made when Jeanne and I first arrived from New Haven two weeks after Alyssa was born. At that dinner he told us he had a .38, practiced with his friend Steve, and was concerned about safety.

"If I hear a strange sound at night, I'll shoot first and ask questions later," he said to Jeanne.

There is an odd expression on his face, ever more expressive as he ages. He knows Jeanne, with young children, goes into the kitchen at odd hours.

No one knew what to say. Jeanne is angry later when we are alone, and frightened. We both realize Gar has gone from odd if not at times bizarre to paranoid. We wonder how long it has been like this: no wonder Mom and Mothie are not coping. We wonder when Mom moved out of their bedroom, or when Mothie isolated herself in her little room.

Now Linda and I hear Gar come from the bedroom and walk down the hall. Our tension turns heavy as potatoes in our hands. But we aren't afraid of zany behavior with the gun: Mom has tossed that out, along with a German Lugar he picked up for show while stationed in Washington, D.C. during his service in the Navy in World War II. He knocks at my mother's door.

"Lucille? Lucille?" he calls. There is no answer. "Lucille?" He knocks again. Silence. He opens the door and goes in. "Lucille? Lucille...Lucille!" He storms into the living room.

"Do you know where your mother is?" he demands. We act puzzled.

"She went to bed early," I say.

"She didn't feel well," Linda adds.

"She's not there. She's stuffed pillows under the blankets and left hair curlers on the pillow!"

We look astonished. It's not hard to appear convincing: I know I am actor and audience at the same time. I'm sure Linda feels the same.

I can picture him approaching the sleeping form in bed.

"Lucille?"

Picture how he hesitates, then reaches out to touch her shoulder.

"Lucille...."

She's not there. He flips on the light.

"Lucille!"

He tears back the covers and bares the massed pillows imitating a body, stares at the curlers on the pillow at the head of the bed.

"She's taken all my bankbooks!"

"What do you mean?" I sound innocent. He explains their bankbooks from banks on the East Coast are missing.

"I check them every night!"

Words rise in my gorge. Did you think you could go on emotionally abusive forever? That you could regale me with tales of your sexual exploits, as you did all through college, and yet simultaneously claim to be faithful? Did you think your serial infidelities were a secret? What about all the arguments you've picked with all of us, with Mom most of all, of the months of tension building to her exasperated explosions year in and out? How much love did you think you could exasperate? How much beauty insult? All those criticisms to all of us, the demeaning remarks to Mom and Linda, to me about Jeanne, about myself, your glowering and unhappy face always certain to find us at fault for something! What of all those excruciating family dinners, the tension heavier than the food? Your bizarre inability to behave normally around children, and especially to the women in the family? What about our own relationship, virtually nonexistent for years during and after graduate school at the Yale School of Drama, when I wouldn't talk to you, and for good reason? What about your demand for the truth combined with your inability to recognize it: what about....

"How could she do this to me?"

"I don't know," is all I say.

I imagine his nightly ritual again, now. A distinguished looking man of 55 in his pajamas sits on the edge of his bed and takes all his bankbooks from the cabinet beside him. One by one he checks their balance. It doesn't matter whether there has been any activity to check. He needs to see the solid, black figures. Done, he stacks them again in the cabinet, turns off the light, and lays down, until recently next to my mother. Every night he does the same. Not long after this evening when the attorney my mother has retained looks at his accounts he is astonished how every expense to the penny is recorded stretching back to the 1930s.

"I've never seen anything like it," he said.

Gar did the same with everything, listing every book he read going back to the same years, and every article, paper, and magazine....

I realize his financial accounting was his wall against insecurity, against the chaos of chance, against the advertising agencies like Y&R where he started, or networks like NBC when he was in charge of programming there after Y&R. The nightly review reassured him about a world where security so often proved to be a mirage; against the stray intruder in the night he now trains himself to shoot. They gave the lie to his parents,' and especially mother's, criticism that he had failed expectations as happened after he graduated from Penn and briefly worked as a sales clerk. His twin Charles, a few minutes older, never faced such criticism. "No," Gar could say to all this, "look what I have, in vaults, beyond accident and criticism!"

Even now I don't know whether to laugh or feel sad.

That evening he is insistent.

"She's absconded with my life's savings!" Absconded, a thief in the night.

"I can't believe Mom would do anything like that," I say. We know she had had enough, seen a lawyer, and been told to go to New York City and close out all their accounts and bring their proceeds to California with its far more favorable divorce laws where all this would be community property, 50-50 in ownership. We knew about her bedroom disguise, of the farce that would be played out, the lines we would speak.

I follow him into his study. He calls airlines, determined to track her down, guessing where she has gone. The airlines refuse to reveal their passenger lists. He calls his lawyer who advises him there is nothing he can do with phone calls to stop the banks from honoring her request to close accounts as a joint holder. When he realizes there is nothing he can do, he sits back with a sigh and becomes philosophic.

"I can't understand such behavior. I've always given her everything, anything she wanted; why would she go take all that money? She'll find me as understanding as ever when she comes home. There is no reason for any of this. I have never loved anyone else. There has never been anyone else. I have always treated her with love and consideration, no matter what the provocation."

I let him go on, still an audience member watching the show in which I perform, as I had so often in the past. Occasionally I chip in with an assurance that I'm sure she'll explain it all once she's back, that she couldn't be up to anything bad. But nothing stops his stream once provoked: he spends hours rewriting history until he becomes the misunderstood hero of the piece, martyred through his own goodwill by the unreasonable people around him. I thought about his wandering the house in the early hours, gun in hand, and of how he had gotten away with a lifetime of such behavior with us, intimidating us all with his aura of violence, if never actually physical. The evening felt surreal, like so much of the rest of our lives, ever deepening with the years.

I try to look through the window to the sweep of Los Angeles' lights in the night. But his curtains are drawn: from his fifties to his end his study, his inner sanctum, was shut off from the world.

When did that start, I wonder? When did the young man who transcended ethnicity and poverty into a famous career become this man? Or the Dream Girl of 1940 become a woman on a night flight to the East "absconding" with her husband's bank books?

How could two so deeply emblematic of the American Dream come to a climax that would have embarrassed the credibility of a soap opera?

PART ONE:
THE DREAM IN OPERATION

> To be ignorant of what occurred before you were born is to remain always a child.
>
> Cicero, *Orator*

MY BIRTH, THEIR MARRIAGES

Arrival

Something was wrong....
When my mother brought me home from the hospital I slept all the time. I never cried. When I was awake, I was happy. After I fed I burped with a contented sigh, and went back to sleep.

Mom and Mothie grew uneasy.

This was the age of Dr. Spock, not the character from Star Trek struggling with his humanity but the real Spock, impervious to reason, dispute, or nature, the prophet leading mothers and children to a proper and perfect antiseptic upbringing. So I am certain my mother and Mothie carefully followed instructions for the right formula mix, bottle-fed me only when I was supposed to be fed, and, thanks to Mothie, not otherwise. It's easy to imagine our kitchen full of bottles upside down on a clean cloth cooling, bottles steaming on the stove, and boxes of formula waiting to be mixed, poured, and delivered to me by the long, rubber nipples judged to be so much better than the real as though the moment's fad had more weight than four million years of evolution.

But after two weeks of my unrelieved contentment Mom and Mothie were distraught.

They consulted the pediatrician without success. Then they consulted the hospital and discovered it sent my mother home with a rich formula for an undernourished, underweight child, anything but what I, at ten pounds, so the story went, should be having. They gave her a new, less nourishing formula.

Soon I no longer slept all the time. I rarely smiled when awake. I cried day and night, desperate for the thing of glass and rubber dispensing the milk that no longer satisfied.

They were happy.

Now, finally, it could be said I had arrived.

What I Believed

Until one late spring day in 2002 as I neared sixty I believed I was born Sunday, August 25, 1942 in Doctor's Hospital in Manhattan opposite Carl Schurz Park and the mayor's residence, Gracie Mansion. I weighed nearly ten pounds, and was named Lance Millard Lee, not Levy like my father. My mother went into the hospital under "Lee" to prevent the publicity that would have surrounded the famous model Lucille Wilds and the revelation she was now Lucille Levy, the wife of *We The People* writer, director and producer David Levy. They were afraid of such publicity reaching Philadelphia, my father's home town, because he hadn't told his parents he was married, let alone about to have his first child. After I was born he sent them a telegram, "Dear Mom & Pop, Stop. Am married. Stop. Have son. Stop. Come see. Stop. love, Stop. David Stop."

No occasional prying had changed that story when I was a child and later a young man. After that the story with all its ambiguities was just one of those givens I trotted out to amuse friends. Not even coming into possession of my father's journals which he began in 1944 helped clear up any questions: I found those unreadable on casual browsing, and never looked up August 25th.

Those journals stretch to 1957, with a few late additions reaching into the 1970s. They should be a treasure trove for writing my family romance. Alas, they are an endless recital of 'who I met today, what dinner attended and show saw and star met afterwards' with only rare philosophical moments or expressions of tenderness as when my father wrote in the 1944 journal that leaning over my crib after everyone else has gone to sleep, sometimes lifting me a little to feel my weight, made his day worthwhile. Otherwise their constant 'me me me' was enough to make me slam them shut.

I knew too after a lifetime of experience with my father that he may indeed have leaned over my crib at night, perhaps prodded me in mystification, and risked waking me to satisfy his curiosity, but that his admirable sentiments were suspect.

Friends urged me to tell my family story when I regaled them with one piece of it or another, but until that spring day I was never able to face the reliving a retelling involves. But my mother was now 87, my father had passed away two years earlier, and my imminent 60th birthday inevitably made me aware of my own mortality. Defiant, I didn't want our lives to disappear, unplumbed and unshared.

My Parents' Standard Versions

So on that spring day I picked up my father's first journal, begun in 1944, and opened it to August 25, 1944 to see what he had to say in his first entry on my birthday, two years after the actual event.

He wrote how the weekend I was born his parents, Lillian and Benjamin (Nanny and Poppy to me) visited him in Manhattan at his Beaux Arts apartment. They would not have spent long at that small apartment where he lived with my mother: the morning of Saturday, August 24, 1942 she went into labor and was taken to Doctors Hospital. So his parents' timing was good: they would be on hand for the great event.

But my mother's labor dragged on, and so my father, always eager to please his parents, left the hospital and took them around Manhattan as he did usually when they visited from Philadelphia. Occasionally he called my mother to see if there was any point in coming back, but I lingered in the womb throughout Saturday on into Sunday. Disappointed, Nanny and Poppy could wait no longer and went home Sunday evening. I was born late that night, almost ten pounds. My father sent them a telegram.

Naturally, he wrote, they returned on Monday. "They were delighted."

I tried to imagine my anxious father and grandparents at the hospital, then their growing dullness as I lingered, until Gar, seeing them suppress their restlessness, took them out to a good dinner and show, and more the next day. How obstinate of me to hold things up like that! How angelic of my mother to give her blessing to my father's need to entertain his father and formidable mother. I imagined Gar's solicitous calls to my mother between courses at the 21 Club, familiarly '21,' the famous restaurant at the center of New York's entertainment society, or between acts at the theatre, and her reassurance there was no reason to hurry back. No doubt Mothie was with her.

Mom knew how anxious Gar was to impress his parents. He was the son who had moved away from Philadelphia, entered a chancy world of writing and radio production and lived to prosper. Not for him the safety of an academic career with an initial sidestep into the Book of the Month Club, like his slightly elder identical twin, Charles. David was making it in Manhattan, he was a man with a future, a Jew overcoming the odds, the second twin defying everything on his way to the top, to first place.... That need to prove how important he was in part explains why his journals are so hard to read as he endlessly name-drops and piles up events and encounters with significant people like trophies.

He met quite a few of these through *We The People* which aimed at bringing representative Americans with dramatic stories and differing backgrounds to a national radio audience. The show, immensely popular at this time before television, brought him into contact with an ever widening circle of stars, producers, directors, and writers in the entertainment world as well as diverse ordinary Americans, and after the outbreak of World War II with individuals ranging from common soldiers to prominent members of the Roosevelt and Truman cabinets and war effort.

Yet even as I read his account of my birth I felt an underlying tug of incredulity. Was my father so driven to keep his parents amused that he took them around the city while his wife was in labor? Would his parents have wanted to be absent at such a time? What could Gar have said to them as he returned to his seat at dinner after he checked in with the hospital?

"Well, Mother, she's still in the early stages and urges us to enjoy ourselves."

"Isn't she considerate."

"What show are we seeing, son?"

"Dad, I have tickets for...."

Ridiculous.

Were Nanny and Poppy, once they were home, happy with the telegram announcing a tardy grandson so that they hurried back the next day, "delighted?"

I had grown up with that other story in which Nanny and Poppy did not know what was going on. In that story my father dreaded his mother. He had promised her never to elope, as Charles had done with his wife Erma two years earlier. It didn't matter that Erma, a dancer, was also a nice, Boston Jewish girl: Nanny and Poppy forbade Charles to marry her.

Angered, he and Erma eloped immediately. Nanny threatened to commit suicide with such fervor it took the entire family to dissuade her. Thereafter she dedicated herself to destroying Charles' marriage. It was during this turmoil my father made his promise. After he eloped in turn he couldn't face her with his betrayal.

Worse, he not only broke his vow, he married a gentile. We think of prejudice running one way: that Jews suffer from antisemitism. Wasn't the Holocaust, unbeknown to us then, underway in Germany? Here the 'Gentleman's Agreement' was in full sway. Nanny and Poppy traveled as Mr. and Mrs. Lee. Charles permanently changed his name to Lee in order to remove the glass ceiling prejudice would have imposed on his career at the University of Pennsylvania. This is all true, yet leaves out that there were Jews like my Grandmother Nanny who despised gentiles.

I learned all this in pieces from Mothie and Mom as I grew up, and for all these reasons believed my father resorted to subterfuges to avoid facing Nanny, like persuading my mother to marry in South Carolina in 1941 by proxy under his nom de plume Peter King, my mother using Lucille Marjorie Widdecombe. Her mother and father knew she was marrying. My mother's fame provided Gar with his excuse for secretiveness from the beginning of their relationship: he didn't want his parents to know he was married until he had time to bring them around.

"They were his parents," my mother said once. "I left him to deal with them. I was mistaken."

The result was that while my mother waited for him to 'bring his parents around,' she stayed with her parents in Great Neck whenever his parents visited after their South Carolina marriage, removing all sign of her married presence from the Beaux Arts apartment. Once Nanny and Poppy returned to Philadelphia she returned and unpacked. Their getting to know her was strictly limited to an occasional encounter at dinner or a theatre. There was no way for them to know when she became pregnant....

That was why in their primal origin story Mom registered as "Mrs. "Lee" at the hospital: the news of the famous model's marriage had only to appear in the local Sunday papers and the cat would be out of the bag. And yet now I had this new version from my father's journal: why had the original story of total ignorance on the part of his parents been allowed to stand?

I let the journal rest on my lap. Their marriage was an additional puzzle. There was rumor of a New York marriage license that expired before the very murky South Carolina marriage by proxies: but why did they need South Carolina for that? Perhaps its distance had the air of a 'getaway,' or the South was 'Siberia' for the New York press. How any of these maneuvers were kept out of the press my mother and Mothie assiduously cultivated was another mystery: my mother was a cultural icon.

At least it was indisputable that I grew up a Lee, not Levy. As I grew older I never got beyond the myth summed up by the telegram informing Nanny and Poppy of marriage and birth simultaneously. By the time I was ready to ask my father directly our relations were so poor and I had so many other things on my mind that the distant past was a buried soreness I didn't want to touch as well as a founding piece of the mythology in which I lived. I knew my family well enough to know no one would give a straight answer to any questions. They wouldn't lie because at this point they believed the lies.

I decided to call my mother.

Revelations

I reach my mother after lunch at The Canterbury where she has her own assisted living apartment. The Canterbury is on the top of the Palos Verdes peninsula south of Los Angeles, and only a few minutes from my sister Linda's home. The views sweep across the Los Angeles basin from the Pacific to the surrounding Angeles Crest mountains from the common dining room. The Canterbury is a series of two-story wings of mostly retirement apartments set in lawns and gardens. One wing is consigned to those needing assistance, and one upper floor for those needing acute care.

My sister and I never thought Mom with her fierce independence would give up her apartment for such a community. Once when I tried to arrange help for her with household chores she wept because she thought I didn't consider her capable of managing on her own. But after a broken hip and hip replacement operation a social worker advised finding an assisted living facility. Mom had known about The Canterbury for years while active in All Saints Episcopal Church in Beverly Hills, which sponsored it. She had even visited there while still in Beverly Hills. To our surprise, she was delighted when we mentioned the possibility. By sheer good luck there was an opening the morning Linda and I inquired. After a short time there Mom likened her experience to "being on a cruise."

At eighty-seven she uses a walker, although the lack of cartilage in her right knee is painful enough to drive her soon permanently into a wheelchair with a sigh of relief. The years shortened her and added weight, thinned her hair, and turned her face into an old woman's, but the years rolled away with her smile and it was possible to believe she was once one of the most beautiful women in America. Friends are dazzled when they see the modeling shots from her heyday.

She is happy to hear from me, now.

"Hello dear." Her voice is clear, and sounds surprised, as if hearing from me wasn't commonplace. In her late years she acts surprised Linda and I extend ourselves for her: we can't imagine why.... We talk about the immediate events of the day, and then,

"You remember Gar's journals?"

"Oh yes. He started writing them in 1944. I was impressed at how he sat down every night and kept them up. But you know him, once he set his mind to something he just kept on."

"Yes, I know."

His relentless pursuit of his career despite all its ups and very considerable downs flashes through my mind, together with his late career as a writer, publishing his last book, *Executive Jungle*, while he lay in his acute nursing facility.

"I've never done more than glance at his journals," I go on now, "even though I got Linda's from her a while ago. They're hard to take, all surface activity and name-dropping of stars or influential people in the industry ('the industry' always meant first radio, and then television) with hardly anything of himself." She laughs.

"That's so typical. We used to float around Manhattan from show to show, cocktail party to party. Mothie was a godsend that way, we could leave you and Linda with her."

"It's all 'me me me.'"

"It always was."

"I just read his account of my birth." There is silence on the other end of the phone. "Don't know why I haven't in the past. Anyway, he wrote—" and I repeat his description carefully. There is a prolonged silence on the phone. Then she blows up in a way I have never heard before.

"None of that is true, Lance," she starts, her voice sharp and clear. "It was never like that. I went into that hospital and his parents never knew. Believe me, they weren't delighted at the end, either!"

"Oh?"

"They used to come visit your father at the Beaux Arts where we had an apartment. Whenever they came in 1942 I would go to Great Neck to be with Mother. They didn't know I was pregnant."

I interrupt with a laugh, and repeat the mythological story about the telegram, "'Am married, have son, come see.' She doesn't laugh.

"Oh no, they knew we married in January 1942, in a public, Jewish ceremony."

"Jewish?"

"Yes, we got married earlier in 1941 in South Carolina, but under the pseudonym of Phillip King he used sometimes when he wrote. Only Mother and Dad knew, and a few friends." I laugh. "But it made no difference. I could never be at the apartment when his parents' visited—he couldn't bring himself to tell them. When I discovered I was pregnant your father counted the weeks: with eight months left you could be premature. But how would he explain seven? At last he realized he had to act. So yes, in a matter of weeks I converted, and we held a ceremony in a synagogue for the sake of his parents so they'd know we were married. Everyone came but them."

"In a Jewish ceremony, converted...."

"Oh yes! But that hardly helped. His mother was already furious at Charles eloping and marrying Erma. Just the fact that another woman dared claim on one of her boys, especially another of her twins, was too much. She certainly wasn't coming to the wedding on a few weeks abrupt notice of someone she hardly knew who was a last minute convert and was taking her other twin! I never realized it at the time, but I was already hated!"

"Well—"

"But your father was so deathly afraid of his mother," she races on, "he couldn't bring himself to tell her I was pregnant even after they knew we were married! I still had to rush off to Great Neck once I started to show."

"And they never learned of South Carolina?"

"Which time?" she laughed. She can tell from my silence I'm stunned. "There were two times! The first time we eloped we got off the plane and your father looked at me.

'Are you sure you want to do this?' he asked. I took one look at him and knew he was having doubts. So I made him turn around and bring me home. The second time is when we did it through proxies.

"The weekend I went into labor," she goes on, "his parents came to visit. I went into Doctor's Hospital near Gracie Mansion, and he still didn't say anything to them! He did what he usually did, explained I was at Mothie's because she or Dad was ill, and sent my regrets. So he took them out to dinner and a show as if nothing was happening! Sometimes he'd disappear and check in on me. Then he'd rush back. I don't know what they thought. Sunday afternoon they went home and I was still in labor: it wasn't until that night that you finally arrived."

I make an inarticulate sound.

"It was only after you were born that your father knew he finally had to tell them. That's when he sent a telegram informing them they had a new grandson. They came up the next day to see us. They were horrified."

"How could he write what he did, then?"

"Your father wrote what he wanted to believe happened. He probably eventually believed it did happen that way. He believed what he wanted to where these things were concerned."

I thought of how Gar always idealized his mother—at a distance, and suffered in her presence.

"He behaved the same way with associates. I couldn't understand how he could warp reality so much. Some of them stabbed him in the back, or he stabbed them—I always thought his business behavior was disgraceful—but he'd remember their birthdays with a friendly card as if nothing had happened."

I remembered how once I sat in his study in Beverly Hills as he consulted the book where he kept such information. He had recently fought bitterly with Alan Courtney, who was still at NBC, though Gar had been fired. But he saw it was Alan's birthday and muttered he'd have to get him a card. He never met a man he wasn't prepared to make an enemy, or an enemy he wasn't prepared to share a warm wish with on a birthday. It was his enmity others remembered.

"So," I say, "none of what he wrote is true."

"No. And you know, when you were born his mother Lily counted back from August and decided with you nearly ten pounds that I had gotten pregnant to trap your father and force him to marry me. From the end of January to the end of August she made out barely seven months. She didn't know about the earlier marriage, and your father never told her. The truth wouldn't have mattered anyway. They all believed what they wanted."

I can't tell whether she is choking with rage or laughter.

"That *I* had trapped *him*!"

"So there was a telegram, but they knew you were married; and you converted, and even held a Jewish ceremony for them, and they refused to come."

"Yes."

The 1944 journal is large and heavy on my lap. Gar's handwriting scrawls across the pages I flip, the lines growing shorter as the year progresses. In later journals the indentations squeeze in at times from each side, and the entries grow ever less frequent. Still, he persevered. The journals shrank in size over the years: detail lessened, and the last, only partly filled, has a few scrawled, lengthy entries that finally, a few years after their divorce, stop. I sigh, almost not hearing her as she rushes on.

"I never knew just how hostile they were of course," she goes on, talking of Nanny and Poppy, "until a few years later. We used to have them come up to Great Neck before your father went into the Navy in 1944 and we moved to Washington D.C., and then again after he was discharged in 1946 and we moved back. Mothie's home was much better than we could have managed on our own! He came to think of it as his. And when his parents came Mothie would turn herself inside out trying to give them a pleasant time."

I can picture Mom and Mothie making the stay in Great Neck as pleasing as possible, a form of WASP noblesse oblige. I'm sure that alone was enough to make Nanny see red, and Nanny always made sure her sons knew how she felt. Phone calls were followed by letters, and Gar's behavior steadily worsened after each parental visit.

"After they went home after Christmas in 1946 your father acted badly. I couldn't understand it because we had given his parents such a nice time! When a letter came from Philadelphia, Mother and I steamed it open."

The kitchen at Great Neck rises to my mind's eye with the two of them holding a letter over a boiling teapot. My mother is dressed with a model's sense of style, while Mothie has the red kerchief tied around her head she sometimes wore when house cleaning. Gingerly they pick at the letter's rear flap until the steam has done its work and they can peel it open. They sit on a bench at the kitchen table near the door out to the yard with a great apple tree, and read. Silence—then their voices burst with incredulity, then anger. For hours they debate what to do, forgetting about the boiling teapot on the stove until the water burns off and the metal begins to burn. From then on there were no details of my mother's marriage not known to Mothie.

"Imagine how shocked we were when we read it. It was a really vile attack on me and poor Mother who only wanted things to go well.

I was "that blond shiksa" who had stolen her boy and poisoned his life, and the unkind things she wrote about Mother! She said Mother flirted with the neighbors, carried on with one widower in particular, and called her a prostitute! Lily (Nanny) went on and on. There was nothing in our background to prepare us for anyone like her."

"What did you do?"

"When your father came home I confronted him. He was horrified, less at my opening the letter than over what we found out. He backpedaled as fast as he could, apologizing for his mother and for his behavior. He always caved in when confronted, but it just wasn't my way to argue with him constantly.

"He knew he was in the wrong, but what could he do? Lily was his mother! He just couldn't see how horrible she was unless confronted with the evidence, and then he would just try to beg off with an impossible parent. She put him in terrible conflict all the time."

She doesn't say, but the thought is clear. He had no backbone. He couldn't face her. He couldn't face the truth. I wonder, as I write this, if that is why he immersed himself in a career of make-believe, one I often heard him speak of with contempt even as he pursued his latest project.

"After that I told him he could go to Philadelphia as often as he liked, but not with you or Linda. His parents could visit twice a year for a weekend. I was firm."

So that was how Philadelphia and the family there became strangers, and the root of why I was brought up Episcopalian. I didn't see Philadelphia after 1946 until 1982 when I was forty.

An hour and a half has gone by. Her voice has not flagged. She isn't trying to convince me, either: hers has been a stream of outrage and long felt hurt.

The year previous—the year after Gar died—Charles visited us with Ruth, whom he married while my father slipped towards oblivion. Ruth was in her early 70s, still beautiful, dottily in love with Charles. She was hungry for family history, and one day during her visit joined myself, my older daughter Heather, my sister Linda and her husband, Pete, my wife Jeanne, and my mother for lunch. It was a lively lunch and Charles, as always, was the epitome of professorial culture and sartorial smoothness although his short-term memory was failing. Inevitably the conversation turned to family matters, and inevitably to Nanny.

"The twins—Charles and David—were always in touch with her," my mother tells Ruth. "They wrote her every day of their lives, and talked to her at least once by telephone every day."

"Isn't it nice they were so close to their mother?" Ruth asks innocently. Charles smiles.

"She was an awful woman," my mother snaps. "She ruined their marriages, and tried to ruin Abner's." She leans across towards Ruth. "The best thing Nana Levy could have done for Charles and David was die young."

We sit stunned.

"She was a terrible influence on everyone in the family through them." Ruth is dumbstruck. "She wrecked Charles' first marriage with Erma, and mine too! After Ben died Nana moved in with Margie and refused to leave. 'My son wants me to stay' she told Margie. She usurped Margie's home until Margie took the kids and left, telling Abner it was them or his mother." Abner was Nanny's youngest son. "Only then did Nana's boys get her an apartment with live-in companionship. She warped her sons, and all of us through them!" My mother isn't being unpleasant, but laughing as she talks. Charles' smile hovers over us, disembodied. He is silent. I've never heard her speak so bluntly.

The conversation turns.

Afterward as we leave I stand next to Charles and Ruth. Ruth is dying to have a moment to talk to me without anyone around. Charles beams at her.

"Wasn't that a pleasant lunch?" he says. Ruth stares at him. "What did we talk about?" It would have been in his and Gar's character to have forgotten already even without short-term memory loss.

But it is only that year Mom grew so frank. She was taking stock, preparing to go, though there were still four years ahead before her real decline set in. But she seized opportunities now nonetheless to square accounts heretofore unresolved.

I tell my mother we've been on the phone for a long time. She is still angry, repeating pieces of our conversation.

"So much for his journals," I laugh.

"He lied and then believed his lies," she repeats. We say goodbye. My ear is sweaty from the conversation. I return the journal to the shelf with the others. Next to them is the book where I keep the blueprints of the family home in Great Neck that fade when I stare at them in the light, trying to recall how it was.

I realize I've begun our family romance.

The Real Story

Immediately after this conversation I found a plethora of material I had pushed aside over the years or only recently obtained, whether my father's journals, later family photos of familiar and obscure relatives he assembled with histories; scrapbooks of his, Mom, and Mothie's, including his own newspaper notices; her modeling shots, press releases, and much else. I discovered and used our current genealogical resources. Included in all this material were items both had preserved, so at odds with their stories, and forgotten. I'm no longer puzzled by the wealth of information, which I keep discovering, but that anything was ever obscure! I have to keep reminding myself as I tell our story in order to be accurate to keep to the moment-by-moment stream of experience with its omissions, deceptions, and half glimpsed truths that shape us.

As for the facts about my birth and their marriages:

On July 25, 1941 my parents flew to Greenville, South Carolina, and married. They saved pictures of themselves standing by their two witnesses, strangers who were involved because they were on hand. My father identified himself as Phillip King, my mother used Lucille Marjorie Widdecombe. From their recollections there must have been a moment of cold feet, but there was no return flight to New York followed by a second, proxied Greenville occasion.

Back in New York my mother did leave the Beaux Arts apartment whenever Nanny and Poppy visited, removing all trace of herself until they left, seeing them only as my father's 'date.' Only Mothie and Daddy Wilds knew the truth. When she became pregnant Gar did realize he had to arrange a public marriage quickly: he never revealed his elopement to his mother. Nanny and Poppy put a notice in their local paper announcing a prospective ceremony at Chapel (!) Beth El in Great Neck. They referred to Mothie and Daddy Wilds as Mr. and Mrs. Louis (not Leonard) Wildes (not Wilds). In my family of assumed identities, spelling matters.

A clue to the controversies that raged is found at the back of an idealized photograph taken before my parents' marriage. My mother and father sit romantically before a fire with Mom at his feet, leaning back against him in an elegant pose full of the then conventional attitudes about the roles of the sexes. On the photo's back she wrote,

> Let's contend no more, Love
> Strive nor weep:
> All be as before, Love
>
> Teach me, only teach, love!
>   as I aught
> I will speak thy speech, Love
>   think thy thought—.
> Contend, strive, weep....

They did not marry in 'Chapel' Beth El but "eloped"—around the corner from her parents' home to that of Mark Warnow, a popular bandleader of the time my father knew. My mother did convert to Judaism, something that survived these events as a rumor she routinely denied. There is a witnessed statement of conversion at Temple Beth El on the morning of her marriage.

For a change there is reliable evidence on these events from a 1941-42 diary my father kept at the time, a diary not written with an eye for later readership as with the journals from 1944 on. Here the decision to marry openly is only made January 6th, two-and-a-half weeks before the ceremony. He doesn't tell his parents until January 9th, hoping "all at home come around—and let there be an end to strife...." Only on the 11th does he arrange with Mark Warnow to hold their marriage two weeks later at his home. On the 12th a note from his parents makes clear they are not coming. On the night before the ceremony he talks with his father and Charles, but in vain: *no one* comes from his family. Mothie and Daddy Wilds also stay home once it is clear the entire thing is a pointless sham. My parents almost bungle getting their marriage license, too: my father forgot some necessary documents when they drove to Manhasset to get it on only the 17th, and it isn't until the 21st they succeed, two days before the actual ceremony January 23, 1942. On the that morning Rabbi Rubin received my mother's conversion, and then performed the ceremony. My father wrote,

> The ceremony was lovely and L. a beautiful bride—and we were all impressed by the sincerity of her conversion and the material sacrifice it entailed.

Even in this account there are grey areas: was 'Chapel' Beth El ever really seriously considered as an alternative to Mark Warnow's? Did Gar, more likely, accept Mark Warnow's offer of his home on the 11th when he told him of his marriage plans, but before he knew his parents wouldn't come? It takes time to organize a marriage and reception, to send out notices and invitations and receive replies even to a sham marriage like this one, and this was already rushed.

The bewildering truth is that my parents made five attempts at marriage. This public one, the actual South Carolina elopement, their memories of a second South Carolina excursion that never happened, and in a later biographical fragment of my father's, references to a marriage license taken out in March, 1941 in New York that they let lapse, and a second 'miss' at getting another license when they drove up to Newburgh where Mom's maternal Grandmother Charlotte lived—but where they arrived too late.

It is easy to imagine Nanny's hysteria in the buildup to my mother's public wedding, together with my mother's anger over the pointlessness of a ceremony and conversion to placate my father's parents. The story of Abner's marriage a few years later gives a good idea of Nanny's behavior.

"What do you think he [Abner] is," she complained to Margie's father when told of the marriage plans, "an apple you can pick off the tree?" Poppy refused his blessing since he had not been asked by Abner to approve his engagement, while Nanny threatened to kill herself (again). Her hysteria grew worse as they neared the ceremony. Finally Margie's father had had enough.

"Lillian," he said, "there is going to be a ceremony. Make up your mind so I know whether to dress for a wedding or a funeral."

Faced with the inevitable, she gave in. Nonetheless she had to be bodily carried into the synagogue. I was there, four years old, but only remember the crowd, and a drummer especially adept at making his cymbals shiver.

Daddy Wilds was even angrier at his daughter's mistreatment with regard to the South Carolinian elopement as well as the disastrous public ceremony.

"He and Mother didn't approve of your father because he was Jewish," my mother told me, "but they made the best of it for my sake." More to the point, and closer to the truth, was the way both Mom and Mothie so often said in later years that had Daddy Wilds not been so sick from heart disease the last three years of his life that "he would have sent your father packing at the start." This became a refrain trotted out in every crisis….

After their public marriage feelings continued to run high, for once my mother's pregnancy showed she did avoid Nanny and Poppy for Gar's sake by again retreating to Great Neck. Marriage he could divulge: pregnancy, no. That July Daddy Wilds died from his heart disease. My birth a month later, seven months after the public marriage, came amid these events.

Nor was my mother in secret labor over the crucial weekend when Gar's parents visited, with my arrival late Sunday requiring their return Monday. Instead, when they came to visit my father that weekend, my mother checked into Lexington Hotel instead of retreating as usual to Great Neck because of her advanced condition. While there, labor began and she transferred to Doctor's Hospital, in the company of Mothie. I was born late Tuesday, August 25, 1942, and weighed eight pounds, twelve ounces.

Gar was not with her in the hospital although Nanny and Poppy were gone. He was indeed at dinner at 21. He raced across a blacked out, wartime city with Burgess Meredith in tow, whom he approvingly records admiring my mother's beauty, specifically not meaning her beauty as a mother. She was my father's ornament, dazzling even exhausted after giving birth.

Then Nanny and Poppy were told of my arrival. I like to imagine a revised telegram,

Dear Mom and Pop, Stop.
Am married—as you know. Stop.

Have son. Stop.
Come see. Stop.
Love, Stop.
David, Stop.

Whether they came to visit immediately or over the following weekend is unknown. Poppy was still at work. There is no known response from them until a congratulatory telegram arrived, two days later. They were not "delighted."

There is also the matter of my last name, Lee—not Levy. The newspaper announcement of my birth a week later (to allow my father time to notify his parents) mentioned me as a "Lee," and my parents as Mr. and Mrs. David Lee. Why didn't they use Mr. and Mrs. Peter King if the idea was to avoid publicity? Telegrams immediately after my birth addressed to "Lucille Levy" had no difficulty in reaching my mother at the hospital. Why was "Lee" maintained when there was no longer any need for secrecy by my father? The answer is implicit: 'contend, strive, weep.' My mother was angered by his and his parents' behavior years before she and Mothie opened the fatal letter from Nanny after Christmas, 1946. Across the years I think it is clear she insisted I be a Lee, and my sister four years later too, and that both of us be raised Episcopalian. Her conversion to Judaism was an act, like one of her countless staged scenes for a photo shoot.

Years later Gar wrote he was "immature" to register my mother as Lucille Lee. But he was concerned "about my parents' feelings about the suddenness" of my arrival, apparently only seven months after marriage. Did he think he could keep me hidden a few months more? In the event my name simply became "fixed," while he "lost my name for posterity." Besides, as name change was common in his family, why not with me?

This is a weak rationalization for he didn't register my mother as "Lee:" she did when she went without him, in labor, to the hospital with Mothie. I wonder if it didn't all come as a shock to him, with rationalizations and revisions of history to follow. Oddly, my father never mentioned his second, open marriage to Linda and myself, but wrote and talked as if their elopement to South Carolina had been open and the start of "us all."

Yet their maneuvers came at a steep price for me. Gar was my father, yet I always believed in some inner recess that I had to find my father, and sought out appropriate figures all my life. I was at once bound to him, and set free to make out of "Lee" what I would. I suppose I am lucky "Lee" was not "King," with all the inchoate fantasies that might have spawned in a child in my situation.

Further Complications

The convoluted story of my parents' marriage leaves out their equally convoluted courtship. My father was not my mother's first choice. At first he unwittingly conspired to give my mother to someone else. There was a Bill Kent she became engaged to in a very public way after a prior publicity coup of having her legs insured by her modeling agency, according to the story, for $150,000, a phenomenal sum then. It was in fact $100,000, and for her figure. At the same time Walter Thornton, head of my mother's modeling agency, insured another model's smile for $75,000.

My mother's feelings for Kent were partly real, partly made up by Thornton for publicity. There is one photograph of her and Bill at a club with others, including Mothie. That immediately raises suspicion that a publicity stunt was underway, for Mothie pushed Mom's career, living it vicariously as a former Gibson Girl from her youth at the turn of the century. It was Mothie who kept the albums of Mom's modeling shots and press releases, removing all dates as she enjoyed a notoriety missing from the settled life she built with Daddy Wilds.

My father met my mother in 1939 during this engagement to Kent, which, in a crescendo of nonsense, was said to be publicly opposed by her father and Thornton. My father, thoroughly duped by mother and daughter, even wrote a broadcast for *We The People* with Mothie and Mom interviewed on air about how a hard-hearted Walter Thornton refused to let Bill Kent marry his star model by enforcing a $10,000 marriage penalty clause in her contract which apparently the lovers could not pay. As a consequence Thornton's wife Judy threatened to leave him, while Mothie threatened not to go home to Daddy Wilds in Great Neck unless he removed his objections to the marriage, too.

Incredibly, after that *We The People* show my father floated a proposal that the 'lovers' actually marry on another episode once Thornton and Daddy Wilds relented. When he got wind they might not actually want to marry, he suggested they could divorce immediately afterwards. He was overruled by his superiors on the grounds that any marriage had to be real. This was, after all, 1939. My mother later broke up with Kent, not because of the $10,000 marriage penalty, but because "Bill," as she said one day when this story came up, "was a Catholic, and he drank."

There was also John Mineke. Mom had "a terrible crush on him" in Great Neck High School, then lost sight of him as she took up modeling and he went off to college. But they met again during the Finnish Relief Ball in 1940. She was now at the height of her fame, the acknowledged "Dream Girl" of 1940. Walter Thornton, James Patterson, and Alex Raymond, the creator of Flash Gordon, performed the ceremony and made sure it got maximum publicity.

John asked her out after the Ball: she accepted, then broke the date, broke a second date, and only after he sent her two dozen red roses, saw him. It was soon intense, and that spring at Jones Beach he dropped on his knees and asked her to marry him.

"I had a lot of beaux, some of them older. I wasn't ready to be tied down, to live in some apartment in New Haven while he went to Yale Law for three years." That was the end of John. Later she admitted,

"I should have married him. But your father seemed such a nice young man, too."

She was with Linda and myself. Linda smiled and said,

"You should have told John you needed someone complicated, devious and deceptive, with terrible parents." Mom laughed.

There was also Pip Waldren, an older man, whom Daddy Wilds liked but considered "fast," and James Hasty, among others. James reproached Pip for bringing my mother to a risqué place, and she dropped Pip for James.

More than a year passed after the *We The People* show before my mother consented to a "serious" date with my father in early 1941. If things moved swiftly then, there were still setbacks, my mother often disappearing on jobs, at one point leaving a message breaking off their relationship in my father's refrigerator in his Beaux Arts apartment. The following gives some idea of her breeziness.

> Tuesday
>
> Dear Dave,
> The fates still seem against us because I have to leave this evening for a Lucky Strike job in Durham———You'll have to forgive me for this last minute note because it was a very last minute booking. But just to be sure you have—I'll call you in a week when I return.
> Lucille

In such a competitive field Gar would not have betrayed any of his own difficulties at home nor any romantic ambivalence. Once launched in pursuit of a goal he was relentless, and my mother was his dream, in and of herself and as the symbol of the world he wanted to move into and master, leaving his poverty and ethnicity behind. He must have been frantic from the emotions pulling him in different directions that he had to hide as she was obviously of two minds about him: all those delays or missed timings for licenses made her reluctance clear.

Beyond this, a Jew was even less acceptable to the WASP gentility Mothie embodied than a Catholic—yet my mother chose the former. She possessed her own streak of rebelliousness, and asserted her independence by marrying out of caste. I never heard my mother say she loved Bill Kent, and however she strung my father along and suffered through him afterwards, she did love him.

Age was yet another undercurrent in their marriage. My father was twenty-nine, my mother twenty-seven, in 1942. He thought she was twenty-two. In a late biographical fragment he gave his age as twenty-six and hers as twenty-one. His confusion about himself doesn't make sense: about her, it does given her and Mothie's lifetime of altering dates. This was also an era when one was a matron at thirty, middle-aged at forty. My mother was certainly aware she was now looking towards that fate. She had no desire then, or earlier, to follow friends to Hollywood for a movie career, so what was left for her but marriage? She strung my father along then married him, startling him with how swiftly she turned into a homebody. My father remained ignorant of her age until she sought Social Security. Once he got over his fear that her check would diminish his own, he reacted in shock as he finally realized only two years separated them.

Another twist to this tale is that although I was certainly adored by my mother and Mothie, my father, as my mother said once, "painfully rejected" me. He was interested in the fact of me, the weight of me, the puzzle of my being there at all, the first born, his son; and he was interested in being in photos with me. Here and there he gives the game away in his journals, referring to how he "resisted" any childish pleas or tears, imagining instead it was his role to discipline, not please. He had no real interest in me until I was older and we could begin to talk. By then I was half a stranger.

I became conscious of this rejection slowly despite the immediate impact of being rejected. As I grew older, first I blindly took my mother's side, then turned away from all of these stories, treating them as curiosities so I could distance anger and grief, until old enough now to know better. I knew a part of me was in the fairy-tale position of the boy who discovers those he thought his parents were not and that, instead, he is the son of others, at least of another man. I was left with the feeling I must have a special, hidden destiny, in which the discovery of the truth is coequal with the discovery of who I am. That's a hard thing to live with amid the world's ever-denying reality, and doesn't compensate for the reverse feelings of inadequacy his rejection generated.

Hovering over these events was Daddy Wilds. He was larger than life in his children's eyes while alive, and grew larger in death. Central to his disproportionate size was Mom and Mothie's belief that Daddy Wilds died young at 58. After his death their belief grew ever stronger that had he lived he could have fixed not just her marriage, but anything.

In the end as a child I 'knew' that my parents had eloped, and that Nanny was mad at my father for doing so. South Carolina figured in that, somehow. I 'knew' my father kept his forbidden marriage secret as long as possible from his forbidding mother, who only learned about everything the night of my birth. These beliefs shaped my childhood and youth as they were maintained by those around me in place of the truth. Over time they forgot that themselves. My truth has been…myth. These are the stories

I told myself to give my life meaning and shape. To alter such a shaping takes the greatest effort, for change sparks the fear of both unhinging our world, and of being unhinged—mad. Barring some sudden crisis, change can take a lifetime of erosion until the truth emerges at last with a sigh of relief mixed with incredulity. We are less free than we think, and hunger for the truth far less than any of us admit in the midst of, paradoxically, that hunger.

In the end the 'truest' story of my birth and their marriage is that Gar sent his parents a telegram one Sunday night announcing both to them.

Letters

My mother rummages through a closet in their Beaux Arts apartment one day during her pregnancy. She pulls down a shoebox she doesn't recognize from a high shelf. There she discovers the letters Ruth wrote my father during their earlier courtship.

Ruth was the girl my father dated for years even after he moved to Manhattan where she routinely visited him his Beaux Arts apartment although, as Gar said to me, "Nothing ever happened. Men and women didn't behave like they do today." What he meant was that in his youth in the 1930s men weren't supposed to take advantage of good girls, however often good girls did get into trouble. Ruth wasn't one of the women in the entertainment industry that came his way and he felt no such inhibitions about: she was a good girl.

Gar continued seeing Ruth even as he pursued my mother, but Ruth soon realized what was happening and at the end of one weekend refused to let my father accompany her to the train station. She stopped him at the steps down to the subway and held out her hand.

"Goodbye, Dave." He was nonplussed as he shook her hand, but understood. She turned and disappeared from his life for forty years.

My mother sits on the floor reading Ruth's letters. My father finds her there in tears when he comes in, Ruth's letters scattered around her. He prepares himself to reassure my mother that Ruth is history and my mother the woman he pursued, loved, loves, but she forestalls him.

"She really loved you," my mother sobs. "How could you let her go? You should have married her."

THE WHIRLWIND AND THE BEAUTY

"Gar"

How does a man get his true name?
We do not go on spirit quests like the Indians, as some still do, their true name appearing in the course of a vision. So how did my father become Gar, a name Linda didn't use but my children did, as well as Linda's, but which originated and remained primary with me?
Was it some innocent version of the inevitable "Dada," my first groping for the inevitable parental name? Did it come from my sense of his always going out or away, something like "dada g'way" somehow becoming "Gar?" In one story—my Uncle Bud's?—my father was imagined leaning over my crib when he thought no one was about and whispering, "God." The best I could manage was Gar.
That stuck.

The Whirlwind

My father is inseparable from his career. One of his paternal uncles, Uncle Harry, spent a career in vaudeville and theatre before he went blind, and influenced my father far more than his own staid, hardworking father, Benjamin Levy, ultimately a foreman at Bethlehem Steel. By the time my father was in high school he thought of himself as an actor, and initially spoke of himself as an actor professionally. But he was a writer, too: in college he entered play contests, and received an honorable mention for *The Genial Tyrant* in one of these.

His first job after graduating from the University of Pennsylvania was a plebian sales position at Macy's in Philadelphia. This was not well received at home as sufficient fruit for a college education. He and Charles went through Penn on scholarships, already materially independent of their parents, but their psychological dependence on them made any criticism sting. Gar went back for his Masters in Business at the Wharton School of Business at Penn, graduating in 1936. He had a tough audience to prove himself to, this secondborn twin.

He found himself in 1936 an instructor of playwrighting at the Philadelphia School of Theatre, a brief post while he churned out at best politely received plays. There was no sign of the social urgency energizing so much Depression era writing in his own: his plays were escapist entertainment. This job too seemed small reward for all his education, and shortly thereafter he was working in merchandising in a general store in Syracuse, New York.

Although Syracuse was his first extended time away from home, he was not unhappy for that reason, but because he was too far from the 'action' in New York, the center of the creative world. He wrote scripts for any radio show that was interested, and in the process discovered a gift for dialogue and the audience participation format. While still in Syracuse he landed a job writing for *Sally at the Switchboard* for Sears Roebuck, his first regular assignment, and when he heard of a contest for new writers staged by Y&R's *We The People*, a very popular human interest show, he submitted his work. He was one of three writers selected out of forty. He moved to New York to work for what was then the largest and most influential of the advertising agencies who dominated the broadcast media into the 1950s, absorbing television when it first arrived on the scene. By September 1938 the first show written by my father aired on *We The People*, and he was on his way.

His boss Adrian Samish was receptive to this young man's energy and drive, and soon permitted him to direct, then produce as well for *We The People*. In my father's second year on *We The People* he wrote and helped produce the show where he met Lucille Wilds. The show's increasing success allowed my father to meet an ever wider array of the famous as well as the unknowns whose stories *We The People* dramatized. By 1940 Max Wylie in his groundbreaking *The Best Broadcasts of 1938-1939* picked *We The People* as the best human interest show on the air, its success materially related to my father's swift rise. *We The People* reached an audience of 12 million sets, a very large number in a population of under 150,000,000 Americans.

By 1940 my father was the assistant on *We The People* for Joe Hill, who succeeded Adrian Samish; in 1941 Gar took charge of the show. One of his coups was an interview with Maxwell Anderson with excerpts from *The Eve of St Mark*, an anti-war play by a playwright then at the height of his Broadway success. Gar deliberately turned the show into a war interest venue after Pearl Harbor, winning *We The People* encomiums even from the *New York Times* for personalizing the war experience for the national audience. In 1942 he was able to reach out to world figures like Winston Churchill because of the show's prominence, now the number one show in the nation and reaching 24 out of 48 million sets. Half the nation listened to *We The People*.

Nothing but a polite telegram regretting his inability to take part came from Churchill, but from then on leading figures in the government and military increasingly appeared on the show. There they became acquainted with the dynamic, multitalented David Levy who wrote, directed, and produced so much of it himself. In 1943 *We The People* assisted the Treasury Department with its war bond drives, staging shows across the country and in venues like the USS Constitution in Boston to launch particular drives. My father became well known to Henry Morgenthau, Secretary of the Treasury, as well as to figures like Admiral DeWitt Ramsey.

He was directing other shows by now as well, including *Midnight at Manhattan*, also for Y&R, as well as a variety of specials, like producing and directing a star-studded variety show for WMCA-4 for the British-American Ambulance Corps in 1942. He was a whirlwind of activity, and had to conduct his romance with my mother not just within her schedule but within his hectic media and social whirl filled with play and film going, dinners, and parties where young professionals like himself mixed with senior to further their careers. No doubt he discovered then the price of being a Jew in a world of marked antisemitism, in which the upper echelons of Y&R and its competitors were run by WASPS.

Antisemitism was a given before and after World War II. Gregory Peck pretended to be Jewish in *Gentleman's Agreement* in 1947 to expose the constant prejudice Jews routinely encountered in WASP America. In my father's world a cocktail party was a business rite, the successful host and his gracious wife entertaining peers and ambitious young men like my father, all expected to be of the 'right sort.' He was too smart not to realize how professionally useful he was to such men but simultaneously unsuited socially to their world.

Part of the release of energy he showed in these years was due to being free from Philadelphia. Charles, except for his brief fling in Boston with Bennet Cerf at the Book of the Month Club, stayed in Philadelphia and began a career as an academic at Penn: Gar had found a larger pond where he could make more of a splash and overshadow his twin. If he (and Charles) remained in daily touch with their mother, Gar at least was a city away and saw her and Poppy only on visits home or when they came to New York.

My father's connection to Secretary Morgenthau proved crucial. In April of 1943 he arranged an Easter Sunday kickoff for a war bond drive with Morgenthau as 'master of ceremonies' in a script he provided for the Secretary from Cedar Rapids, Wisconsin. In August he visited Morgenthau in Washington to arrange a follow-up engagement, and in September produced another war bond drive special, this for the Third War Bond Drive, from Monticello. There are photographs of my father and Morgenthau touring distinctive places in the Charlottesville area together.

The *National Radio Magazine* wrote of my father's activities in 1943,

He is only thirty, which is arrestingly young for one doing such important work, yet his ability has called forth admiring comment alike from listeners and government departments.[1]

He was becoming someone.

He was still writing on his own account, too, like his *Tag #1,184,463*, a script on the Unknown Soldier first broadcast on radio, then later written up as fiction and transformed into "I Belong to You in the August," as part of a 1943 *Radio Mirror* magazine of radio romance.

His involvement with Morgenthau deepened. They kicked off the Fourth War Bond Drive from Bridgeport, Connecticut in January 1944. By March 1944 my father had reached out through his now myriad contacts, including Admiral King, Secretary of the Navy, and arranged to enter the Navy as a Lieutenant, JG, technically in the Reserve. There are photos of my mother and Mrs. Ramsey socializing, for what can never be forgotten is that through all this activity after July, 1941 my mother is present by his side at socially critical moments with her grace, beauty, and manners of a kind familiar to and accepted by the establishment, in which she was free to mingle after my appearance because of Mothie's presence at home. Living in Great Neck after August 1942, Gar had both the wife and setting to entertain successfully on his own account. He was no longer a social outsider. There would not be a glass ceiling for him. Life in Great Neck was "Far better," my mother said, "than he could have managed on his own. Yet he never once remembered Mothie on her birthday, or on Mother's Day during these years, or later."

The omission is glaring when you consider that Gar's black address book listed the birthdays equally of friends and enemies he remembered with equally friendly cards and notes.

He began to debate entering the Navy feverishly with my mother in the months leading up to his commission in May, 1944. He was, in fact, afraid of being drafted into the Army, where Bud was already serving. One of the first things he did after marriage was go to the local draft board to be reclassified from 1A. He preserved a number of his draft cards, and although his rating was lower after marriage and fatherhood, it was subject to constant review. Joining the Navy through his new contacts and being assigned to Washington avoided the peril. At first he was assigned to the

Training Film Branch of the Navy's Photographic Division of the Bureau of Aeronautics to make training films. This lasted a few months only, as Morgenthau soon requested his services for the Treasury Department to assist with the Sixth War Bond Drive through Thomas Lane at the Treasury War Finance Committee. My father remained with the Treasury thereafter, although repeated requests had to be made for that purpose to the Navy.

"He lived in dread of being called to active service in the Pacific," according to my mother, "and worked feverishly behind the scenes to stay with Morgenthau. I was called into service with Mrs. Ramsey and other wives I met in Washington to help him. He even applied for active service once, but only once he was sure it would be denied."

This reflects poorly on him, and there is no record I have found to substantiate my mother's story. But she was amused telling the story, not vindictive, and it certainly fits with my father's machinations to work at the Department of Treasury where he was a protégé of Morgenthau's. Service in the Pacific was enough to make any thoughtful man blanch, while there is no doubt he rendered great service on the home front at the Treasury where he became head of its radio division and was directly involved in the production of the war bond drives. He also, as he broadened the Treasury's exposure on network radio, extended his range of contacts in the broadcast industry.

By 1945 he worked directly with officials ranging up to President Truman to forward war bond drives, involving the President in the kickoff of the Seventh War Bond Drive in May, 1945. He became head of all Treasury radio programs, supervised all material going out to other stations, and made himself available to help other networks during the war bond drives. One individual he worked with at this time was Mark Goodson, whose later shows like *What's My Line?* my father materially assisted reaching the air. They became lifelong friends.

He expanded the radio division, increased its personnel, and took on *Treasury Salute* programs which dramatized the Department of Treasury's work and needs, including adding *Music for the Millions*. But by late 1945 he was planning a Victory War Bond Drive under Secretary of the Treasury Fred Vinson. Morgenthau was prone to periodic bouts of depression and insecurity, and all through his tenure at the Treasury under Roosevelt he would at such times offer to resign, offers Roosevelt always declined. When he did this with Truman, to his dismay he was taken at his word and let go. There is no comment by my father on this turn of events despite his closeness to Morgenthau, although he remained friendly with him. There is an unmistakable sense of Morgenthau having served his purpose, and mention of him disappears from my father's journals.

By late 1945 the urge to return to civilian life was a national obsession, with my father no exception. He was back at Y&R by May of 1946 after protracted negotiations befitting his new eminence, and was elevated to chief of daytime radio after maneuvering out of a more limited West Coast assignment. He had done well by the country and himself at the Treasury. He was already thinking of civilian life before he was formally discharged, pushing a quiz show at Y&R in early 1946 called *Chance of a Lifetime*.

Once free, the family returned to Great Neck. But Gar was still ascending at Y&R, and in 1947, hardly a year into his role as head of daytime radio, he switched to the new video staff, for he saw that the new medium of television would replace radio as the leading broadcast medium. We had an early TV in the dark corner made by the stairs that led up from the living room to the landing above, and I can remember flashes of disturbing war and postwar imagery from its flickering tube, including one image of a dead, white horse, legs in the air beside some bombed carts. There has never been a time since then when violent images were absent from television or my home, and soon from most other American homes.

Now a period of great innovation began for my father. He continued at Y&R to assist the Department of the Treasury in bond drives, producing, often directing and writing key shows for the drives. He took on soap operas, trying to make *The Second Mrs. Burton* socially responsible for CBS, the start of a lifelong effort to encourage 'family values' on television. He directed Harriet Horne's interviews of celebrities, worked with Fred Rickey at CBS to keep advertising content relevant for news broadcasts, and helped pioneer broadcasting political conventions, beginning with the Republican Convention of 1948. He assisted NBC and *Life Magazine* with their convention coverage, working with a staff of eighteen at the time. Over the years he had a hand in Arthur Godfrey's *Talent Scouts*, *Father Knows Best*, *The Life of Riley*, *I Married Joan*, *Our Miss Brooks*, and *Maverick* while still at Y&R. He survived a shakeup that saw Pat Weaver brought in because of account losses in the late 1940s, and helped with projects as diverse as Eisenhower's *Crusade in Europe* and *Hollywood Screen Test*.

He was in perpetual motion, noting in a journal entry that I realized the only time I got to see him was on a Sunday. By 1950 he was elevated to Vice President in the Television Department at Y&R, one of the 'in' set, a maker of popular taste and public attitude. By then we lived in New York in an apartment near Gracie Mansion with spacious living and dining rooms ideal for entertaining his peers and selected young men on their way up, all put at their ease by my mother's polished manners, graciousness, and beauty. He had arrived.

Dream Girl

In 1940 Lucille Wilds was crowned the "Dream Girl" of America in Atlantic City. This followed her 1939 crowning as the Models' Miss America. The term wasn't in use then, but she had become America's preeminent supermodel. It is hard to take in the blend of frivolity and wish fulfillment involved in such a role, or to imagine her feelings of being ogled, her image nationally pervasive in the printed media and in gossipy news tidbits generated by the publicity machine at the Walter Thornton Agency for Models. In a certain sense becoming the models' Miss America and America's Dream Girl must have felt at once an excursion into fairyland or Hollywood and, equally, self-confirmation on a mythic scale.

She was the ultimate success of the Wilds Myth (see Part II), a perfect, proper daughter to go with a perfect, proper son and recognized as such by all. Her brother Bud was a model in his own right of American, WASP propriety, doing passable academic work at Great Neck High, participating in musical productions, and excelling as an All League halfback in football, one of Long Island's best. Tall, handsome, he went on to the University of Alabama where he continued to play football and to win drinking contests of—milk, duly reported in his home newspaper. Mom was molded by the indulgence of her father and drive of her mother for stability and place. Becoming a model might expose her to a risqué world, yet becoming the queen of the models confirmed her preeminence in fact which was so indulgently granted her by her father Daddy Wilds and striven for by Mothie. How delicious when dream, myth, and reality coincide.

Little detail survives of her youth in Brooklyn, always in growing affluence, or then in Long Island. No traumas or whispers of dark secrets have come down in the family lore, and to write a history of her would be to write a history of the times those privileged to enjoy them would recognize, but all others recognize as a Hollywood (or later TV) idealization of white, Anglo-Saxon, protestant middle-class life.

She was not touched by World War I, the influenza epidemic, or the Red Scare. These were distant events encountered by hearsay or through magazine images, or heard referred to on the radio from the 1920s on. She knew none of the poverty and driven striving of my father and his twin: she was not on the receiving end of ethnicity. Prohibition and escalating crime were also hearsay and newspaper images, or exotic items on radio news broadcasts or streams of silent images on the burgeoning cinema screens. Jazz as it bloomed and affected dance and popular music, and the upheaval in women's styles from the 19th Century dress to the first recognizably 20th Century Flappers' short dresses were more immediate experiences, albeit all to be flirted with from the safety of a protected environment. A home might be downsized because of Daddy Wilds' losses in the Great Crash of 1929, but the family's lifestyle was hardly affected.

That style should matter to a beautiful girl or a fashion conscious mother is not surprising. Nor is the concern trivial or some fault involved in life's greater unpleasantnesses being held at arm's length. We should be slow to judge, having watched the Vietnam body counts become a taken-for-granted part of the evening broadcasts in the 1960s and 1970s, and news itself turn towards entertainment until today much of what we see is performance, including some of the violence that takes advantage of the television camera to stage what has become its genre. Too many now cannot tell what is fake or real and are encouraged in their confusion from the top down. Why depreciate a lifestyle so free of the world's traumas when it is for just such a life others less fortunate hunger?

The mood of the country did not turn uniformly bleak with the onset of the Depression, either. That event sparked a great deal of socially relevant film and drama and, equally, a proliferation of ornate stage and film musicals that coincided with an outburst of often zany comedies by writers like Kaufman and Hart. The heart has many more chambers than four.

Comedies and musicals provided momentary escapes from hard times in stories of lives purged of suffering or in which suffering became humorous, complementing dramas that descended into the depths of human nature. Glamorous women like Greta Garbo, Marlene Dietrich, Jean Harlow glowed on the screen opposite handsome newcomers like Jimmy Stewart, Cary Grant, or Clark Gable. Joan Crawford and Bette

Davis were young and romantic. The talkies arrived with the bad times and helped make them bearable.

We need our dream girls who embody the ultimate reward of the American Dream no less than our Eleanor Roosevelts who widen the range of equality and opportunity for women. We may look askance at the empty smiles of our own super models in our feminist era, but they are as much a fact of life if not more so than women corporate executives or Ph.Ds, and speak to us less ambiguously than do these others of success and its glamour.

The worst punishment my mother remembers suffering fits her idyllic world. She was sent to clean each spring supporting the master mattress, in those days not covered as now, if she annoyed Mothie sufficiently. It took hours, was tedious, demeaning in a minor way, resented, and effective. Two pages that survive from her diary at fifteen give a sense of her life then in Great Neck.

January 2, 1930

I awoke late this morning and had my breakfast and lunch together. I haven't done anything much except read a very interesting novel by Booth Tarkington entitled, 'Women.'

Skippy is barking his brainless little head off because he is tied and can't come in. Really he is the most provoking dog. I've tried and tried to teach him tricks and he just won't learn them he rolls all over and just plays. Oh well, perhaps when he is bigger he will develop more gray matter! I know Miss Chisholm would be shocked at my use of English but who will ever see it but me! I've broken the E string on my violin and it was because I didn't want to practice either…I guess it decided to retire from old age. I've been studying Algebra because I've absolutely got to pass the test. The Biology region doesn't seem to worry me as much as the other girls & insignificant boy.

Skippy broke loose and vanished with another dog and I in my bedroom slippers was forced to run after him to recapture him.

January 3, 1930

I arose late again this morning and after straightening my room I descended to ma petite dejeuner and afterwards just loafed around doing anything I could think of. This evening I listened to the radio and Buddy and I had a scrap about which of us he liked best, resulting in him calling me a pig and I a sale bete whereupon ma mere slapped me and I retired to my room for a sound cry. I took a bath and washed my hair. Today I also painted the top of a candy box to use as a handkerchief box, it turned out quite pretty. I'm so disappointed, there isn't any sleigh riding or ice-skating because of a sudden fancy of old Mr. Temperature to register warm feelings! And besides I've got a big black and blue mark on my thigh from bumping into the handle of our refrigerator. Ho. Hum!

Today I've finished all the books I brought from the Library and the thought of the Algebra test has me all nervy. The radio is playing "If you haven't got a girl." I'm going to make a cover for this little diary friend of mine.

    And until tomorrow night.
    Bon Soit

The air of privileged indolence is amusing, and the affected rhetorical flourishes, as if she is a belle much put upon by those around her, or a character out of Oscar Wilde's *The Importance of Being Ernest*. There Cecily replies to her tutor, Miss Prism, who is urging Cecily to study her German.

Cecily
(coming over very slowly)
But I don't like German. It isn't at all a becoming language, I know perfectly well that I look quite plain after my German lesson.[2]

She and Cecily could have been sisters.

Revealingly school is taken as a necessity, but just passing is enough, "I've absolutely got to pass the test," she wrote, but felt no need to drive herself to achieve academic excellence as Gar and Charles felt necessary to do for their impossible to please mother. If Charles became student body President, then Gar received the special service award. Bud might play football, one of the boys—Gar participated in track, and in one meet when the only other competitor defaulted, ran the high hurdles alone against the clock. Neither Mom nor Bud had anything to prove. It was sufficient to be oneself, to meet academic and or social responsibility adequately. To pass.

The back of my mother's second entry has a drawing of steps. A stick figure of Einstein falls from the topmost step, symbolic of the difficulty of his theory of relativity, while standing on a lower step is a stick figure of John Mineke with a big "O.K." under his name. Her unrequited high school crush on him was not so strong that when rekindled years later after their reunion at the Finnish Relief Ball it carried her through to marriage. It was my father who touched her to passion and rage.

My mother began to model by the end of high school in 1934 facilitated by that idealization of herself Mothie held in her youth as a turn of the century Gibson Girl. Daddy Wilds accompanied her on assignments before he became ill from 1939 on, at first in New York when she started at NYU, intending to become a teacher (not at Barnard as she claimed later). She is unmistakably young in her earliest modeling photos, her blonde hair coiffed by herself in a style that endured for years. But as her success grew her hair assumed a variety of professional looks and colors. Her modeling career was so successful that after two years at NYU she broke off her studies and signed with the Walter Thornton Model Agency in 1936. She was a professional success at twenty-one, typically American in the belief in self-transformation allowing someone to be whatever he or she wanted to be, regardless how much of that was simply image.

Thornton's was the preeminent agency for models in these years; Thornton was sometimes referred to as "The Merchant of Venus." When he celebrated his 35th birthday he included fifty of his models including my mother besides his wife. The artist McClelland Barclay was asked to choose the most beautiful girl present, and it was Lucille (the second 'l' popped in and out of my mother's name) Wilds he selected: in three years she rose to the top of Thornton's models.

A rare versatility led to my mother's rise. Some models might do well for the "rollicking juvenile," according to Thornton in a newspaper article. Others might do for the "sweet, wholesome American woman," or be right for the "pert, smart debutante," or be perfect for the role of "sportswoman," while still others might be right for the "glamorous, exotic lady of fame," but "when a model turns up sufficiently versatile to portray any or all of these roles, I acclaim her Queen among Models.... Lucille is Number One."[3]

This versatility stood her in good stead as she got through her public marriage in January, 1942, affecting my father and Mark Warnow with the depth of her 'conversion' to Judaism. She was, in short, an actress, like some of her early friends such as Susan Hayward, but without the ambition to transition into film.

Someone so prominent loses a certain amount of privacy, and though there were no paparazzi trailing my mother, her measurements were public knowledge as a template for true American beauty: 5' 7", 118 lbs., a 34" bust, 35" hips, 25" waist, with a shoe size of 5A. Measurements for gloves and hats were also given publicly. In our own age these figures point to an appearance of elegance, not to the ripe, bosomy sexuality of Victoria's Secret models parading down runways in briefs and bras. Conversely, there is no suggestion of the kind of bulimic thinness typical of many high fashion models now, either.

The marriage of The Models' Miss America and The Dream Girl of 1940, as well as the ridiculous *We The People* episode broadcast nationally about the famous model with the $100,000 figure whose mean agent and father jointly prevented her from marrying her true love, was indeed news. My father had good reason to fear some item reaching his parents in the Philadelphia papers. My father had married the American, not the Jewish, Dream Girl, who thereafter was his bridge to WASP acceptance.

But it would be unfair to think this was one-sided, a beauty and the beast act: he too was handsome, polished, bright, and spoke well. In Bud's memory, so often mocking or unkind where my father is concerned, he said they turned heads equally entering a room: they were "dazzling."

Modeling did not stop with marriage, if it did slowly taper. She was still regarded as a leading "international cover girl" at age 30 when she modeled for the ladies of Truman's Cabinet in 1945 while my father was at the Treasury. One of her most famous portraits as an American Madonna was for Prudential and shot not long after I was born and could be safely held in her arms before a camera. She continued to model when my father returned to Y&R after the war, in particular as the model of choice for decades by Elinor Ames' "The Correct Thing" in *The New York Daily News*.

There are caveats. Successful as she was, if my mother danced the Black Bottom in a Harlem night club, she went to bed at the family home in Great Neck. If a racy beau, or one too old, called on her, it was at the front door of that home where he was confronted by an appraising Daddy Wilds. For all her enjoyment of café society, theatre, balls, the 'in' social life of Manhattan, dawn found her sleeping upstairs in her Great Neck, childhood bedroom. She was away only on out-of-town modeling assignments, and those were chaperoned. In a sense, she never left home, a home that she moved my father into after Daddy Wilds' death and my birth in 1942.

She absorbed him.

One consequence of her fame compared to my father was that her income was far greater than his for many years, freeing her of dependence on him. When my father signed at Y&R in 1938, Poppy wanted to know what he made.

"Fifty dollars, Pop," he lied. That was his father's monthly salary: he couldn't bring himself to say he now made as much in a week. But that paled against hers, and in their early years together she rarely asked him for money for any expenses. When her modeling income decreased she borrowed at need from Mothie. Only towards the end of the 1940s did she accept and routinely receive money from my father. He was at first puzzled at her refusal to take money from him, probably insulted in his amour proper, and equally happy to have marriage cost so little. Only later did money become a poisonous issue, one from which her earlier independence at first insulated them.

As I reflect on their marriage, my birth, the myths each lived within and tried to develop, it dawns on me I was a child of beauty and a handsome if alien-edged presence full of ambivalence, and I wonder what they truly saw in each other or, if, looking in the other's eyes they saw their own image and desire looking back.

First Flight

Their inevitable rude awakening came quickly: in October 1943 my mother abruptly took a three week modeling assignment in Phoenix, Arizona, her marriage to my father tottering. I was 14 months old, a toddler entrusted to Mothie's care in Great Neck. My father saved my mother's letters from this separation, with one earlier letter that serves as a prelude. She saved none of his.

That earlier letter of April 22, 1943, gives a glimpse into my parents' domestic reality. He had gone to Cedar Rapids to launch a war bond drive, and she is eager to keep him abreast of life at home. She has a new avocation, she informs him: forging signatures: "The one I did on yours was a work of art" on some necessary form she took to Y&R for him. That skill would grow in importance down the years, and be passed on unwitting to me to exploit during high school.

She adds that their maid has a fractured ankle, and is worried about her ability to work, but Mom has told her "I'd keep her busy polishing silver and doing the things that she can do sitting down." She and Mothie had had a tiring day, grew grumpy, and went to bed without speaking to each other, a scene that will be played out many times over the years, including the aftermath the next morning when "all's serene on the home front." She's priced a fence for part of the yard, though she's not sure it will work for me or Smokie, our black cocker spaniel. "I think I told you" that Lance has had a smallpox vaccination, which should take by the coming Sunday: she is worried I might be cranky or a little fevered. She ends,

> Well—nowadays I fill a letter with household chit chat—I don't know whether that's good or bad because I used to use the same amount of space just to tell you I love you.

and hastens to reassure him,

> "Incidentally—I still do—I love you—and I miss you—and I wish you were back—That I was there or you were here——anyway—
> All my love
> Lucille."

His distance as a father is clear: she's not even sure he knows about his son's smallpox vaccination. All on the domestic front is in her and Mothie's hands. From Great Neck Gar commutes daily to the city, or goes off on work-related trips; once home in the evening, he spreads his work out on the dining room table, or sits on the phone in the living room with business calls that consume the evening, as time went on adding watching select TV shows to his routine. Outside of photo ops, as when he posed in front of our Victory Garden, rake in hand, or bottle-feeding me in another, there is little connection between him and the new family life surrounding him. There is no diaper changing for him. Instead America's Dream Girl does these, arranges pediatric appointments and vaccinations, prices fences to restrain the dog and myself, and deals with injured maids.

How does he react to these inevitable and natural changes? In a way that profoundly hurts, angers, then drives my mother to accept a last minute assignment in October, 1943 that sees her leave child, husband and home behind after so brief a time together.

That assignment is so last minute she reveals in an initial letter of October 22nd that she and four other girls reach Chicago on that date with neither train reservations onward to Phoenix nor hotel reservations in Chicago. Fortunately one of the girls has a fiancé with connections and gets her and another model, Carol, a room in his club, the Union League Club of Chicago, and the other two girls a room at another club. It takes three days to get train reservations from Chicago to Phoenix, days during which my father bombards her with angry phone calls and letters she responds to on October 25th in the single most open letter of hers that survives.

She begins with how she has spent another sleepless and unhappy night thanks to his latest phone calls. My father doesn't want her to take this assignment, when in fact "I would have stayed home had you told me too—it seems to me that Chicago was a little late to make up your mind—."

If her decision to go was abrupt, he was unable to speak his mind until after the fact. He never could be direct and honest about his feelings to a woman once in a settled relationship unless driven to an extremity, a characteristic that emerges now with my mother for the first time as he confronts the consequences of his inability to speak directly to her except when in crisis.

She goes on in her October 25th letter to point out she will make more on this one trip than she could on a number of exhausting dashes around New York studios, which, implicitly, she has been doing since resuming her career after my birth. But that is not why she left.

It's not in her nature to complain, she explains, so maybe he just doesn't realize the strain she's been through since at least their public marriage. She had to deal with his fears about his parents while pregnant: in fact "at a time when I needed your reassurances you were off with your parents while I was put up at the Hotel Lexington" so they wouldn't see her pregnancy. Her resentment at his absurd behavior finally comes out. Daddy Wilds' death a month before my birth was a "dreadful blow" whose impact on herself she tried to shield him from so as "not (to) inflict you with it." What was so fragile about him to make such critical grieving a burden to keep to herself at such a time? The absence of sharing essential emotions and experience is painfully clear. Mothie too has been a problem on top of this, having lost both Daddy Wilds and earlier that same year her mother, Lotte, and yet Mothie "worried about my having the baby more than you did."

Their move to Great Neck, she reminds him, resulted because she felt leaving Mothie in the house alone was too much in view of these losses, especially with Bud in the army, and so "knowing even then David—how you felt—we moved out." He didn't want to leave his constant urban whirl, and came home in a bad humor without sympathy for her needs at a time when his primary thought should have been for her and their coming child as well as the loss she had endured. Consequently, my mother never got the rest she felt she needed after I was born, instead working hard to make you feel the way mother felt—that this was our house to do with as we pleased—hoping that you'd understand that I realized how you felt—that you'd understand why I was torn—how much I want you to be satisfied.

I needed more money—I wanted to take care of my mother—I wanted to please you—I couldn't model I didn't want to endanger your draft status in any way and I didn't want to burden you financially so my mind went around in circles—trying to figure everything out—

but

Instead of growing together, talking things out—our life together grew more difficult—Perhaps because of the fact that lots of times I was more exhausted than you knew—I discovered I couldn't cope with your moods—I felt that you no longer thought me attractive, glamorous, desirable....

In a rush she paints the picture of a burdened woman and a moody, self-absorbed man she felt a need to protect from reality when he should have been her greatest supporter.

Worse, it's been a long time since he said she was attractive, or was even merely "pleased" with her. It's been "a long time since you've said, I love you———." When they go out together it's a struggle to be part of the group for her, because "you felt that the other people were more fortunate than you—whose wives appeared more attractive!" He exerted himself for others, but not for her. It all "built up to a point of near desperation————."

This is a devastating picture of a husband too frightened of his parents to stand by his wife during her pregnancy, and so rejecting before and after my birth that he made this beautiful woman feel the opposite: unloved, unwanted, unattractive. He comes off as emotionally out of touch, if not crippled in his self-absorption, and blindly critical at the same time in an inappropriate and baseless manner—certainly no one to approach for money!

His most recent unpleasant phone calls to Chicago ironically have shown "the liveliest interest or concern" towards her since they've been married! She can't believe all his unpleasantness over the trip when he knows she needs money, and that Phoenix will at least be a healthy climate where maybe she can get some rest. Is he worried about her having a "gay time?" Well, "You ought to know me better." What she needs besides rest is, by the way, $400 dollars for deferred dental work.

Some of this is disingenuous—she took the job in anger and despair to strike back at him, not merely for rest or to make money, the latter of which she could do with far less disruption in New York. It's impossible too at this point not to wonder how one-sided this may be, but unfortunately the man emerging from this unhappy portrait is the one I came to know later so well, a man of instant criticism for any failing, satisfied in Linda and myself or my mother only in those moments we were picture perfect, as though idealized images come to life from the popular family and women's magazines of the day. Any failing, especially any physical falling from perfect cleanliness and health, provoked biting sarcasm and immediate rejection. So it is easy to imagine his growing repugnance as my mother swelled in pregnancy, then for a brief time displayed the usual swollen, postnatal belly before she regained her figure and resumed modeling.

Gar had a horror of normal bodily smells and functions. One of my strongest memories in Great Neck and especially later in Manhattan was of the amount of cologne he and his friends wore, always immaculately dressed, sporting expensive rings and cufflinks for their shirts, which left me with a lifelong revulsion towards male scents and jewelry.

What a negative inversion of beauty and glamour her pregnancy and domestic concerns must have appeared to him, mingled now with the smell of the cotton diapers of the day, or bottles rattling in the kitchen as they were sterilized as he tried to work at the dining room table in the adjoining room. This wasn't the dream image he'd pursued but a real woman he hardly knew.

A story from some years later is illustrative. It is long after my sister appeared in 1946. Now she is twelve, I am in high school, and on this particular weekend evening the four of us have driven from our house in Weston, Connecticut to Westport for a family dinner out. Linda goes to great pains to be the perfect daughter, dresses nicely, does her hair, and is perfectly turned out. After we park and start to walk out of the parking lot to the restaurant we split apart to avoid a large puddle. Gar watches Linda approach as we come back together. She has a worried half smile on her face: what could be wrong?

"Dear," he says, "I never realized until now what big feet you have."

Linda stops, the half smile frozen on her face, her clown feet still.... She can say nothing.

"Oh David," my mother laughs, "there's nothing wrong with her feet." Linda's eyes are luminous with tears she controls: her smile has gone. It does not reappear for the rest of the evening. My father can't understand what he has done wrong.

I realize now as I read my mother's catalogue of complaints from her October 25th letter that she has encountered this aspect of my father for the first time. Confusingly, despite how unpleasant he could be, there was an essential naiveté about his criticism, based on his inability to share normal perspectives or feelings with us except when shocked by our reactions which normally we repressed, for he was emotionally intimidating far beyond his words. He emanated an aura of potential violence when he was in full, self-righteous stride, which combined with his naiveté gave him an emotional license we found daunting. He would persist in his criticisms no matter how unhappy he made us, attacking anything that unsettled his constant idealization of experience, until restraint and fear gave way to completely exasperated reproaches on our parts that forced him to deal with our all-too-human reality.

It is just this evocation of the drumbeat of his criticism and neglect leading up to her anger, and his first self-righteous reaction when finally confronted with the consequences of his behavior (her anger, and in this instance, flight), that constituted the first stage of his repetitive behavior at home.

My mother continues in that seminal letter that thanks to those unpleasant evening calls and belated reproaches, this trip to Phoenix has become an unhappy and unfortunate necessity, meaning he has done nothing to remove her resolve to go, only made things more unpleasant. Worse, with its three day delay in departing for Phoenix, the trip will be longer than planned, yet all he can think of is imposing a deadline for her to be back, so "I shall be under constant strain and pressure during the rest of this awful trip." He doesn't get it. Then she mocks his not wanting her to be at social engagements with him, and adds because of his pressure she won't be able to get the rest she needs, after all. He ruins everything. She receives a phone call from the desk downstairs to say a letter of his has arrived, but can't face going down to get it.

> I'm too exhausted—too miserable—I feel that a love that can make me this miserable—that you can upset me so [crossed out: "without thinking of"] because you're upset yourself—needs a little explaining...."

She imagines tearing up this letter now that she's expressed her feelings: maybe she sounds "hysterical"—after all, she's been awake all night, and "I don't know if it tells you what I've tried to——" or even if "having been written it matters," and she breaks off. Unsigned, her writing at the end degenerating into a scrawl, she sent the letter: it survived down the years in its postmarked envelope.

After a cursory letter and a postcard from San Antonio after she and the girls are finally able to leave for Phoenix, she writes more seriously again on October 28th. At least one more of his letters has reached her, and there have been additional unpleasant calls. She reminds him of his dour face each time she drives him to the Great Neck train station to commute to Manhattan, unless they pick up an associate like Dan Miller, when Gar becomes cheerful. She wonders if he's catching on, as she quotes a sentence from a letter to the effect of 'how dismal it is not to have the one you long for at your side.' Maybe some "distance" is working, she adds. She defines her ideal marriage:

> I always wanted a marriage where I'd grow together, in love and understanding, with my husband. One in which he'd love and admire me as I would him—and not be afraid to show it. Try to work towards a complete understanding of each other and work out together any problems which might confuse us.

Instead, all she has experienced is "constant friction" despite being sure he does, in his misguided way, love her. This trip should help them attain a clearer outlook, as she also knows she can take "a selfish point of view." She closes with a warning that sometimes, in her dreams, he is "the bogeyman!"

This collision in 1943 shocked them both, for they were young, in love, had a young child, noted and promising careers, and thought a full life lay ahead. But here the profound, revelatory disappointment of a young wife emerges and meets the fear that the life, love and future she has given herself to body and soul is an illusion.

My father had discovered the glamorous woman he pursued was, actually, just a woman, unhappy, with a child, and embedded in a real household with well-founded marital unhappiness. Even more shocking he found she had the strength of character and a limit to her toleration of his bad behavior, even to the point of being willing to leave him.

So now he revealed the next part of his pattern whenever he drove my mother to such desperation that she explosively forced him to face the reality and unattractiveness of his actual as opposed to idealized behavior: he backpedaled swiftly and surrendered abjectly.

Return

Mom said more than once that Gar wrote "beautifully" when he wanted to, his letters peppered with literary quotes and allusions and graceful sentiments. Uncle Charles wrote in an even more literary vein. In an earlier letter to my mother apparently Gar alluded to Shakespeare's Sonnet CXVI, writing, "love does not alter when it alteration finds," which is actually: "…Love is not love/which alters when it alteration finds." His version shows love endures whatever the circumstances, a banal, American romanticism. Shakespeare shows love is not love which changes under the impact of circumstance—which is precisely my mother's reproach to my father despite her despairing feeling he probably does love her in his own way, one which she finds impossible to understand.

Her unhappiness and firmness and the force of her charges finally dawned on Gar around October 28th, when he sent off a letter she received on the 30th. By then, abruptly, the crisis is past as she writes,

> Darling!
> It's so pleasant to have all that unpleasantness behind us and for me to be able to write you with a heart filled to bursting with love.

They had talked the previous night on the phone, and she "felt so relieved, as though a dreadful burden had been removed" by his words. Then in the morning she got his "wonderful letter" of Oct. 28th. He has pleaded for sympathy, evidently, but also reassured her on all the matters he had raised doubt about: loving her, and finding her glamorous and attractive.

It's sad his letter is lost. He was a master at belated submission, supplication, reassurance, and lovingness. Often he shifted the blame for his behavior to the unrelenting pressure of his mother with a helpless shrug: "But what can I do? She's my mother" he told my mother once after another blowup, a phrase that became a catchphrase down the years.... It must be remembered he was in daily touch with his mother who did all she could to undermine his and his brothers' marriages.

No matter: he has reassured my mother so convincingly, abandoning all his previous positions, that now she is anxious to get home. She feels they've reached "a better understanding" and is "so happy" "because we've so much to treasure and build between us." She begs him not to "hoard" any future unhappy thoughts, nor will she:

> ...anyway David, I love you very dearly and our future together is very important to me.
>
> I can't wait to get home—to see you—to love you—oh David—I miss you dreadfully—and I am getting home-sicker by the second—
>
> Darling—take care of yourself and love me as I love you—
> Lucille

She is manic with relief, ready "to kiss his fat stomach" until he tells her he has been on a diet and lost 14 pounds, at which point she tells him to keep his waist trim and looks forward to kissing that.... By November 3rd she

> ...just can't wait darling—to see you and kiss you————well darling—I love you, love you, love you————

He's to save his strength for she will soon be home, and then—but she can't say, given the sexual restraint that endured throughout the 1940s and 1950s, 'to make love with you.'

Now they write each other as often as three times a day. One day two special delivery letters reach her from him, and three of hers reach him. Her letters turn into descriptions of the shoot in Phoenix, happy references to tanning, and dreams of trips they might take together. Phoenix is now a "bad idea," and she tries to speed up her assignments, make early train reservations, or even find a flight out. On October 31st she sends another special delivery letter.

> Darling, I miss you dreadfully—I do everything with you participating really, because I'm always sharing things with you mentally——I know that the girls are heartily sick of hearing about my David! I'm sure they think we're a couple of fatuous fools—but they're also very jealous——all except Carol—who has her Robert———

They're jealous, she reflects elsewhere, because they are looking for a divinely happy marriage just like hers!

He even loosens up on money, his ultimate unbending, and sends her $500, dwarfing the $200 her friend Carol receives from "her Robert." Yet among these happy gushings she intersperses realistic asides, mentioning here her impatience at catering to his moods, there that they've "profited, I hope, by this unfortunate experience." At another time she reminds him how hard and unsuccessfully she struggled to get him to say 'I love you' to her on a regular basis. On November 1st she writes,

> Well my pet—please take care of yourself—Eat your meals— [she doesn't want him to diet too much] and don't worry and fret darling——because I shall rush home to you as quickly as possible and I'll just stay very close to your side forever after—— Darling miss me and love me as I do you———

She tells him in another letter of Miss Fratkin fainting, the woman responsible for coordinating the shots, then adds,

> Honestly David, you shouldn't have let me go on this trip—you should have known better! Here I am at the mercy of fainting Miss Fratkin!

There's an odd shift in her protestations of love to reassuring and worrying about him: she can't protest her love enough, worry about his weight enough, urge him not to "worry and fret" enough, or express her concern about his draft status warmly enough, an ongoing worry until he receives his commission in the Navy and is safely ensconced at the Treasury. By caving in and begging for sympathy he has shifted the attention from the person he has injured, to himself. It is one of his techniques, one spectacularly on view years later when his mother dies and he debates going to her funeral.

"I don't know if my heart can take the stress," he worries to me at the time, and to Uncle Charles. Days filled with worried phone calls between himself in Los Angeles, where he lived after 1963, to Charles and Abner in Philadelphia, until it is his health that everyone focuses on, not the death of Nanny. Remarkably, he doesn't go, either, an absence that bulked large after the attention he had called to himself. Here, in 1943, he instinctively plays on my mother's release from anxiety to draw her into worrying and coddling him. He has the unending need to be first in the eyes of those closest to him, combined with an undying ability to alienate them.

But now they are again able to dream together, to imagine the same illusions and consider them reality. They can again feel they are actors in the same story. The fear of their lives becoming unhinged, of becoming unhinged themselves, goes with the feeling that their story, made self-conscious, can't bear scrutiny and must lead to unknown, frightening change.

She will be the best of wives now.

He will be the best of husbands.

AN EARTHLY PARADISE

Poseur

I start nursery school in Washington, D.C. during my father's Navy-cum-Treasury service.

Mothie and Mom smile at the woman running the school my first morning, leaving for home as soon as they can after a polite exchange. They expect this experiment to fail and when they come to pick me up are apologetic before the director can say a word

"I hope Lance wasn't too difficult," Mom begins.

"He needs to be with other children," Mothie explains, as though this excuses all failings.

"Even though he doesn't speak the social experience here should help him," my mother hurries on.

"Oh no, Mrs. Levy," the woman replies, "Mrs. Wilds. Lance was no trouble at all. He speaks just fine for his age."

They are dumbfounded. I barely speak at home. Even when past four and back in Great Neck I use grunts and gestures with only an occasional word. I remember one meal there in 1946. I sit at the kitchen table, a plate of food before me, my mother next to me. I won't eat.

"Watch, Lance!"

A red bandanna wrapped around her hair, Mothie kicks a leg high over the pots she bangs together. My mouth opens. I let in a spoonful. I point at Mothie and grunt something inarticulate. Proper, matronly, Prussian-backboned Mothie kicks her other leg and clashes the pot and lid again.

I accept another spoonful.

Tales of Great Neck and Washington, 1942-1949

By Great Neck I mean: 138 Baker Hill Road, Great Neck, Long Island....

Our house was on the corner and included an adjoining empty lot where I was free to run, where the family established our Victory Garden in one corner in the early War years. A tall hedge divided the two lots, so tall that it fell over at one end to form a dark cave perfect for childhood fantasies, games, and hiding.

The house was a roomy two story stuccoed home facing Baker Hill Road with the garage on a side street. Large hydrangea bushes bordered the walls, and several large fir trees broke up the front and side lawns. Outside the kitchen was an old apple tree I was sometimes harnessed to when old enough to wander. Even in drought-prone Los Angeles where I live now I struggle to grow hydrangeas along one side of my home, while at the garden's rear an apple tree struggles to bear fruit: the house too is stuccoed, although Spanish in style. Though the front door faced Baker Hill Road it was rarely used. A side door led into the living room, another from the garage into the kitchen, and a last from the kitchen into the yard.

Downstairs a large kitchen and adjoining dining room took up half the space, with a large, two-story living area the other. A staircase went up the far wall to the second floor landing that ran above the far end of the living room to the bedrooms. There were four of those, and when we moved back from Washington, D.C. I was given the small one closest to the landing where unknown to me Daddy Wilds had died. Linda must have been in my parents' room when she arrived in 1946, with Bud and Mothie each in theirs.

So it was not large in the number of rooms, but each room, except mine, felt spacious. The distance between the dining room across the living room to the stairs up seemed especially large to me after I heard Prokofiev's *Peter and the Wolf*. I was sure a wolf stirred in the dark corner under the stairs as they reached the second floor landing. I imagined I could feel his breath on my heels as I leaped onto the first step after I dashed across that space.

Gar tended the Victory Garden in the adjoining lot before we left for Washington, D.C. in 1944. That is, he was photographed on weekends holding a rake, while during the week Mothie did the gardening. In those first two years I slept in a crib in my parents room where, according to Mothie, I was kept too long. What could they have been thinking as they lay spent after lovemaking, with me only a few feet away? Years later I used a dream about that in a poem.

BECOMING HUMAN

> The dog's tail pounds the crib's bars,
> black and ominous, waking me—
> or the moans do from the nearby bed
> where my parents couple. Slowly
> my eyes move up the wall,
> but where the ceiling should enfold,
> star beyond star pulls me deeply
> into the night. Fear swells,
> and my heart throbs—I gulp the
> breathless vacuum, and thrash—
> then wake, swallowing
> great gulfs of air like milk.
> Slowly night spins down
> and topples over.... I see the terror
> that fills my heart so suddenly, so often,
> is just the memory dreamed here
> of how I learned I was alone
> and became human.
>   That terror lies
> at the root, nutriment and gnawing tooth:
> it is the life I must not wake from, now.[4]

This primal scene made its impact before I was old enough to take things oedipally or verbally, rooting my awareness of self-consciousness in fantasy and dream with the perception of separateness in a not hostile but indifferent universe. Being in that room those years was like the milk I was given when I came home from the hospital: at first too much, then too little.

One day I rocked the crib across the room so it blocked the bedroom door. Apparently I thought this a huge joke. Another time I made my mother gag when she discovered me eating my feces. We have to be taught to hate any part of ourselves: I 'remember' a sweet taste. I have a perverse wish to claim this for memory even though I must have been teased with this story later.

I recall none of the neighborhood children those first two years that later became my friends. Even so I made my mark on the neighborhood, for I stripped and dashed out to the street from the kitchen yard once I could walk if not watched closely. One of the girls in the neighborhood would bring me home to my embarrassed mothers. Soon I was harnessed to the apple tree, though even then I managed to shed my clothes and tried to run free, now as my amused parents filmed me. When older they threatened to show this film to enforce discipline, for I hated the thought of anyone seeing me like that.

My first memories are at the nursery school in Washington, D.C. Once I discovered a chocolate bar in another child's coat and ate it. He saw me and threatened to have his mother call a doctor to cut it out. I was afraid but didn't tell Mom or Mothie afterwards: we start keeping secrets very young from shame and fear. One day I tripped on a flight of stairs, rolling down a step or two. When I realized I was unhurt, I rolled to the bottom pleased to be the center of attention at its foot and to go home early.

Apparently I schooled Mothie and Mom to continue pushing me in a stroller well past necessity. On one such outing in nearby Lafayette Park a woman with a child walking beside her came up to us.

"Poor boy," she murmured, assuming I was crippled.

"Oh no," they assured her, "he walks fine. He's just tired."

I got up and hugged the child.

"Isn't he nice."

Then I bit him.

The woman retreated hastily with her child: I got back in the stroller as my flustered mothers tried to apologize and reproach me simultaneously.

Somewhere in the Washington, D.C. apartment there was a large wicker basket full of my toys that were doled out to me. One evening despite its darkness I went into the room with the basket and pulled it over: the toys were all mine. But these Washington memories are like slides projected with a weak light.

Curiously, I am not afraid of the dark in these memories; sometime later, after our return to Great Neck, that fear emerged and had to be fended off with lights, or a toy that let me project animal images on the dark walls. For our distant ancestors darkness was the safe time, when the great dangers of the day slept and we moved through the dark with great eyes. Did we have to become human to dread the night, to add nightmare to dream? To fear phantoms of our mind, so transparent in the light? Or just grow up enough to have events going on about us that we needed to repress, then fear their emergence at night? We are torn on this. We worship the clear night sky when the Milky Way pours across it extravagantly, while few things please us more than fire, invisible by day, hypnotic—at night.

These remembered fragments are from the lost wholeness of experience that endures somewhere in the mind, part of all those preverbal experiences we can only act out later, like an ingrained sense of the world's capacity to alternate feast and famine. Even that sharp jolt of emotion I felt within a month of birth as Daddy Wilds died before Mom could bring him his pill left a residue. Some of these fragments we recall after we are old enough to attach an evocative image to an inchoate sense.

None of this is a statement of knowledge. Those who presume to know what goes on in an infant's mind from birth through its first two years, as in those complex psychoanalytic theories sprung from Melanie Klein, project their own adult, ingrained attitudes and presumptions on the blank slate an infant provides in his preverbal years. Then they use these ex post facto 'discoveries' to confirm their prejudices. Mind you the blank slate is an adult's baffled perception of infantile life, not an infant's experience. The infant experiences an immediate marvel of passing experience, all literally new, and if not integrated as we think of integration, nonetheless full and vibrant. 'Being' is every bit as satisfying as 'knowing' or 'acting,' and more fundamental than our later more mature sense of cause and effect. We lose this immediacy and fullness, however benign or confused, when we grow up.

I do know in my Washington, D.C. years I was taken to parks by Mothie and my beautiful mother. I know Mothie potty-trained me, bribing me with the candy I have found nearly irresistible since. I even know what my transitional object was in Donald Winnicott's term, the innovative British psychoanalyst who invented that term for the crucial object almost all children become attached to, a Teddy that becomes battered with the years, a pacifier always near to hand, or some other object that symbolizes simultaneously the mother and her absence. For me this was a small, knitted blanket with which I consoled myself for Mom's frequent absences and my father's rejection.

I know too that the constant presence of Mothie acted as a primary reinforcement of the trust and sense of security at the root of play, one of the prime roots of my inner sense of security. Having dual mothers countered the trauma of my father's behavior. That double nurturing also provided the basis for an intensity of private play such that I hardly needed another, and friends have always been, despite close ones I think of as 'family,' unnecessary for the richness of my inner life and imagination.

It's an odd gift, these counterbalanced feelings: to be so secure, to find my own reflection and fantasy so encompassing, the environment so unable to impact these negatively, yet at the same time to be shy and insecure—self-sufficient, and full of hunger for contact I feared I would disappoint. This play of opposites tormented me into adulthood, alternating confidence with abrupt assaults of shyness. They are still there, if controlled and muted.

Beyond these memories and tales was one inexplicable element that has conditioned me from the beginning: an innate perception that life is tragic, that love is all in all but cannot prevail, and that loss is inevitable. Only Daddy Wilds' death in that upstairs room in Great Neck, and the shock that rolled through my mother's system and so mine, a month before I was born, supplies an experience that could have left me with such a sense, certainly not Gar's behavior, so amply compensated for my mothers. In the end, all these unrecoverable, formative preverbal experiences and fundamental perceptions are the personal equivalent of the 'dark matter' still to be explained in the universe that conditions the lives of galaxies and stars and so, ultimately, ourselves.

Memory Awakens, 1946

Once back in Great Neck in 1946 memory moves to surer footing. At almost four we are recognizable individuals and, as evident from my nursery school experiences, becoming players within the greater stories around us. I'm sometimes amazed at how much I can remember so early.

Each spring a neighbor's driveway was lined thickly with tulips....

One spring Alan Glaser, my friend from a few houses up the street, and I picked them all for our mothers. I needed both arms to hold the half I carried home, beaming as I came around the garage path past the cherry tree into the yard with the apple tree facing the kitchen where I found Mom. She was horrified. Mothie was as horrified. After a quick debate they tossed the tulips into the dark cave the great hedge made as it fell over into the empty, adjoining yard. Then they waited.

It was not long before the neighbors showed up, furious. Both Mom and Mothie acted surprised.

"What a dreadful thing! Who could have done that?" they commiserated.

"Well, we just want to make sure it wasn't Lance—"

"Oh no, we've only just gotten in, and he's been with us all morning."

I saw they were not believed. The neighbors left reluctantly. I don't know what Alan's parents said, or if they were even questioned. He was a well-behaved child: I was the one with a reputation thanks to my earlier naked two year old jaunts through the neighborhood.

But Mom and Mothie were suspect, too.

One day they backed out of the garage too fast, shot across the street, and drove in the side of another neighbor's car. They took one look and hurried to the garage Daddy Wilds had used for Bud's mishaps with cars in his youth, and had every sign of impact removed from their car. Later, when the neighbors came by to tell them what had happened and ask if they had seen anything, they acted with similar sympathy.

"What a dreadful thing! Who would have done that? It must have been a workman."

"Did you have any at the house today?"

"Oh no, not us."

One day I was with Georgie, Alan, and one of the neighborhood girls.

Georgie was four. Alan couldn't lift him: I managed to carry him on my shoulders. How strong I was! How manly! How swollen with pride from their admiring looks! Why couldn't my father see me now? Surely he'd applaud, too! I swaggered ahead, staggered, then fell, Georgie scraping his face badly on the sidewalk as he shot forward from my shoulders. Everyone was mad: what did I think I was doing? Didn't I know my own limits? Was I the boy with two mothers who could do what others couldn't, or one in some sense without a father who could do little?

I was told how I used to press my face against the window and watch Gar leave, although that leaving was something my mother participated in too.

For my mother was always going out at night.

One night I blocked my mother and father at the door as they prepared to leave for the evening. I begged them not to go.

"You always go out," I complained, "please don't go tonight!" My pleas and objections were directed only at my mother. I took Gar's leaving for granted. At moments like this I hated him beyond words however at other times I jumped at any opportunity to please him. Even at forty I did things solely to have an experience with him, like take a trip to Philadelphia after 36 years of absence. On another occasion I went with him to Las Vegas for the same reason. I even coauthored a script with him in my thirties, one about identical twins, which I stuck out despite how difficult he made the experience. Now, at the door, however, I clung to my mother as Gar grew impatient. It must have been late autumn, for he wore an overcoat over his suit, my mother a similar coat over her gown.

"I don't want you to go. Please don't go!" I repeated over and over. I started to cry. Mothie tried to pull me away.

"Don't be silly darling, I'll be back later," she smiled. I could feel her warmth through her gown, smell her perfume.

"You're always going," I blubbered, holding tighter.

"Don't be so unreasonable darling," my mother said, "stay with Mothie. We'll be home later."

"Lucille," my father said in the background, "really, we have to go. Let your mother go, Lance." It was his firm, slightly exasperated tone, with its indefinable threat against anyone presuming to inconvenience him, the voice that believed childish blandishments should be resisted, that used "compel" and "should be compelled" routinely in his journals with respect to me. A child should not be encouraged to be a child but a little adult, perfectly dressed, perfectly behaved, such as he must have felt were his best moments with Nanny.

But now I was beyond reason, clutching my mother, sobbing as Mothie half pulled half pried me loose. I flailed hysterically. They went out the door.

I cried for a long time, slowly giving way to shudders, sniffles, finally to silence.

That night I didn't need to project images on the walls to see them. A fox's slyly menacing head lifted above the radiator.... A bear lumbered across the ceiling, as though in his own dim bubble of light....

The truth is Mom continued the "café life," as my father called it, stemming from her days of freedom as the models' Miss America and the Dream Girl whose life was a continual celebration, now on his arm. Their beauty I took for granted: that was how parents should look because, of course, it is how mine looked. I found its absence in other families a puzzle until I was older and more tempered by 'reality.' So 1946 begins years of paradox: an expanding, secure sense of self, and an endangered one touched by a sense of the tragic; of a house full of people, yet one pervaded for me with loneliness and abandonment.

Apples and Irises

The autumn after our return to Great Neck in 1946 I set off up Baker Hill Road with a composed, proper, formidable Mothie. I walk as if wearing a costume, like when I walked up the block to show off a new cowboy outfit I got for my birthday that summer to my friend Alan, afraid a sudden movement would make the Stetson, vest, cowboy shirt, gun belt and holstered gun, chaps, pants and boots all fall off.

Mothie carries a large sack and a long pole. I know what is coming, appalled. Uphill to the left is a large apple orchard behind a low stone wall. The trees are close to the wall, full of apples, though not close enough to pick by hand. Mothie stops, looks both ways, and when she sees no one knocks choice apples from their branches with her pole. I watch them give the ground a hundred red eyes. She hands me the bag when she is satisfied.

"Climb over now Lance and get the apples."

I clamber over and rush stiffly from apple to apple, stuffing them in the bag, although some slip from my cold, awkward hands.

"That's enough. Give me the bag."

I can barely lift it over the wall.

"Hurry up!"

I feel eyes pressing against the back of my head. I am in a story now, the wall between the real and imaginary erased. I am Peter Rabbit discovered stealing carrots by an angry farmer with a rake in hand. I scrape my hands and bruise a shin clambering hastily to safety.

Mothie walks home looking neither left nor the right, sack of apples in one hand, pole in the other, heels clacking on the sidewalk.

She makes a superb apple pie. No one ever matches her apple pies. No one will ever have such forbidden fruit on hand. No one so proper will ever show such magisterial disdain for propriety.

Years later when we live in the country in Connecticut my mother drives a station wagon with two shovels, bags, and some old cloths in the back. She and Mothie are besotted with Tiger Lilies. They stop the car whenever they pass a clump growing wild, although 'wild' sometimes means a clump of lilies at the end of a well-tended row in front of someone's house. Quickly they scan the road, woods or yard for signs of life. Certain all is clear they get out, the car left running, open the trunk, grab the shovels and swiftly dig up the desired lilies, slip them into a bag or wrap them in a cloth, stash them in the cargo space with the shovels, slam into their seats, and gun away, sending a spray of dirt behind. I have to help their larcenies until older, rebellious, I refuse, certain they will be caught, embarrassed, fined, even arrested.

They are never caught.

They never steal.

What they want is always, somehow, already theirs.

Second Flight

What I Remember

When we returned to Great Neck in 1946 from Washington, D.C. I still talked at home as little as possible, rare words sufficient to set Mothie dancing or Mom in motion to satisfy some desire, notwithstanding my outburst at the door that night. I began to know others: Alan, Georgie, the girls of the neighborhood, Joan, Carole, Mary Jane, Barbara who praised me as a big boy when I stopped taking enforced naps, and Beth Bell whose name still rings in memory. My mother's brother Lenny, Unk to me, Bud to others, came home a hero from his military service. He barred my night solace with Mothie, as Gar had already with Mom, but was otherwise amused by me, and sometimes as 1946 passed and summer 1947 arrived took me with him to the beach with whatever girl he dated. That was the price Mom exacted for his borrowing a car, but he did it with such good grace I longed for repeat experiences.

Once in kindergarten in 1947 my experience widened in fits and starts. I remember playing a game in which we divided into flocks of birds who had to run from one side of the yard to the other. Suddenly I felt such pain in my legs I had to sit down and watch everyone else, acutely conscious of not being one of the 'flocks,' instead experiencing my 'self' as someone unique and apart, just as in the dream recaptured in the poem "Becoming Human." That year in a park neighboring the school groups of young boys gathered around charismatic figures to form 'gangs.' To my great surprise I was asked to form one. I failed dismally to know what to do as they gathered around me. One by one the boys trickled off to other gangs until I was alone again.

I recall cross-dressing as a girl one day after my sister Linda's arrival in November, 1946, and off and on for some years after that, to Bud's dismay. Gar however wrote what a pretty a girl I would have made. He didn't realize I had come to the conclusion at four that what my father paid attention to was women.

But cross-dressing in those years immediately following 1946 wasn't my only confusion: I must have experimented with alternate identities, the present one having proven to be so ineffective to get my father's attention. At one point I decided I was a dog. Our black cocker spaniel, Smokey, was doted on without question. For a number of years I took a fancy to dog biscuits.

What I Forgot

Yet the key to understanding those years was in what I chose to forget. For example, I have no memory of Mom's pregnancy or of Linda's arrival in November, 1946.

Years later my mother told me Gar did not want another child, and four years went by before she became pregnant with Linda. At one point she took sugar pills to please him, which he thought were some kind of birth control measure, though of what kind I can't imagine twenty years in advance of the pill. I must have been talked to as my mother's pregnancy developed. She must have disappeared into the hospital. Perhaps I visited, and even saw Linda through a glass wall in her newborn nursery, but not until 1950 do I remember anything of my sister, with one exception.

I made a clay snake and wound it around the umbrella pole one warm day in the spring of 1947 next to Linda in a baby seat on the garden table. I recall the snake, and how plump Linda was.

Crucially, I don't remember how in the fall of 1947 my parents' marriage exploded. I have no actual memory of how in early 1948 Mom again took flight with a modeling job, this time for six weeks in Scottsdale, Arizona. Now I know Mom grew suspicious of my father's frequent late work at night. She couldn't always be at his side in his whirlwind of engagements, despite my feeling that she was. Added to her growing suspicion was the revelation of his parents' opinion of herself and Mothie in Nanny's letter of Christmas 1946.

Both Mom and Mothie grew so suspicious of Gar's social whirl and late homecomings that they hired a private detective.

He shadowed my father who proved to be both a business and womanizing whirlwind. He also experimented with homosexuality. My mother reviewed the dossier with its incriminating details and photos. It takes no imagination to guess her and Mothie's shock.

My mother confronted Gar.

The house must have resonated with angry, rising voices as happened so often afterwards as Gar denied her charges adamantly although she had him chapter and verse. He pulled one surprise out of his hat in self-defense, however, and revealed he was seeing a psychiatrist by the name of Carl Binger. When I repeated that name many years later to an analyst friend of mine, it rang a bell—he thought there had been such an analyst in New York at that time, which went through a brief fad of 'spouse blaming' in popular therapy. I was bemused, as I always was, when some detail of the family romance turned out to be factual. Carl Binger was actually a respected psychiatrist of the day who taught at a number of medical schools, including Harvard's, where he continued as a consultant after his teaching days.

Even more extraordinary, Gar arranged for my mother to see Dr. Binger. Years later he did a similar thing with me when he insisted I come with him to an appointment with a psychiatrist he was seeing in Beverly Hills, Dr. Nathan Rickles, both of them in their 80s.

Dr. Binger chose to level with my mother. He was revelatory.

Yes, my father was serially unfaithful.

Yes, he had experimented once with homosexuality.

Worse, he added, Gar would never grow up: his personality was arrested at twelve.

Consequently, he split himself into separate selves and ignored their contradictory natures.

The best thing for her to do, Dr. Binger told my mother, was to divorce my father.

"He must have seen what an innocent I was," my mother said years later, trying to explain his extraordinary breach of doctor-patient confidentiality as she related all this. "Really Mothie and I were innocents. We had never come across anything in our experience like David. I didn't know what to make of it all."

My mother exuded freshness and innocence even at her most sophisticated, and it was not just an assumed air. However free or daring she may have seemed as the most famous model in the country, that was only her image. Her reality was anchored in her home in Great Neck with Daddy Wilds at the door.

So Binger must have judged. My mother left the good doctor's office in a state of shock. At home Mothie refused to believe he had said these things. She had Mom call him again, with Mothie and the detective on an extension. It takes no imagination either to reconstruct that call.

"Hello Dr. Binger. Thanks for taking my call."

"That's quite alright, Mrs. Levy."

"I came home in such a state—I can hardly remember what you said. You did tell me David had been unfaithful, didn't you?"

"I am afraid so. Serially."

"Oh dear.... And—excuse me, I can still hardly believe it all—that he had experimented with homosexuality."

"There was one episode."

"Do you really think his development is arrested at twelve years?"

"Yes, I'm afraid so. He is locked into his relationship with his twin and his mother, with an early adolescent need he will never get past to prove himself in some way that will never actually be sufficient for his mother, or, in fact, allow him to surpass his twin by becoming the firstborn."

"Never is very harsh, Dr. Binger."

"Yes. Unfortunately your husband's resistances are too great to overcome barring commitment to an extended analysis on his part, which he is not prepared to undertake."

"I see.... There really does seem to be little left but to divorce him."

"I'm very sorry to agree with you, but that is my opinion for your own sake and the children's."

It would have been impossible not to hear her explosion that night when Gar came home. He still denied everything. Mom believed nothing. Shortly after Christmas she left for Scottsdale. Mothie took care of me and Linda.

We have her first flight in 1943 and her correspondence to alert us to her deep distress and devastation which could only be worse, now.

Added to her despair must have been a profound sense of insult and depreciation from his promiscuities as well as his usual unrelenting drumbeat of criticism undermining her sense of worth, attractiveness and desirability. She would have been emotionally exhausted, as in 1943, and in a deeper sense of doubt about herself and him individually and of themselves as a going concern this second time around. All of her mythicizing, shared dreams, and hope appeared to have collapsed. Love would have appeared futile, happiness a delusion and mirage, her attempt to create the perfect family a perfect failure.

Bitter reproaches must have flown back and forth, my mother's reproaches beating against my father's denials and attempts to justify himself, the phone lines humming, multiple letters crossing one another, often daily, as during her first flight, but for twice as long. Her stature as a supermodel was still sufficient in 1947 to land a quick job, her beauty still a desirable commodity despite all his depreciation. She still didn't need him, materially.

And just as in 1943, when the depth of her anger, so much deeper this time after these betrayals, broke through his denials, the moment came when Gar realized he was about to lose everything he in fact wanted. An abyss opened under his feet as a moment of terrible self-perception grounded in reality instead of fantasy swept over him, leading once more to an abject surrender, begging and repeated apologies meant to close that void.

He said all the things such men say: I won't do it again, I'll be a changed man, I've learned my lesson, I'm a fool, give me another chance and, in his case, repeatedly, "My mother is at the root of it all, what can I do? She's my mother." He would have said again and again words to the effect that their dream of family life wasn't a myth but a reality they could attain. At some point in Scottsdale as he capitulated and begged for yet another chance relief again flooded my mother, if more subdued now, with no effort made on her part to come home early. A far more hard-headed evaluation was underway, as Gar was to discover. Towards the end the moment must have come when he tried to intimate it was now her blocking reconciliation, and he would have tried to find some way to make his own sense of well-being or health a matter of focus, as he had in 1943.

This was his lifelong pattern, naked in 1943, and as true in 1947 and in their later explosions, that showed up even when his own mother died. Revealing just how devastated he was is the complete collapse of his diary entries and almost complete absence of scrapbook entries. For unlike 1943 nothing survives from 1947: no letters, no notes on conversations, nothing: all went unrecorded and/or were obliterated. The man noted for decades of tracking his least expense to the penny tracked nothing.

Behind the scenes Mothie inevitably played her by now predictable role—at first freeing Mom to leave, excoriating my father's faults before she left, but once Gar abjectly backpedaled, constantly reminding my mother of the difficulties of being a divorcee with two young children, and now, of getting older. My mother was 32.

"After all," I heard Mothie say on another occasion, "he doesn't smoke or swear, Lucille."

Mothie expected very little from a man.

And, of course, in the 1940s divorce was an admission that what had been lived, dreamed, and presented as real to others was in fact a fantasy, a lie, and would involve humiliating public disclosures of private matters. In the end, as with her first flight, Mom found these arguments persuasive.

During this same period Gar wrote to Dr. Binger, lacerating him for betraying his confidence, and making him guilty for the trouble he now was having with his marriage! But he didn't deny the substance of Binger's revelations to my mother. 23 years later Dr. Binger wrote the 25th "What I Have Learned" essay for *The Saturday Review*. In that he advises, "Make a decision, if you can, even if you have to settle for third choice." Gar saw the article and wrote an angry To The Editor letter, ending:

> I agree with Binger's comments about courage and compassion, and his expressed wish, "I hope that I may yet acquire something of them." Since he is 80 and never showed any sign of these through his first 79 years, this again is another example of his immoderate and synthetic modesty.[5]

The experience still rankled, and his need to blame Binger instead of himself for his difficulties with my mother.

As she returned from Scottsdale Mom was courted by one of the Astors, which she let on to Mothie—who quickly told Gar. Mothie recalled many years later how that touched off a storm of letters, telegrams, and flowers that met my mother at every stop. Terrified, Gar got on a train and met her in Chicago, and escorted her home as ardently and romantically as he could, interposing himself between her and anyone else.

The Long Return

Reconstructing their emotions this way seems, on the face of it, the least difficult part of revealing these 'lost' years. Reconstructing the chronology of events is less difficult than might be thought so long afterwards, too.

I know the first confrontations started in November 1947—that is when my father's journal breaks off after four steady years, not to resume until 1951. His scrapbooks contain only a few mementos kept from the earlier part of the Presidential campaign of 1948, although that was when he played a major role in pioneering the Republican convention on new-fangled television. The baby book my mother kept stops with my fifth birthday August 25, 1947.

My father never mentioned any of these events. He did promise to catch Linda and myself up with the last four years' events when he resumed his journals in 1951, but wrote only of current events. In 1951 we now lived in New York in an apartment on East 86th Street, across from the park containing the mayor's mansion. We now had a beach house in Westhampton, Long Island. He doesn't explain how these changes happened, but only mentions the speculation surrounding a possible run by Eisenhower for the Presidency. He doesn't think a military man should hold the position, although when the time comes he will be a strong Eisenhower supporter.

He dwells lovingly and sentimentally on myself and Linda, although I should be "compelled" to continue piano lessons. He is delighted at how happily Linda and I play together in the room we share. When I recount this to Linda, she laughs.

"I don't recall our ever playing together happily." Neither do I. Our childhood relationship was marked by unrelenting rivalry.

He recounts our putting on a show with music and drawings, and of how "I was moved to tears." For a time after reading this I wonder if I am mad, if all my memories of childhood with him are false—how could he write all this loving regard and none of it be true? It is on a par with writing how his parents reacted when they heard of my birth and came to see me: "They were delighted" instead of: 'they were appalled.'

I share this too with Linda, and she shakes her head.

"I can't imagine his ever behaving like that."

It's the ideal world he wished to exist, the ideal father he wished he was, experience revised on the go into its opposite then believed was true. Once, in my thirties, he struck me dumb as we were driving together by asking what kind of father I thought he had been. He wasn't fazed by my expression.

"I think I was a perfect father," he said, with a smile. I searched his face. He was serious.

I, and Linda, lived in an atmosphere of stark untruthfulness.

To grow up this way with a reality constantly altered from what I knew to be true was crazy making.

That both the Levy and the Wilds dream machines could yet be set spinning again for over another twenty years speaks to the toughness and necessity of the stories we imagine we are living. This is how we see our lives: to give up one's story or myth is to give up one's life to that moment. How many of us can do that?

Now, too, the loss of Daddy Wilds fed a deepening sense of his potency in my mother and Bud: mere mortality had stopped him from fixing their lives! Just by existing in our minds this way Daddy Wilds became a shield against all efforts to derail my (as it developed) and my mother's versions of reality. Death was at fault, not them; Gar was at fault. Daddy Wilds was a figure my father could not belittle, try as he might.

One revealing, shared written record alone exists from these troubled years. From 1941 until the end of his life my mother and father exchanged the same Christmas card. Sometimes years might pass without new entries, but altogether its entries stretch over thirty years, if one-sided. In 1947 my father wrote, "It was tough but we made it—," which indicates their full explosion didn't come until 1948 when my mother left him for her Scottsdale assignment. But 1948's is a fuller statement.

> Dear,
> The sentiment holds for '48 as it did for '41 when I first gave you this card. Marriage has its trials—but reason and love should triumph. I love you—I always have and always will. But my love cannot overcome insurmountable obstacles that place an artificial barrier between us—one that we eliminated in '41. Reason it out with me. You've always been first—have I?

Predictably, now she is at fault for prolonging difficulties, revealing that after her return in 1948 a great deal of coolness continued, unlike the relieved, almost manic young wife from five years earlier. Nor does he refer to her first flight in 1943, but only to his 'less' controversial campaign to marry her! Now, in 1948, she clearly had made a cooler calculation with abiding reservations of emotion and thought he continued to feel as an "artificial barrier" to their full reconciliation and resumption of mutual dreaming. That lasted, as we saw, until 1951 when he was at last able to resume his fantastic journals.

My mother did not reply in 1948 on their Christmas Card. She was in fact silent until she wrote in 1971,

> —And so it continues, and for the first time in many years I am able to send this card to you in liking, friendship, and deep devotion.

She had at last just divorced him.

It was as if she had heard Dr. Binger in 1947 advise her to make a decision even if it meant choosing a 'third' way. She had not divorced nor merely reconciled, but proceeded to upend our lives as we had known them. New homes, new locations, and as would become apparent over time in New York, new goals.

I was five at these events' start, seven at their end in 1949 when we moved to New York, eight before any full memory returns. Hereafter our lives set into a pattern of steadily increasing periods of tension over misbehavior by my father until my mother exploded, followed by that backpedaling on Gar's part full of avowals of devotion and abject apologies, especially where his mother was concerned if she was involved (which was usual), until each storm was past. Then the buildup resumed after a few halcyon weeks until the next explosion and retreat, but all now within the new conditions created by Mothie and my mother.

My father did not learn from my mother's two flights to moderate his behavior. On the ensuing occasions down the years of climactic blowups, only accidents of external circumstances led my mother to endure further reconciliations. Tension was always in the air.

It was during these events in Great Neck someone thought it a good idea to play Prokofiev's *Peter & The Wolf.*

Everywhere I turned in those years that wolf was waiting.

Our upheavals and the cold aftermath consumed four years. I must have thought the story about the sky falling had come true. There it lay in pieces all about me. After it was patched together there was a great difference: now I knew there was a villain in the family romance, my yearned for, rejecting but now increasingly rejected father. I also knew despite all my parents said that our lives were untrue under the resumed surface. They were wish fulfillments, not facts. My mother and father's desire for the perfect family of their dreams to be true, and, improbably, their continued love, however damaged and despite all the 'reasons' against it, obscured the 'untruth' of our shared reality even as the division between fantasy and reality steadily deepened, growing ever more explosive.

Two direct results that were not subjected to my forgetting were, first, an increased sense of my 'self as separation,' and, second, a deepening of my underlying sense of the tragic. At that age no one would have thought to attribute such a sense to me; instead, I seemed a child with an unusually serious edge. A reinforced sense something can happen out of the blue that cannot be understood or integrated and is profoundly unhappy became an integral part of myself. If this reconstruction implies my forgotten memories finally rose to the light for reconciliation, then nothing could be further from the truth.

I began this narration when I was 60 but only now at 79 understand that my obliteration of these years made it possible to avoid the deadly pull of the black hole in my life created by their destruction of *my* world. Who, I wondered, would be where, when, or even present again? What would happen to me? A child feels with a primal urgency any void opening underfoot.

The majesty of my forgetting left me with the ability not just to survive, but despite these events to say:

I had a happy childhood.

THE WOLF

1

A wolf lived beneath the stairs:
when I ran across the living room
his breath singed my legs before
I leaped to the safety of the steps.
I was four, the year they told me
I had one mother, not two:
the year my sister was born and
bemedalled Uncle came home
and barred me from his mother's room
as father had already from mine.
I listened to Prokofiev's story
about the boy who cried wolf too often,
and thought, alone at night
despite those softnesses just down
the hall that teased my mind,
he has nothing on me
with my own wolf at my heels....

2

An early TV stood before his lair,
screening him with images.
I remember one, a white horse
at war's end, legs splayed
topsy-turvy in tattered snow,
staring back in fear like me

whenever I crossed that room....
The house felt frozen yet feral,
springing again and again
from some deep trance
as Mother, Father, Grandmother, Uncle
smiled and smiled and smiled
over girlfriends, infidelities, rivalries.
Snowy images lingered on those early TVs
from *Father Knows Best*, or *I Remember
    Mama*,
and all the other waking lies we echoed
as though the black true beast was not
the dark screen our family idyll
    glimmered on.
*That was the war to me, not the
wide, slaughtered starving world.*

3

Grandmother sold that house
to stop our warring masteries.
I thought then to cross rooms wide as years
    without pursuit:
that such hunger I felt, desire
turning on itself, anger
the world could never match a boy's dream
were just my childhood lot. But now
I am in the middle wood, winding
    in the trees,
hurrying through the clearings, I know
the rage desire and anger feed and form
    is not put by—
*for the wolf runs in the heart:
there is nowhere to hide.*[6]

The Earthly Paradise

How can I write "I had a happy childhood" after these events, or call this chapter "An Earthly Paradise?" In what sense could that be true?

It is true in large part because I turned outward and away from this troubled family realm into a greater world.

My parents' arguments disappeared in the astonishing light slanting through a tree, or making a flower's petals translucent. How amazing the dew seemed to me in the way a lawn or bush could turn into a brilliant universe in the early light able to match the star littered night sky. How riveting to watch the light become imbued with yellow and gray and a strange luminosity seen only as good weather gave way to storm. And storm! How clouds piled white range on range in the summer sky as the air stilled and the heat leaned on my shoulders—

and the leaves' undersides turned white—

and distant flashes lit the sky—

followed by a faint thunder, like a woodpile falling over in a neighbor's yard—

then the sound of silk being torn and finally—

the whoosh of wind through our trees and hedges with the abrupt hard slap and deep rumble of thunder overhead as lightning tore through the yard and rain slathered against the windows....

How marvelous in autumn to watch low-lying clouds scud under a gray cover, eager to coalesce and bring a rain whipped horizontally by a cold wind, the trees bending, the hedge nearly toppling to that invisible force.

Or snow....

What did it matter how impure the world within the house was and how much traumatic experience needed to be forgotten there so I could maintain my necessary illusions of family and safety when outside snow drew a blanket of perfection over everything? What an eerie thickening in the air before snowfall, the first flakes coming down as if released reluctantly, the wind growing until driving snow with a dry rattle against my window. In other snowfalls the snowflakes magically materialized and thickened in the still air until the night turned darkly white, snow mounting on leaf and limb, windowsill and ground. Going to sleep on such nights was special for I knew I would wake in a transformed, purified world.

There are moments in Beethoven's *Pastoral Symphony* that evoke such experiences, the build, the tension, the flowing release, the real storm behind the romantic storm leaping into memory.

One winter after a heavy snowfall a day dawned bright and warm enough to melt the topmost layer of snow that froze with nightfall. The next day I laid on the snow's surface without breaking through, moved my arms up and down, then carefully moved away. The outline left behind was that of an angel.

Another storm closed Baker Hill Road…. Even plowed it was snow-covered, with a chest high ridge of snow down its middle. For hours I dragged my sled uphill, then sped down in a joyous rush, the wind searing my cheeks. I couldn't bear to go in when gray seeped into the sky and the cold honed its edge.

Robinson Jeffers writes of how as an adult he managed his conflicts by imagining characters in his epics to embody them, set against the natural grandeur of Big Sur. William Wordsworth went back to childhood itself and saw how nature, even to a four year old, could be a separate, better universe than the "fretful" adult world. In the two-part *Prelude* he writes,

> …For this didst thou,
> O Derwent, traveling over the green plains
> Near my 'sweet birthplace', didst thou, beauteous stream,
> Make ceaseless music through the night and day,
> Which with its steady cadence tempering
> Our human waywardness, composed my thoughts
> To more than infant softness, giving me
> Among the fretful dwelling of mankind
> A knowledge, a dim earnest, of the calm
> Which Nature breathes among the fields and groves?[7]

It is the narrowness of our social life Jeffers decried: it is the fullness of nature, a natural field for the release of childhood wonder and freedom, Wordsworth celebrated, and lamented his growing loss of down the years.

Let me tell you how mysterious it was to see the first sharp, green tips of bulbs pierce the spring earth as I knelt on the cold ground. In what dark, through what privation, did such life endure? To what did it start to respond to renew itself? One day bare earth, the next a green shoot, as though something from nothing? Questions felt, not verbalized.

Or how convey the sense of fingers cold enough to hurt from scrabbling in that earth, refusing to come in? How could I say how immediate, how present those cold fingers made me feel, or the red tip of my nose, or how my face burned in the kitchen's warmth?

How can I communicate the sensual, heady smell of freshly cut grass in summer, the way its piles, left untended under a hot sun, ferment? Or the smolder of fall leaves through a rainy day, carpeting the ground in a colorful mosaic, or gleaming from some internal fire through the gray and cold air? Or the salt tang in the air by a seashore, the restless rhythm of waves whose song drowned out the cries of children playing? How relate the way light swelled one morning until it passed through everything, even through my fingers held before my eyes?

There was too the mystery of other living things, birds inscrutable in their coming and going, their indifference to our lives, their fear of our nearness. Were we so frightening? Was I, so large, to be frightened of spiders? To recoil from a Black Widow in a woodpile so quickly I fell backward? What was there about a fox and a bear that made them my heraldic animals, the one quick, untrustworthy, sharp, the other shambling, stalwart, manly? I lived in polarities and found natural symbols to express my experience. The natural world from which these came became my world, my solace, my inspiration.

I did not need to name each thing to 'know' it, to catch every butterfly, and mount them—nature wasn't something to number, catalogue or control as for so many adults, but a fullness to be within and experience.

Children's stories sometimes catch the way the world can transform as some child hero finds a new world in the back of a closet, or through a door, or at the end of a rainbow, or where a storm deposits them. A child is never wholly sure what will appear around a corner, or be found if he or she abruptly spins on their heels and looks back. No doubt this was part of my immature attempt to grasp reality, my rationalization and projection of the adult behavior within my home. *But reality also has just such qualities.* This sense of the potential to meet the unexpected at any moment is the perception at the root of a great scientist or artist in any field—that there is more than meets the eye, more than can ever be found, listed, created, experienced or written about; that reality is an unfathomable, inexhaustible storehouse of the marvelous.

Lay on your back one clear night along a shore, listen to the ocean. Take in the Milky Way, feel your acquired knowledge and prejudices shrink against these immensities, and deny what I have said. How could my parents' troubled world compete with this greater, natural one? They never guessed its existence, confined to their narrow adult activities, and so never suspected how it trivialized them in my eyes as it supplied a richness in place of their failings, rejections, and absences.

Nature does not go out, does not turn its back, does not go away. We do those things,

> ...for nature is not jaded—
> there are only cruel or worn out men.[8]

We speak of childhood as a smaller world, its sense of size much reduced to an adult eye—and there is truth to that in a conventional sense. But what I discovered in my turn to nature was an infinitely greater world exists, one I experienced immediately, physically, sensually, viscerally. We lose so much immediacy and wonder as we mature until we arrive at those adults so narrow and prosaic that the heart wilts at the poverty of their emotional and imaginative lives. This first sense of nature's immediate wonder and transformative being is with me still, together with that innate sense of the tragic underlying our smiles that layers and gives maturity to my sense of nature. These intuitive perceptions are at the root of the poet I became.

It is the paradise in which I still walk, if often only after a struggle to push aside adult illusions and choices. Great Neck remains my shorthand expression for this ability to step, even now, however briefly, into the earthly paradise.

This was childhood's great gift to me, and the intensity with which I have held to it the unintended gift of those deceptive, warring, loving presences around me.

Night Solace/Mothers

My father barred me from Mom's solace in their room if wakened by nightmare after our return to Great Neck in 1946. I don't know how far back into our Washington days my father's injunction stretched. Thereafter, however, in Great Neck Mothie provided consolation once I made it down the dark hallway to her room. But when Bud came home from the Army he barred me from her in turn. I doubt if I cried—that would have been normal, but even then I was too impressed by my uncle to cry in his presence.

I was also firmly convinced I had two mothers.

Some time during that first year back in Great Neck after the war I was taken aside and told I did not. Was it Bud who told me as part of his campaign to be the man of the house in Great Neck, determined to set my father and myself straight? Or Gar determined to discipline my fantasies?

Yet Mothie remained Mothie after this enlightenment, and Mom, Mom: my belief in two mothers was rooted in preverbal and continuing experience, inaccessible to reason. I felt too in that part of me always looking for a true father that two mothers were my due in compensation for the loss that search revealed.

That duality shaped the story I felt was mine.

MANHATTAN STORIES

Leaving Great Neck

Bud was scarred by the tumult in my parents' lives as well. After his return from the Army in 1946 my father at my mother's urging helped him find a job with Mark Goodson in the days before Goodson became famous for *What's My Line* and his succeeding run of hit television shows. Mark was no different from my father in behavior, having one set of standards for home, another for what liaisons might come his way as a producer. He became famous later for his use of the casting couch in his office, according to my father. One day during our upheavals my mother asked Bud for help with Mark's wife, Blooma. Blooma was sure Mark also was being unfaithful. Bud knew where Mark kept his 'little black book,' actually a list he kept under the blotter on his desk. Naively he gave that to my mother, believing she would keep it to herself: she passed it on to Blooma.

Far from leaving Mark, as Bud and Mom expected, Blooma reconciled with Mark after the inevitable explosion. But Bud was no longer part of Mark and my father's 'man's world' and a prospective partner with Mark, but instead was unemployed and needed to find his own career path. All this must have generated a secondary set of heated arguments between my parents, for my mother always strongly supported her brother. All signs of this conflict too were consigned to my forgetting of these years.

Simultaneously Bud and my father contested for mastery of the house. Although the home wasn't his, Mom revealed in her earlier letter she and Mothie had encouraged Gar to think of it that way to overcome his reluctance to move in, in 1942. Once in residence my father swiftly asserted a proprietary right, which Bud now challenged. The full tension in the Great Neck house during those years can now be imagined. All were at each other's throats. Mothie put her foot down with Mom's backing and sold the house out from under the warring parties.

Paradoxically, much as Gar had resisted moving to Great Neck in 1942, he now took his comfortable Great Neck lifestyle for granted and didn't want to move. He never wanted to move. His reaction to any initiative that might involve change, let alone cost money, long after that ceased to be a real factor, was "No." But in the late spring of 1949 we moved to an apartment in Manhattan on East 86th Street across from Carl Schurz Park where the mayoral mansion is located, and not far from the hospital where I was born. Mothie got her own apartment two blocks away, although she also had quarters in the rear of our new, spacious accommodations on the seventh floor. Bud found a bachelor pad that Mom and Mothie outfitted ideally for him.

One late spring day in 1949 I sat on the back of a moving truck in Great Neck, swinging my legs, then moved out of the way of men carrying a piece of furniture. Just this memory survives the forgetting I visited on all the traumas of those years: of the packing and arrival of the moving men I remember nothing, nor do I remember moving into our apartment in Manhattan. Only one Great Neck memory remains after our move; a few weeks later I returned for Beth Bell's birthday party. Beth ran down the driveway when I arrived, flung her arms around my neck and kissed me passionately. Even now I see her run towards me in her party dress, feel her arms go around my neck, her soft lips press against mine.

I never saw Beth or any of my Great Neck friends again.

Manhattan

Our new home was 544 East 86th Street where our apartment split the seventh floor with another, running the length of one side of the building. It was a large, comfortable family cocoon sharply divided from the rest of the world. At first I shared a room with Linda down the hallway from my parents' room decorated with charming murals painted by Mom, one of a cowboy on his horse above my bed, a feminine image above Linda's. After a year I moved to the far end of the apartment past the living room, foyer, my father's study, dining room, through the swinging door into the 'back.' To the right was, for Gar, the mysterious, feminine world of the kitchen, to the left a small dinette area, a small bedroom that became Mothie's room more often occupied by her than her own apartment, and then finally my bedroom, long and narrow, with a view to another building across the courtyard far below. It was my haven, a part of the apartment rarely visited by Gar, where we kept Mothie's black cocker spaniel, Smokie.

I had no idea moving meant leaving behind the natural world around me I could walk into so easily in Great Neck. The hydrangeas along the side of the house were in bloom when we left, the tulips and daffodils had come and gone, even those along the neighbor's driveway Alan and I plucked that spring three years earlier. The dogwoods had had their moment, and the cherry and apple trees were at the end of their blooms. There was the superficially ideal family world in the house with its dark undercurrents, and the ideal world just outside the door where promises were kept, fruit followed bloom, and each thing marked and filled its own time in natural rhythms that had become part of my sensibility.

Granted those rhythms were harder to find in 1949 Great Neck as it filled with post-war development like so many other places in America. Its own version of Levittown spread where there had once been farmland, the American dream of home ownership and middle-class family life mushrooming explosively. The lack of variation home to home in all these developments was not from a lack of imagination or simply to keep costs low—something more essential was at work. The sameness of design only confirmed these homes' underlying ideality. They were snapped up eagerly. And why not?

Hadn't my parents' generation paid its dues, suffered, overcome the Depression, transformed the country into a modern, regulated state with essential elements like Social Security, the SEC to keep unrestrained capitalism in hand, unemployment insurance, and a sense that sometimes we must act together through government for the common good, no longer blindly trusting an idolized market or a 19th century idea of limited government? Wasn't this the generation that in the fullness of time, even as its values were being torn apart, would in 1965 create Medicare?

Weren't they also the ones who put an end to fascism in the greatest of all wars—then devised a scheme to contain Communism? Didn't they bring the world the atomic bomb—and atomic energy? Wasn't this enough suffering and achievement to earn any generation the sobriquet "greatest," which later it received? Now this generation was entitled to homes for the middle and working classes, cars, peace, good schools for their children, economic security, and prosperity for all.

So the last hurrah of the American Victorian settled in as a deliberate dreaming imposed on a world whose harshness and danger were denied as strenuously as possible, however we children soon found ourselves drilling against nuclear attack by ducking under our desks. To call that era the '50s' and think of Ike, or Adlai Stevenson showing a hole in his shoe from campaigning, or Marilyn Monroe with her skirt blown into the air in *The Seven Year Itch*, or of the camera panning her perfect, sequined figure in *Bus Stop*, or singing *"Diamonds Are A Girl's Best Friend,"* is to remember a reassuring surface that embodied the national hunger for the perfect, happy life where even sex was given a glossy patina to cover its capacity for rawness, transformation, and subversion.

With this ideality my parents' moods and needs and mythicizing were in perfect accord. The move to Manhattan gave them a second chance to renew their dreams, however they had hurt each other and endangered these before. That urge would resist their conflicts well into the 1960s, echoing the nation in this perfectly as well.

Lending this added piquancy for my mother as the second part of her 'third way' decision was her determination that Linda and my lives should be as normal as possible, despite Gar's self-absorption, negativity, and infidelities. 'First' was our upheaval in living arrangements. For this second part she found an unexpected ally beyond Mothie's support. Gar might have broken off treatment with Carl Binger in 1947, but in Manhattan he found someone else to confide in routinely on a casual basis, his cardiologist, the then eminent Charles Friedberg.

My father never realized how completely he gave himself away when he spoke with what he thought was candor to another he thought sympathetic. He had little ability to see himself as another might except on those rare occasions when Mom turned on him in rage and held up a mirror. So Friedberg took his measure as they discussed sources of stress, discussions that inevitably led into family confidences. Gar tried to turn all his cardiologists into friends and counselors. So it was hardly surprising it was to Friedberg Mom turned for advice as we settled into New York, knowing Gar talked to him. She repeated this conversation to me later when I was in college.

What he said both evoked Dr. Binger, and went beyond him in sympathetic, practical advice.

"Lucille, David is permanently arrested at twelve years old," Friedberg told her as she recounted her marital difficulties, and added in Linda and my growing needs and Gar's inflexibility.

"What do you mean?"

"He will always be twelve or thirteen, emotionally, for all his brilliance. You need to understand that and act from that knowledge."

"You make him sound like my third child! He is so difficult about everything I think necessary for the children he isn't used to."

"Yes, I know. But he is emotionally a preteen in a troubled relationship with a twin, and with an overbearing mother." She knew this only too well.

"What should I do?"

"Do what you think is right and proper and especially, the normal thing to do."

She never repeated this to Gar, but those words from a man my father respected validated what was already her impulse. The result was that if Gar opposed any activity that was normal in her eyes, he would simply be ignored or, given enough time, maneuvered into acquiescence. She was determined we were going to have the ideal life they dreamed however Gar actually dragged his feet over any 'normal' activity.

But how could their marriage go on under such steady duress? Powerful as was the opprobrium against divorce in her circle, powerful as were the ways in which they mutually sustained one another's mythicizing or echoed the greater national, these alone were not enough to compensate for the stresses he continued to inflict or her rebukes and retaliations. Something else held them together. I discovered what that was one day during our first Manhattan year as I looked for my mother in vain. Finally I turned down the L-shaped hallway towards the master bedroom at the front of the apartment next to the living room. My father had just come home from a trip, and as I barged into their room I was stunned to find her on his lap in the armchair by the bed, in tears, sharing a moment of tenderness. On another such search I came into their room just as Mom finished showering. She thought only my father was present and emerged naked from their bathroom, pink, beautiful, smiling, only to see me and reach for a towel.

That was not out of modesty—Mom and I continued to take baths together far too long in New York for her nakedness to be anything but familiar. For equally too long I was taken into the women's dressing rooms at Macy's or Saks Fifth Avenue or Bonwit Teller or Lord & Taylor on Mom and Mothie's shopping expeditions until finally complaints from the other women put an end to this when I was a eleven. No, the towel was to cover an offer I wasn't meant to witness. Love and desire still bound these two despite all their self-inflicted damages. Further complicating this was that Gar, despite his philandering, suffered from the most primitive sexual ideas. He informed me as I turned twelve that I had to remember the sex act involved the mingling of areas used by our bodies to excrete, particularly on the part of women. Sex was dirty, a neat jibing with Mom and Mothie's outlook too.

And so we settled into Manhattan....

Immediately I learned that 'to walk out' meant taking an elevator down seven flights and walking out a long entranceway to a city sidewalk. I was not allowed at first to cross the street to Carl Schurz Park without an adult: this was The City. Once in the park, children had to be guarded. This is so common a feature of urban life we forget how hideous a comment it is on the potential evil of individuals in a city. There was no yard to run to, no tunnel of overgrown bushes for games, no vegetable garden, no children's pool for respite from the heat, no garden sprinkler to run through, no familiar friends up the street I could visit without supervision.

When I was taken to the park many children came from rougher streets, and as I explored our area I discovered how a neighborhood could change in a block. Seven years in Manhattan left me with the permanent ability to walk down some streets without a second thought, and turn from others with an instinct it might be unfashionable to put into words.

I might have felt an actor in a farce in Great Neck as I walked up the street to Alan's in my new cowboy outfit: in Carl Schurz Park I was gulled by strange boys into a Cowboy and Indian game in which I was tied to a tree and my guns stolen. In Great Neck I might sled downhill with my neighborhood friends after a severe winter storm closed the roads, but in Carl Schurz Park it was down a slope beside steps leading up to the East River Esplanade in a crowd of strangers, with Mothie vigilant or Gar reluctantly present. This world of concrete, buildings, strangers, its substitute of office rhythms, café life and artifice in place of natural rhythms, was the ideal setting for the feverish activity of a man on the rise in the fantastic worlds of advertising and television, but deeply alienating to me.

If in 1951 Gar's journal speaks of he and my mother talking over the need to find a house in the country so Linda and I could sink "roots" and build up a stable continuity of friends, this was no more than a token offering coupled with a passing favorable reference to the virtue of our new summer house in Westhampton, Long Island—which in fact he hated. In the same entry he moves on to a more congenial matter, an extended account of the death of Count Carlo Sforza, once a defier of Mussolini and later the Italian foreign minister.

One image sums up my first summer in Manhattan. One day, bored as I had never been in Great Neck, I took the elevator down seven flights and bounced a ball off the side of the apartment until humidity, heat and my sweat drove me in, somber as the elevator carried me to our landing. Mothie looked at me in surprise when I came in, then marched me into the closest bathroom. Black rings circled my neck. She wet a washcloth and started to scrub.

Seven black years stretched ahead of me.

42nd St. Drive

One night we drive downtown to pick up Gar at Y&R. Linda and I see his new office befitting his 1950 promotion to Vice President in the television department. It is a lush combination of wood and leather and fabrics, the walls covered with costly Civil War battle prints. Linda and I are impressed: pleased with our effusive admiration, he finishes his last phone call and we leave.

Driving home the traffic moves at a crawl. Ahead of us Gar notices an attractive woman walking down the street, blonde, elegantly dressed, shapely. Anyone would notice her. I do, at eight.

"I bet she's a beauty," my father guesses as we creep forward just enough to keep her in sight. My mother rises to the bait.

"I don't know why you say that, David. Appearances can deceive."

"Where do you think she got that suit?" he asks the expert.

"Lord & Taylor's, maybe Saks. Definitely not Macy's."

For a moment we draw almost abreast of the woman, then fall back again.

"Do you think she's married?" he asks.

"Certainly, and with two children." I can hear the clash now in the joking, in my mother's too light tone.

"She looks too young," he guesses, "too shapely." He is oblivious to the implication of that to Mom, with Linda and myself sitting in the back who think of her as permanently young and too beautiful to describe. And doesn't she have us? The traffic lightens and we are able to draw ahead and see the woman's plain face. Gar shakes his head.

"She isn't what she seems."

"Oh David," my mother laughs, "she's probably a nice young woman doing the best she can."

The rest of the drive is silent.

Machiavelli on Park Avenue

The Scurrilous Letter

These years were the start of 11 golden years professionally for my father, for the 1950s were the high point of the advertising world's creative responsibility for television content, and he was ideally situated as a Vice President in the television department of the largest and most influential ad agency. The ad agencies proposed and developed shows for radio and TV that they then found sponsors for, or developed in response to specific requests from prospective sponsors, then placed with one of the three dominant channels, CBS, perennial second-rate NBC, and far behind both, ABC. Television journalism was at its height with Edward Murrow, not yet a form of entertainment with staged news, or panel shows whose participants outshout each other to be heard. These years too were the golden age of live TV drama like Paddy Chayefsky's *Marty* broadcast by shows like *The Hallmark Hall of Fame* or *The Alcoa Hour*. Milton Berle ruled comedy, Ed Sullivan the variety show for American families' Sunday evenings, the latter with such influence that a performance on his show by Elvis Presley or Barbara Streisand or near the end, The Beatles, instantly made them acceptable to the large middle-class audience in his thrall. My father throve in shaping this new, soon dominant medium.

In pursuing this career he held an image of himself as one who acted honorably at all times. He saw himself as a noble fellow however tawdry the business world might be. He was conscious too of the television world's shallowness, a perception mostly in abeyance in these years but growing steadily under the surface. There is an episode in the later show *Madmen* where a character in a drunken hallucination is told the only thing he has grown is "bullshit." How else should a man behave in such a medium but with incorruptible personal integrity?

But one day in late 1952 Ginny Meade told my mother my father sent a scurrilous letter to a colleague at Y&R, Dan Seymour, that shocked her husband Ev, my father's boss. No one ever explained just what its details were, but 'scurrilous' is not a word that springs casually to our lips. It means, according to Webster's, not just language that is "abusive," but "vulgar." It seems uncharacteristic of Gar. But even if such accusations accurately described the letter, what was shocking wasn't the attribution of abusive or vulgar behavior in a world full of men exploiting their influence and power, but making that behavior explicit.

Ev remained my father's best friend throughout his life: at the beginning of the 1950s he was also among the handful of powerful men who ran Y&R, the head of Gar's television department, as well as the Virginia epitome of a WASP. Transcending the usual pecking order, Ginny and my mother had become fast friends as well.

"David would never write such a letter," was my mother's first reaction.

"Oh, Lucille, don't be so silly, read this." Ginny handed her the letter. Incredibly, it was clearly his. No one was in doubt about the author, despite Gar's denials and the letter's anonymity.

"He had the worst morals in his business dealings," Mom told me years later. "I couldn't believe how badly he behaved towards others."

Among all that has survived from these years, even unflattering letters from my mother to him, this particular letter has been lost. As she spoke I remembered how often he was surprised by the animus of others towards him, never understanding why he deserved such treatment. I've mentioned how periodically he pulled out his black address book to check birthdays and send a card to someone regardless of the true state of their relationship, as he did once before me with Alan Courtney at NBC. The truth is that despite his overall pattern of success, the Levy dream machine did not run smoothly at Y&R. There his aggressiveness and self-idealization sparked resistance.

Yet if the one thing the ad agencies grew was "bullshit" of one kind or another, that was done by men and women all, to varying degrees, fantasists like my father. Their struggles played out with an air at once down to earth—money was changing hands—and unreal, given the nature of the business. This came to a head for Gar in 1953 when Nat Wolf succeeded Ev as head of television just after this 'scurrilous' letter surfaced.

Ev's departure was unexpected. He was good at program development and supervision, but an innocent with women. One day he kissed his secretary and with a chivalrous resolve hard to credit decided he must do the honorable thing, and marry her. His wife Ginny had none of it. She was the force behind Ev and now yanked him back to Charlottesville and an opening at the University of Virginia. There the temptations were fewer and her job of surveillance easier. He filled his spare time by writing novels.

Gar's timing couldn't have been worse.

A Struggle of Signs and Symbols

Nat Wolf was a friend of the defamed Dan Seymour, and one of the rising wave of Jewish executives relegating the WASP leadership to history. Ev saw what was coming and in early 1953 suggested to my father that he keep a diary of activity at Y&R to track

> the situation that began last Nov when Dan Seymour decided to quit because "Levy doesn't like me." I had advised Ev and Nat at my home that this was a bluff—and merely an effort to embarrass Ev and force him to choose or compel him to take it to SSL. Dan, counting on support from SSL and Nat, was willing to precipitate a crisis. Dave Miller intervened and "persuaded" Dan to stay 'til Jan 1 which he gladly did, thus demonstrating the fact that he didn't want to quit.

My father wrote this on March 9, 1953; the crisis lasted until June 30, 1953, with two entries thereafter spaced a year apart. "SSL," Sig(mund) Larmon, was then President of Y&R. Ev of course had no idea Gar was an indefatigable journal keeper, his own best devotee.

None of my father's reflections touch on causality or why Seymour thought "Levy doesn't like me." It records a power struggle over position and precedence in a vacuum of underlying causes. More startling is the reflection that this kind of office politics does not need a "cause"—all that is needed is a hothouse, competitive environment characteristic of the upper echelons of any large business. Storms are always ready to burst out having as their goal a change in position, i.e., power. One need only feel another's success makes him a threat and a psychic alarm bell sounds: not substance but perception is all.

So, as my father perceives it, Seymour simply has this 'idea' he, Levy, doesn't like him, so in turn Seymour is out to get my father. Nor does my father point out that Nat Wolff turned on him in retaliation for this attack on Seymour. No, instead, Nat without cause decided my father's work was not up to expected standards. The diary continues about efforts to meet with Dan, Nat and Ev together to confront the situation, and the maneuverings that forestalled this. Other colleagues are brought in: Dick, Brad, Rod. Each reveals a different version of what Dan said or thought about my father, with Nat growing irritated that his efforts to adopt an 'above it all' stance fails.

Such a struggle doesn't turn on rational debate. All that matters is the struggle itself however pointed or pointless with, finally, a winner. Ev remained only to smooth the transition for Nat, who was initially deceptive in my father's presence. He knew there were those who supported my father.

> When Ev resigned in Dec, Nat rushed into my office as Ev was telling me and said, "You're going to run the department." Two days later, again in Ev's presence, he repeated this. A bit later he asked me to think about organization.

But once Nat was in charge my father found organization charts were organized without his participation. Accounts he had been assigned were challenged before accepted. Casual look-ins to his office decreased, and then ceased, small signs in this world that betrayed larger realities. Since his performance was under question, although no one had ever challenged it directly, my father promised to keep Nat closely informed of all his activities, to Nat's satisfaction. Little did Nat know this meant a daily, unrelenting stream of long, typed, single-spaced, highly detailed memos.

A typical day for my father began with his discussing an extension of a radio show with Pillsbury, and a spot deal on a current project. After a morning of calls to clients on existing projects, lunch followed with Sam Schiff to discuss *You Are There*. After lunch he discussed another Pillsbury project, *Balance the Budget*, with Simmons, a show Pillsbury couldn't decide on: subsequently, he reviewed *Four Star*. For *Time Magazine* he reviewed a problem in Atlanta with Dan Seymour, concerning yet another show, *Women Are People*. There was a problem with Arthur Godfrey for Lipton Tea: Godfrey was due for an operation, and my father had to advise one of his superiors, Ed Barnes, about who would replace Godfrey during that time. For General Foods he discussed a set of problems with Ted Adams, and for Kent Cigarettes reviewed further talent problems. Simmons, again, wanted a new news program. The day ended with an interminable memo for Nat, with a copy for my father.

Every day one account or another had a show reviewed, talent determined, a new project reviewed and evaluated, a crisis managed, or ongoing program discussed with clients and sponsors to keep them up to date. Each day a similar memo went to Nat Wolff. The clients varied, stars were replaced, Presidents Truman (earlier) or Eisenhower (now) placed in public announcement spots for bond drives he again organized for the Treasury. His stream of minutely recorded hyperactivity never stopped. His memos must soon have grown into an uncomfortably large pile on Nat's desk.

Now Gar began the practice—or I first became acutely aware of it—of coming home late, going immediately into his study and reaching for the phone. As he talked to one colleague or another dinner appeared on a tray set before him on his desk by Mom or Mothie. As he ate he reviewed one momentarily critical TV show or another. Thought and immediate action were inseparable: reflection was an unexamined luxury.

The ritual elements of this contest for power continued to emerge. On March 16th he is tipped off by Brad that Dan will have the #3 office—while my father is specifically denied the #2 office with its organizational implication of being more important than #3. Brad is a friend, and warns Nat on March 17th "to watch out for Dan—he's not to be trusted," but to no effect. On March 24th the teletypes my father received to keep him updated with the latest events went instead to Dan, who now told my father what he must do. When Nat returned from a West Coast visit on March 25th, he gave my father only a "fairish greeting." He paid no attention to a discussion between my father and Dan, and failed to look into my father's office on his way out at the end of the day. A tribesman in Africa surrounded by animistic spirits could not pay more attention to every shift of wind or flight of bird or fall of leaf than does my father to these events.

At a stockholders' meeting my father's floor was referred to as "thieves," and no one spoke up for his contributions—among others, he had just closed a deal for *Favorite Husband*. Astonished, he discovered that Dan Seymour was now a vice president on April 7th. No one discussed this move with him or gave him any warning. He was close to being 'out' if such moves, which normally fuel the gossip machine for weeks or months in advance, dropped from a clear sky to him. In response he made sure Sig Larmon heard of his part in making the deal for *Favorite Husband*. The same day Nat's reorganization chart came out, although "no one saw fit to discuss it with me." He discovered Dan was getting credit for *Favorite Husband*. Shortly thereafter the carpenters were at work fixing up Dan's new office.

By April 13th he discovered meetings were held omitting him, and that he was now accused of sending two, not one, scurrilous notes to Dan Seymour. He denied both self-righteously. If my mother saw the second, it left no impression—I never heard her say: 'I read that one too, and it was his!'

Gar took comfort when Ev characterized one of his opponents as a "trickster" without any "real guts." He did manage to have a rare meeting with Nat on April 14th, concerning some projects for *Life Magazine*. Happy, he heard through Ev that Larmon knew that my father was, in fact, productive. But Larmon might like Dan, who was "elegant and careful of every detail" as opposed to Nat, a man "coarse in speech and detail." Appearance counted, and the god on high in the office atop the corporate pyramid weighed taste with achievement, that WASP sense that 'clothes make the man.' Credits ('properties,' shows sold and/or produced) weren't everything—. My father, always well dressed, upgraded to Italian suits after the trips abroad he took with my mother from the early '50s on. He was as dapper as any Dan could be.

But Dan, sure of himself now, in the words of another "protests too much," that his new office was too big! At least in another office, that of Peter Levathes, my father heard he was praised by higher-ups for his role in a renewal achieved with Goodyear.

Peter Levathes became a lifelong friend, although their rivalry sharpened in the future at Y&R. For now my father was busy with his accounts, including screening *Name That Tune*, which he would get on TV for Harry Salter. Pillsbury weighed *The Orient Express*, and he started to write a presentation for *Healthy, Wealthy and Wise* for Metropolitan; he adjusted those working on Godfrey's Talent Scouts. He discussed a 3D experiment being considered for *Life Magazine* on ABC, and screened a series for Loretta Young. Each day ended with another memo to Nat.

By April 30th this stream of material affected Nat, who "was more chatty today than heretofore." It is impossible not to think of Gar's meteoric rise on *We The People* and relentless activity at the Treasury during the WWII. His many irons in the fire were a virtual 'who's who' of 50s TV, that which was proposed, that which was produced, that which succeeded and ran forever, like *What's My Line*. "I believe I note a friendlier tone," he noted on May 1st, "but I'm not certain." The most bizarre part of this game of shadows was the feverish effort to 'produce,' so that a struggle absent of any meaningful content led to additional shows booked, proposed, stars retained, staff shuffled.

Again a friend told Larmon of my father's part in closing key deals, and, typically, Gar congratulated Nat for his birthday on May 8th. He told Ev to make sure he was not 'uninvited' to a key meeting with Paramount: on May 13th for the first time in months he was included with Dan and Nat at lunch going over more details on the 3D proposal. He had been helping the Eisenhower people amid this at Y&R's behest, and hears Larmon has received a letter from them praising his efforts. A TV drama of his own for Y&R was okayed, and again Larmon was notified. Still, he found out at second hand that he was supposed to handle *Circle Theatre*. But the winds were shifting, and in another meeting Nat praised my father to clients in his presence.

Things were not going as well for Nat and Dan, either. For the first time a Y&R colleague directly criticized them to my father about a deal they had pushed as two "peddlers." Dan, who denied being able to take a vacation to my father, revealed to others he was off for a month to Cape Cod. Brad "also told me that Miller [a superior] was 'aware' of Dan's drive to power and for the first time Brad sensed an indication of a coolness coming." What omens augured this are not revealed.

By June 1st Nat and Dan's position eroded further, with a superior asking my father for the "truth," namely "didn't I think Nat and Dan were disinterested in this account," referring to the Remington account, a major account for Y&R. There was a cooling visible among those at first solidly supportive of Nat and Dan. Commercials designed by Nat were attacked by another Y&R figure for their intrusiveness on *Treasury Men*, Nat's responsibility. Nat shuffled off responsibility for commercials to another figure. Nat was forced to clear involvement with a show proposal for Kent Cigarettes (one of my father's accounts) with Larmon; when, on June 5th, my father gave Nat a set of paperweights, "he is very pleased." On June 11th in an Executive Committee meeting my father urged Larmon that Y&R should produce shows to justify its percentages. That Friday (June 12th) Nat indicated "he knew things were coming to a head—and that he was prepared for it!"

All through this Tony Geohagen, who would succeed Larmon, moved steadily from supporting Nat and Dan towards doubts, so much so Nat by June was surprised Geohagen supported an idea Nat was for, too. A colleague advised Tony on June 16th that Dan was "sneaky," and Y&R needed "organization men," suggesting Dan was out for himself. The winds had so shifted that on June 17th,

> I was floored today when Nat came in to tell me he had wanted to say several things—and proceeded to say I had scored with him—that I was the most valuable man here—that he'd leave others—any other—go before he'd lose me! He said he told this to SSL, to Brock & Bill Howard & would continue to tell it to others! He said that all my values stood out—…that I really had a tough time of it—that I had handled myself very well—and that he meant every word he said! Frankly, I am floored—moved—and once again hopeful.

Colleagues again drop by 'spontaneously' on their way out in the evening.… Meetings no longer go off without him. Accounts are no longer challenged. Ev, still at Y&R was "very cool to Nat" one day as they all headed off for lunch. The journal starts to taper off. Either he or Ev told Tony Geohagen that "the 'climate' had changed," and Tony revealed Nat had been to see him to tell Tony that he, Nat, had been wrong about my father. Tony added he urged Nat to say that to Larmon, "which Nat last week said he'd done."

My father's scurrilous letter(s) were swamped by a tidal wave of memos, successful activity, and clever infighting, helped by Nat's overstepping himself and Seymour proving an unreliable 'organization man.' There was no word from my father to indicate he had atoned, or had anything to atone for, no sense he wounded himself and then with a Herculean burst of activity proved he was too able to let go.

Instead there is a jump to January 24, 1954 to record that his "private thoughts" were requested by another executive before a key meeting with Larmon and Geohagen. The following June my father pushed for the post of Director of Operations, sure now of Geohagen who thought Nat's man was inadequate. In a follow-up meeting Geohagen attacked this executive for betraying his confidences; he needed to be moved 'upstairs' to counsel as a way of easing him out of responsibility. Brad, on June 30, 1954 revealed Nat had hoped he, my father, would resign during the previous year. By now Dan and Nat were trying to "scoop" each other before other executives, and an attempt by Dan to insert himself into the Commercial Department, and an attack on Peter Levathes, both failed. My father carried these tales to Geohagen, who was glad to be informed.

Two last entries finish this diary.... On December 29, 1954 Nat told my father he would be on a new "top" council but told another, Bill Howard, the opposite. Again Nat felt my father would be better outside Y&R, but by now my father's position was so safe Nat's view just seemed "a lack of judgment" concerning "a true Y&R man," one who had proved he was an organization man first. His last entry reports hearsay that Dan "is out to get me"—still—but by now his position was safe with Larmon. There are no further entries.

Aftermath

I might have misjudged these maneuvers or found them impenetrable if not for the experience years later of teaching in the Department of Theatre Arts at UCLA in the early 1970s. As I sat in one faculty meeting after another my eyes were opened. One meeting in particular wore into a second hour with a ferocious debate about which amendment to the amendment to the motion was on the floor, in a faculty hopelessly divided between tenured men with no respect or liking for each other, and those without tenure who dared offend no one. I realized no educational issue was afoot, only a maneuvering for power. It didn't matter that the victory would be trivial in an academic setting: it was the victory that counted, the psychological reinforcement of prevailing, as being seen as 'the man.'

So the concern over organizational charts, or Dan Seymour's office size or his attitude towards it, reveal themselves as just so much froth hiding that underlying struggle, to be 'the man.' No great principle was at stake, only whether one group could victimize another and so gain the victory. Success in managing an account, proposing an idea, closing a deal took on the coloration of this struggle, for business had to be done, paradoxically, as we saw, because each side had to prove itself more able.

Yet these shows that made up 'business' could be without intrinsic merit. That was the steadily lengthening shadow that struck my father. All this power, but, for what? Success here meant being more important than another, at work and in the social world and, finally, of having more money—for cars, luxury apartments, mink coats for wives, private schools for children, Italian suits for work. Y&R was a microcosm of the larger business world, and behind it all lay the forgotten Calvinist belief worldly success was a sure sign of being one of the elect, a view by now built into American business culture, pan-religious and determinative to this day. If you are one of the moneyed, you are blessed: everyone else can feed off the crumbs from your table. Today we call that "trickle-down" economics.

Once we made money making things, but 'planned obsolescence' was a phrase gaining currency in the 1950s, referring to a 'making' designed to fail quickly and need replacement. Style overtook substance throughout the 1950s, an additional falseness that fed the rebelliousness of the 1960s. If Gar felt this loss of value in the shows they worked so hard to create and get on the air, then his was an experience in microcosm of the tremendous social and technological revolution through which we are still living that separates effort from outcome, and reduces any value judgment to one of purely transient and monetary utility. This divorce between an individual and the outcome of his work *and* the sense that his work has some necessary value is profoundly alienating.

As for my father's struggle with Nat, that individual discovered he had bitten off more than he anticipated with my father, who knew too many people in the firm and behind the scenes had a beautiful wife staging successful cocktail parties unnoted in his diary but entertaining and influential for those who counted, a wife moreover who was the friend of the wife of the departing but still powerful Everard Meade. My father, the successful Jew from Philadelphia, might have had trouble fitting into the Charlottesville scene of the 1950s, or the tweed and pipe set in the upper echelons of Y&R, although for years he affected at least a pipe, but not Lucille Levy nee Wilds, the former Dream Girl of the country, the WASP princess personified.

Still the byzantine, selfish maneuvering is hard to take and was so for my father precisely because of his underlying doubt of the value of his work. For the last twenty years of his life I met him routinely for afternoon tea in one or another fancy haunt in Beverly Hills, and he frequently spoke resentfully of the TV work he had devoted so much time to which he knew almost from the start was worth so little. I remember that new office he so proudly showed to Linda and myself, and how proud he was of the great Civil War prints that lined his walls, as though he were a politician or historian and his office was the focus of great issues.

The Good Wife's Guide

Housekeeping Monthly, May 13, 1955

Have dinner ready. Plan ahead, even the night before, to have a delicious meal ready, on time for his return. This is a way of letting him know that you have been thinking about him and are concerned about his needs. Most men are hungry when they come home and the prospect of a good meal (especially his favorite dish) is part of the warm welcome needed.

Prepare yourself. Take 15 minutes to rest so you'll be refreshed when he arrives. Touch up your makeup, put a ribbon in your hair and be fresh-looking. He has just been with a lot of work-weary people!

Be a little gay and a little more interesting for him. His boring day may need a lift and one of your duties is to provide it.

Clear away the clutter. Make one last trip through the main part of the house just before your husband arrives.

Gather schoolbooks, toys, paper etc., and then run a dust cloth over the tables.

Over the cooler months of the year you should prepare and light a fire for him to unwind by. Your husband will feel he has reached a haven of rest and order, and it will give you a lift, too. After all, catering to his comfort will provide you with immense personal satisfaction.

Prepare the children. Take a few minutes to wash the children's hands and faces (if they are small), comb their hair and, if necessary, change their clothes. They are little treasures and he would like to see them playing the part. Minimize *all noise. At the time of his arrival, eliminate all noise of the washer, dryer or vacuum. Try to encourage the children to be quiet.*

Be happy to see him.

Greet him with a warm smile and show sincerity in your desire to please him.

Listen to him. You may have a dozen important things to tell him, but the moment of his arrival is not the time. Let him talk first – remember, his topics of conversation are more important than yours.

Make the evening his. Never complain if he comes home late or goes out to dinner, or other places of entertainment without you. Instead, try to understand his world of strain and pressure and his very real need to be at home and relax.

Your goal: Try to make sure your home is a place of peace, order and tranquility where your husband can renew himself in body and spirit.

Don't greet him with complaints and problems.

Don't complain if he's late home for dinner or even if he stays out all night. Count this as minor compared to what he might have gone through that day.

Make him comfortable. Have him lean back in a comfortable chair or have him lie down in the bedroom. Have a cool or warm drink ready for him.

Arrange his pillow and offer to take off his shoes. Speak in a low, soothing and pleasant voice.

Don't ask him questions about his actions or question his judgment or integrity. Remember, he is the master of the house and as such will always exercise his will with fairness and truthfulness. You have no right to question him.

A good wife always knows her place.[9]

The World According to "The Correct Thing"

As my mother became homebound to a disappointing husband between flights these conventions she had flirted or flouted as a model tightened around her, while Gar's demand she continue to remain a dream girl created an unresolvable tension in their relationship. What baffled Gar was the speed with which this transformation from Dream Girl to the Perfect Mother took place.

Some modeling continued through her relationship with Elinor Ames who ran "The Correct Thing" for decades in *The New York Daily News*, a column embodying the American craving to know how to match improving circumstances with improved manners. This craving to be proper was part of our national self-idealization which was inevitably exploited in these same years by figures like Betty Page, whom Congress investigated for pornography, or by the appearance of *Playboy*, and created the repressed audience for whom Marilyn Monroe was a sexual fantasy to enjoy vicariously.

In this era Edward Murrow was thought heroic—for telling the truth. This belated American Victorian was the force behind the rants and character assassinations of Senator McCarthy even more than our fear of communism. No true American would doubt his country or his government when with victory and the return of prosperity we lived in the best of both. A knee-jerk patriotism accompanied such an attitude, much like that of Queen and Country in Britain in the 19th Century. To maintain this worldview my parents dismissed or denounced the imperfections around them. Children who became adults in the 1960s steeped in this era with its wholesale distortion of reality were only too aware how out of joint with the truth it was. They reacted to that betrayal with the fury of disenchanted innocents. Their upheavals turned figures like Elinor Ames with her *The New York Daily News* columns or Emily Vanderbilt with her books on etiquette into curiosities. Those years too were the end of even the shadow of my mother's former glory.

"The Correct Thing" gives a revealing snapshot cultural history from the late 1930s into the early 1960s. Every week Elinor prepared situations fraught with potential social miscues for these Neo-Victorian Americans with a brief description of a problem and its proper solution, accompanied with a suitable photograph. My mother was hardly in all of these, but she was in the majority; after a time I and Rosemary Ames also appeared in some of these imaginary tableaux.

The implication of "The Correct Thing" was that Americans had no idea how to behave 'politely,' and from the point of view of the countless etiquette books of the time, they didn't. In one late 1930s "The Correct Thing: Manners At Home," the reader is reminded, "Remember, the courtesy you extend to others should be shown to members of your own family!" In "Manners At The Movies," a young woman is advised to stand aside while the man buys tickets. Chauffeurs are to be called "Smith or Jones," another reminds us, while the West Point Manual of Official Courtesy is quoted as a man in uniform helps my mother from a taxi: "A gentleman always alights from a vehicle whenever a woman is getting in or out and assists her by opening the door and proffering the hand." There are no soup lines in this world, no 'Hoover Cities,' no explanation of why the young man is in uniform, a subtle distancing of World War II.

"Since the gentleman in the party must rise and remain standing if a lady stops to speak to any one at their table, the lady should not enter into a lengthy conversation" advises "The Correct Thing: Don't Linger" as my mother stops by a table, interrupting a couple. "Let's Go Swimming!" advises a bathing suit should be in "good taste" and "appropriate" to a woman's figure: men, now they're wearing one pieces, should give some thought to theirs! An appropriately tastefully clad, carefree couple (one my mother) happily cavort in the waves.... A casual meeting while out walking requires, in "Good Morning," a gentleman to bow to anyone to whom his companion bows. Of course, "no real lady or gentleman repeats a story damaging to another's character" "Don't Gossip" advises under an appropriate tableau. There are rules for whether or not a girl should assist a man putting on his coat, whether or not she can go to a bachelor's apartment (yes, with another couple, so each couple can act as chaperone for the other), and under what conditions an engagement ring for Christmas can be bought.

A late 1940s "The Correct Thing: Selfish Youngster" warns a child has to be trained early if you want him to have good manners…. Someone who misspeaks must not be corrected in public: that would be too embarrassing. You should not be too opinionated, or, if a girl, slip your feet out of your shoes in company or, if in a short skirt, cross your legs. "Put It Out" even admonishes a woman to put out a "cigaret" when done, for the "stub is annoying and can prove dangerous." "Borrowed items should always be returned promptly" in "Hint To Borrowers!"—even if you have to return it by messenger. Of course one's maid should not be scolded in "the presence of guests" in "Hint For Employers," as a maid is shown standing demurely before her seated employers. The hostess should leave the tip in "Hostess Leaves The Tip" in a restaurant, while guests should know to leave a luncheon after the dessert is served in "Guest Suggests Leaving." Perhaps the heart of all this is in the advise at the end of "Visit A Bachelor's Apartment?" There the "wise young woman is guided by the conventions in the group in which she moves."

As late as 1963 my mother is shown curled up reading on a couch with her shoes on under a caption, "Protect Furniture:" "when you are in another's home, don't 'curl up' on the sofa." Even in your own home remove your shoes. The guardians of manners have Superman's x-ray vision and see even private misbehavior.

We needed also to be told how to get married. My mother ponders an address book under the heading, "A Friend Gives The Shower" because it isn't "considered good form for the bride's sister or any member of her family to give a shower for her, but her girlfriends…." In 1941 my mother broke an old taboo by wearing a wedding gown while modeling before her marriage, a prescient event given my 'early' delivery, as an article almost ten years later notes that three months later she became Mrs. David Levy. There is an accompanying picture in that article of Linda and myself at Gar's feet, while my mother smiles down adoringly at him from the arm of his chair as he reads to the family. It could have been another "The Correct Thing: The Perfect Family." Brides are told that "Satin" is "always correct," although in the spring "tulle, organza, [or] chiffon" can do. At a home wedding there is no recessional: "After the ceremony is completed, the bride and bridegroom turn around and greet their guests." In "Honeymoon

Start" the bride and groom quietly slip away from their guests, "ready for the best man to signal that the car is waiting for them." The contrast with the reality of my parents' weddings is apparent.

In one 1950s "The Correct Thing: Dress Appropriately" I and Rosemary Ames are photographed.

> School is a preparation for adult life. Blue jeans, unpolished shoes and stained or wrinkled clothes lower the tone of the school day. Pupils who dress carelessly, who give no thought to their appearance when going to school, are forming habits that will be hard to overcome when they later seek jobs. A tailored or sport coat (polo reversible, chinchilla, etc.) is the wise choice for a girl. Boys wear windbreakers, car coats or overcoats. Well brushed hair, polished shoes, general neatness should be "musts" for both of them.[10]

By the end of the '60s we would rewrite this as

> School teaches us lies. We must live free of our parents' conventions. Wear blue jeans, don't polish shoes or press or wash your clothes: burn your bras. Pupils who dress carefully, who give all their thought to their appearance are forming habits that will be hard to overcome when they later must cope with reality. Tailored clothes betray an enemy of truth, a McNamara sending more soldiers to a war he knew at the time was wrong. Well brushed hair, polished shoes, general neatness is a dead giveaway we are dealing with the deceitful and inhuman.

These innocent admonitions and idealized interactions of beautiful, handsome, superbly well-dressed models enacting little dramas of everyday life provide a handle on how the larger dream machine with which Gar's steady falsifications of reality or Mom's desire for the perfect home life accorded.

Yet under what now appears absurd were real lives, real distortions, real guilt over any nonconformity or individualism and the heart's hunger in its dance with the unsustaining realities of the world for a better life.

One day in 1963 Elinor called to speak to my mother. She wasn't in, and Gar answered the phone. Afterwards my mother was puzzled Elinor would not return her phone calls or answer her letters. They had been friends for more than 25 years.

"I don't know what David said to her," she told me later, "but I never heard from her again."

I don't know what passed between Elinor and Gar on the subject. He would, of course, have denied everything with increasing vigor as Mom neared the truth had she confronted him.

Hairdresser

Mom was on good terms with her beautician, a man who saw to it she was always immaculately coiffed. One day he disappeared. No one offered an explanation. A new beautician did well in his place, and Mom kept coming to the salon.

One day she was assigned to another new beautician. She was annoyed because the new woman spoke with an offensive intimacy. Mom finally said so. The woman recoiled.

"Oh, Lucille!" she exclaimed, "Don't you recognize me?"

My mother stared.

"I've had the operation," the woman said proudly. "I'm a woman now, too."

It was her old beautician.

Mom chatted away gaily, but it was one thing to transform herself constantly in various modeling roles, another to confront this. Her transformations after all were all superficial. Or were they? Was there anything under her surface that wasn't as malleable?

Years later when she told me this story after the upheavals in her marriage and the transformative impact of the Sixties and Seventies she was amused. But she never went back to that salon.

Master of the House

Two years passed in Manhattan with the slow erosion of anger over the events of 1947-1948 before Mom and Gar's myths synchronized again. While we shared a room together Linda and I pressed our ears against the wall to our parents' room to listen to their debates and Gar's periodic retreats, that now familiar pattern of our lives. We knew the perfect family they tried in their different ways to assemble around us was an illusion.

Mom pursued a course in interior decoration and received a license to compensate for her declining modeling, but did not then pursue a new career. A working wife as opposed to one of the most glamorous women in the country wasn't seen as a great social benefit by my father as he moved increasingly in a crowd where women ran expensive homes and were not among the 'help' who designed their interiors. Nor did my mother wish to work steadily; being the country's "Dream Girl" was a heavy burden in practice; a daily grind of work would only make things worse. She designed a few friends' apartments only as favors.

So her decorating failed to relieve her growing financial dependence on Gar, although wasn't that dependence on the master of the house her proper place in the mythology of the day? But in practice Gar made that dependence almost uniformly unpleasant. Thus now their arguments shifted from fidelity to finance.

Gar gave my mother what he believed was a generous allowance that eventually reached $600 month in Manhattan, and this in 1950s dollars. But everything came from that allowance: groceries, clothes for Linda and myself, school supplies, the countless miscellaneous expenses of running a home, normal monthly bills, her clothes, entertainment costs, home repairs or the costs of home redecorating of any kind.

Mom learned to avoid daily arguments over money by decorating or painting walls or rooms herself rather than trying to hire someone, by sewing drapes herself instead of purchasing them ready made, by recovering couches and chairs herself rather than purchasing slipcovers or having them done professionally, and by mastering and carrying out a myriad of minor handyman-type chores rather than persuade Gar to pay a professional.

So we sat with caution on the living room couch from fear of an unsewn seam still artfully pinned together waiting to stick the unwary. It was no surprise as drapes swooshed together to see one hem finished, another still pinned. A kitchenette chair grown wobbly was glued together temporarily; a hinge come loose rescrewed or replaced. A screwdriver, pliers or hammer became as common in her hands as tube of lipstick.

Gar complained Mom never finished anything, yet he undertook nothing. He was always impeccably dressed, especially in his hand-tailored Italian suits. His cologne had already sparked my revulsion. It was impossible to imagine him hammer or paint brush in hand. Even posing with a rake in his Victory Garden vanished in the 1950s. He left arranging for someone else to do necessary work to Mom.

So it was not surprising that as the year wore on she sank into debt.

Her dependence and debt were softened by Mothie whose inheritance from Daddy Wilds and sale of her Great Neck home gave a reliable income. She steadily 'loaned' my mother money that could never be repaid, going through her resources until by the mid 1960s she was largely dependent on her daughter for daily expenses. Even this wasn't enough, however.

Inevitably Mom was driven, desperate, to ask for more money. Gar's reaction was always an emphatic "No," with an exasperated shake of his head—followed by a protracted, reluctant giving in on his part after repeated pleading.

Inevitably, bill collectors appeared at the door to demand payment.

In the larger context of the great issues of the day, this is all trivial; in the immediate context of day to day living, this sort of behavior and the monetization of relationships kills love with a million featherweight blows. Eventually Gar's parsimony created two practices: first, at Christmas, my father's primary gift to my mother became enough money to pay off her bills. She could get even, but not ahead. Second, it soon occurred to Gar how much more fun this giving would be if in the form of a treasure hunt. Soon each Christmas was marked by a hunt from hiding place to place, each revealing a $50-100 bill and a clue for the next location. Mom scoured the apartment as if embarked on a childhood Easter egg hunt, our hilarity as we trailed after her obscuring the degrading nature of this behavior.

Christmas became a phenomenon. Our trees touched the ceiling, ornaments and lights and silver strands hung from branches aglow as though in fairyland, waves of presents spilled out on all sides. Each year the display was enlarged and perfected further, and after an awed stare by Linda and myself, all tore into the cornucopia spreading across the room with a frenzy that soon sheeted it with torn, glittering wrappings as we assembled our piles of gifts. This once a year munificence was to make up for all earlier shortcomings. Gar tried to slow down unwrapping to view individual gifts, but that was only a means to whet desire further, which he soon was as much a victim of as the rest of us.

Only when the wreckage was complete did the climactic treasure hunt begin. Once done, we quietly assessed whether anything had been left off our long Christmas lists. There followed a flurry of trying on clothes by the women, while I regarded my new books and latest crop of lead soldiers. Christmas dinner followed later in the day when Bud was present, and perhaps some others. After Bud's marriage he and Jill would both be there, followed by a new round of gift-giving. Mark Goodson and his family lived a few flights up from us, and Jewish backgrounds notwithstanding, Christmas was a fact of life there too, and Toasty and Jill appeared sometime during the day to exchange gifts. The material splendor of the occasion was all that mattered, and showed how successful was the master of the house.

This materiality was behind those endless shopping expeditions undertaken by Mom and Mothie they dragged me to, book in hand, watching phantasmagorias of outfits succeed one another as each woman pursued the perfect fit and look. Mom and Mothie and these women expected to emerge flawless, their image in their husbands' eyes on a par with the images presented in fashion magazines. It was all part of a wife knowing her place. Everyone's reality was another's image.

So Mom became the housewife who kept up appearances par excellence, driven to cut corners to save money until she became the 'help' as well as the hirer. Day might find her power saw in hand as she cut down a table to use in the living room as a coffee table, evening reveal her as the epitome of elegance as hostess to a cocktail party for the power brokers in advertising and television. When I moved into my first college apartment, she built the desk, bookcase and cabinets. Gar was not asked for money, or consulted. Step by step my mother and father became ever more entwined in ever less romantic ways.

For something was wrong. She was in her thirties, beautiful, but no longer a twenty something dream girl. She had migrated into the reality where most of us live, yet the shadow of Gar's own growing consciousness of the worthlessness of much of what he did coincided with Mom's growing disdain for their project. Periodically she put on weight, or increasingly, except for 'occasions,' showed a casualness of dress once unimaginable. At times Gar sniffed the air where she had been, and shook his head.

If love and uncertainty overrode the Great Neck explosion and for a time allowed their slow reconciliation to gather force in Manhattan, Gar's infidelity did not stop, and for a woman like my mother that was unforgivable because who could he prefer to her? In the 1950s this misbehavior was not allowed to influence home life overtly. It was purely a 'workplace' event, part of the sordid world beneath its glitter in which Gar moved with his scurrilous letters and Machiavellian behavior. But she knew and that knowledge joined with her growing financial dependence and both Gar's negativity and the ongoing stress stoked by his unrelenting, daily contact with Nanny as well. His mother always hovered in my father's immediate daily background, always critical, always beyond appeasement.

All this paradoxically strengthened my mother's drive to normalcy. Wherever Gar was lacking she filled in, growing ever larger within the family while he, forbidding as he could be, diminished.

It was now Mom began to punish him with coldness in the marital bed: how better to show her disdain? If Gar wanted satisfaction, it had to come increasingly from the very behavior that undermined his marriage. They were caught in an unforgiving loop.

Inevitably their repetitive cycles of argument with the added weight of household disagreements led to ever greater polarization. What emerged in Great Neck became overt in Manhattan and extreme in Weston later. Friedberg's advice to enforce the normal whatever Gar said became canonical: no doubt he would have been taken aback if he had seen its eventual results. They must have thought at first Linda and I did not see, and if we saw, did not judge, and if we judged, did not understand: later they jockeyed for our support.

Each step Mom took following her cool 1948 reconciliation drove her farther down a road she could not have anticipated. The compromise made one day opens the door to a greater tomorrow. Yet how else are we to get on? Purists are saints, and repellent in all the daily proprieties they ignore. Most of the time what we want seems so simple, love returned for love, work rewarded, a family grown to a sequence of generations grateful to one another. In practice our constant 'little' failures baffle and accumulate, compromises grow, and disappointment grow to a fatal dimension.

Day by day America's Dream Girl became the 1950s Master of the House. She was hostess, and help; beauty queen, and mother; buyer, decorator, designer, and executor. Gar blustered, and folded: Mom governed. These were the normalcies in which Linda and I swam.

The Cat

A Siamese cat appears one day as a pet as part of the campaign to establish normalcy. She is kept in the back of the apartment beyond the dining room door with Mothie, Smokie, and me. But sometimes, being a cat, she gets out and wanders, sometimes when Gar is home, who always angrily demands Mom take it away.

One day it escapes before Gar is home, skitters through the foyer into my father's study, and leaps to the top of his tall, red leather chair, 'The Throne of Pain' Linda and I dub it after years of lectures from Gar seated in it. There the cat sits, watching Mom approach, then slides down the leather back, claws leaving long scratch marks, and runs for cover as she gasps in horror.

Nothing hides the scratches, no matter what she tries.

Gar comes home and hurries into his study. Linda, myself, Mom and Mothie sit poised in the dining room across from the TV on the far wall.

"Lucille!" he shouts. She goes to the study door. "I told you to keep that cat out of here!"

"What are you talking about? She's never allowed in your study."

"Look!" He gestures at the claw marks.

"Oh, David, I'm so sorry," Mom sighs. "I scratched it with my nails when I was cleaning earlier."

Her face is guileless. Does he remember how often he sits on the living room sofa she is never quite done recovering, only to jump up when a pin jabs him? Does he wonder if it's possible for someone to be so clumsy? Does he weigh the consequences of calling out her lie? He makes a choking sound and turns away. So ends the perfection of the one area in the apartment kept for himself.

Only when the cat goes into heat, head to the floor, bottom raised swaying in half circles, yowling with raw sexual hunger, do Mom and Mothie decide it must go.

MIDNIGHT IN MANHATTAN

War Games

When Gar is promoted Vice President of Television at Y&R in 1950 I insist we celebrate when he comes home. To please me Mom prepares a table with a cake and party hats, letting my father know as he walks in how much I want to celebrate this great news. He sits with ill grace, impatient to escape to his study as soon as he can. I am eight, but I never make such an effort again. One night succeeded the next with the ritual of dinner served in his study as he watched some show, while Linda and I ate in the kitchenette. Rarely did we gather around the dining room table. Those occasions became intolerable.

"Don't slouch," he'd tell Mom. Or, to me, "Your nails are dirty." He'd eye Linda, who stiffened. He'd look again at Mom: "Don't chew your nails." He'd grill Linda and myself about our school day, but soon cut off our answers to talk about himself as a model child and scholar, and of how the lessons he'd learned applied to the business world. Then he'd be off on his Y&R activities, talking over our heads to Mom. When he left to answer the phone, we sighed in relief.

Saturdays were no different, the phone in constant use, and usually some social event to occupy he and Mom in the evening. Mothie spent most nights in the bedroom in the rear of our apartment to allow Mom to keep up with my father, now a necessity in both her and Mothie's eyes.

Mothie was the point of stability for Linda and myself, most so when we were ill. Mothie oversaw any treatment while Mom blew in with a cheery kiss, a present, then rushed off with my father. Only if Mothie's homeopathic remedies proved inadequate was a doctor summoned and medication given.

Only on Sundays did Gar's attention turn to us, usually for an obligatory family outing to a museum in the winter, or a drive in warmer weather. It was duty to go, duty to endure, and a relief to be back and shrug off our immaculate Sunday best. These outings were exercises in uplift requiring an ideal performance from Linda and me: 'Look! We are perfect children!'

Nanny's steady stream of letters were now routinely steamed open, read, and resealed. However forewarned, the familiar pattern of tension and criticism from Gar built steadily against Mom's attempt to maintain normalcy. As I grew older I realized Gar was afraid of his mother and reproached by his father, who constantly urged him to think ill of his shiksa wife, WASP children, and facilitating mother-in-law. I saw how faced with Mom's anger he spluttered in self-righteousness, then caved in abjectly until his mother's letters and his daily calls to Philadelphia again took their toll. The tension emanating from Y&R aggravated this pattern.

As Linda and I advanced from bystanders to players in the family drama in those years Mom and Gar actively recruited and seduced us with charm, self-justification, or presents. We were unequivocally on Mom's side, for it was never her with an aura of restrained violence and overt criticism, never her with "no" on her lips as her first response to any request, never her building criticism to an intolerable point. It was clear who was the problem.

Unsurprisingly given this world of argument and tension I developed a fascination with war games.

First I gathered a multihued array of marbles that I marshaled into 'countries' on the expansive floor of the living room, eventually filling its green carpet with warring empires. Hours passed on Saturday mornings or on holidays when I was left alone as I imagined realms where first one then another country fielded armies, struggled, lost, until a great empire was faced by a small, hardy remnant determined on independence that took up arms reluctantly but decisively overcame all odds....

At the same time I received sets of lead soldiers at Christmas and on my birthday, first English Guard types, then, increasingly, Confederate and Union soldiers and cavalry. Cannons firing lead pellets could knock over an erect soldier at two feet: soon there was enough artillery and soldiers for Gar and I to organize competing armies, moving the soldiers according to strict, ritualized rules. A log set led to forts and defensive structures. Now if the time was available on a Sunday afternoon we marshaled our armies, built our positions, and set a battle into motion that lasted hours. Battle was our way of being together.

He notes in his journal that when asked what my notion of an ideal day was, I answered, "To play soldiers and chess with Gar." Another time he notes,

> Lance and I indulged in a battle with his Union and Confederate soldiers and one game of chess. In this latter, you already show signs of talent and it shouldn't be too long before you trounce me.

In battles with lead soldiers we could argue safely whether or not a pellet struck a soldier in a recumbent position, in which case he was dead. Winning and losing in these battles that linked us over the course of nearly seven years was far less important than the channeled emotions, and so different from a battle with Bud. He was all for dashing movement and extemporized play, and ignored the careful rules Gar and I used, making our ritual battle impossible. There was no need to ritualize my relationship with Bud. When we moved from New York I kept the soldiers, though by then Gar and I no longer played. When I went to college and the family moved to Los Angeles I gave everything to Bud. The soldiers and artillery filled a trunk, and were stored in his screen porch. They lingered there a few years, unused, rusting, then disappeared.

Gar taught me to play chess at the same time our battles began. I took to it enthusiastically, and eventually at McBurney, a private school I attended for the Seventh and Eighth grades, I joined their chess team. I never learned the formal gambits and defenses except in a most cursory way, but was a surprisingly creative, opportunistic player able to tie up the best of players in some of our tournaments.

Winning mattered in chess. I wanted to defeat Gar in what he considered an intellectual match. I improved steadily, playing deliberate games with him, and fast, cutthroat games with Bud. I became good enough that on one occasion Bud deliberately set me up with a good friend of his who boasted of his chess skills. He took me on as a favor to Bud. I resented his attitude and insisted on playing without my Queen. Bud was horrified. His friend was more so when I won.

Soon after this I played Uncle Charles on one of his visits to New York. The twins competed in chess as in all else, so I took a vicarious pleasure one night in beating him, taking each piece with a decisive snap. Uncle Charles took it in good kind, although he was sheepish in front of Gar, who was pleased at thirteen I had beaten Charles while he still always defeated me. But one night Gar and I played and steadily, remorselessly, I wore him down and, for the first time, won. I was ecstatic. I dashed out of the study to find Mom and Mothie and Linda and let them know. Gar was angry and embarrassed.

When you came to it, losing in anything to me was unbearable for him.

We never played again.

Kidnapping

One day as I push my bike up E. 86th Street towards Third Avenue instead of Carl Schurz Park a small, older man comes up to me diffidently.

"Are you lost?" he asks.

"No."

"Well, your mother and father are concerned. They sent me to look for you."

I look at his seedy jacket, worn shirt, and smell his breath, the kind that takes a lifetime of drinking, smoking, and despair to achieve.

"You should come with me," he says, kindly, stinking. "My apartment is just in there," he adds, gesturing at a nearby brownstone. "I can call your parents and let them know where you are."

I don't brush off this stranger who makes no effort to restrain me, but instead simply shrug and go with him, tugging my bike up the steps and inside after he opens the door. I'm prepared to lug it upstairs to his apartment. I have crossed a boundary effortlessly.

"Better leave it here. You can get it when your mother or father comes," he says at the first landing.

Silently I lean the bike against a banister, and start up another flight. My mind is filled with a white noise, for I know I am walking into something bad without protest. I pause at the second landing.

"You don't want to make your parents angry," the man breathes in my face. He moves close to me. He caresses my ass.

"No," I say finally. He sighs. He understands. He makes no effort to stop or follow me as I go downstairs, get my bike, and go out to the street. Nothing comes of it when I tell my story at home. He is never seen again.

To inheritance and nurture should be added accident as an equal creator of identity—and, as I felt on the stairway when I stopped, the terrible freedom of choice. For those strange moments with that seedy man all the unrealities surrounding me struck home which made any reality appear plausible, any impossibility, possible, any settled life and character transformable—just like that. The collapse and rebirth of worlds between one breath and the next is no more mysterious than the movement one moment towards evil and the next, away.

An Awkward Boy

A childhood picture of myself with my mother shows her perfectly turned out, smiling; I am equally polished, but grave. How alike that expression is to my father's as a child alone or in the presence of his twin, the expression of the second-best boy, the one who somehow didn't measure up. I was not second best, but did not measure up for Gar, invisible to him for most of the week and then, in Manhattan, at war for those ritualized hours on some Sundays.

Still, I had my 'two mothers.' Besides, didn't I have a different name? Was he really my father? Now, in the 1950s, the mythologies to explain this strangeness became evident to me. It's no surprise I veered between extremes, a leader one moment, an outcast the next; confident, or painfully self-conscious and indecisive.

On rare occasions this tension rose to revolt.

A dance was arranged when I was twelve. My date was Rosemary, Elinor Ames' daughter, a friend. At times we played together, so she was not some strange girl I was being brought to meet the night of the dance. But a wave of insecurity rolled over me in the taxi on the way with my parents, who would be chaperones with the other parents at this precocious event.

"I don't want to go," I declared abruptly. My mother smiled reassuringly.

"It will be fine, darling."

"I don't know how to dance."

"No one there knows any more than you."

"We're almost there," Gar added.

"I don't feel well," I said, resistance growing: "I want to go home."

"Now don't be difficult darling...."

"It's too late for that now," Gar said, "We've already made arrangements with the Ameses, and Rosemary is expecting you."

That moment each word of what was arranged for me or expected of me drove me into rebellion. When the taxi stopped at the entrance I refused to get out.

"I'm not going!" I insisted.

"Now Lance—" began my mother.

"Let me handle this dear," Gar broke in. He took my arm. "This is all arranged, Lance, what will people think? You are going to do this now." He couldn't have chosen worse words.

He pulled me while Mom waited on the curb, but I planted my feet against the door's threshold and held onto a handhold, refusing to budge. Gar shouted in anger and yanked with force: I stuck in place. My nose began to bleed. I was subject for years to bad nosebleeds, not fixed until college when a doctor at last cauterized the guilty veins, so now, added to tears and anger, was a quick flow of blood swiftly staining everything.

"Jesus!" Gar's rare curse.

"Oh, Lance."

I didn't care that others stared from the entrance, including, by now, the Ameses. The evening now represented all the falseness around me and, however absurd in timing and place no threats or blandishments could get me out of that taxi. Defeated, excuses rushed with the Ameses, my parents got back into the taxi and I went home, handkerchief to my nose, head back, wet faced and somber in pyrrhic triumph.

This scene like the memory in Great Neck of my clinging to my mother to prevent her from leaving yet again, with my furious wail,

"You're always going out!"

stays in mind with original force, too.

After Sixth grade it was decided I would not continue in public school, but enroll in McBurney. Didn't I take an IQ test and score exceptionally well? Weren't the next few grades in the local public junior high school too rough and too poor academically and socially? I was soon in the habit of riding one bus up 86th Street across Central Park, then catching another down to McBurney around 63rd Street, then on Central Park West. There were no girls at McBurney, an old-fashioned bastion of boys and men, whose Lower School headmaster, Mr. Bam, regaled us with stories of his isolated youth as a teacher in South Africa.

There each night he had brought out his single bottle of whiskey and promised himself that if he could get through another meal of beans, he could have a drink. Each night he downed the beans—and put the bottle away untouched. We marveled at his stoic self-deception. I liked him, and the other teachers for the most part, including Mr. Giocara who once slammed my head with his math book as I whispered with another. There was a Mr. Ball with whom I first began to express my interest in history, who singled me out for my excellent extra work, and a Mr. Spencer who destroyed mathematics for me with his elderly, spaniel face and impossible drone. The following year a Asian-American of great height inspired all to 'A' level work in math, expounding algebra with a novel, inspiring clarity between hilarious interruptions from his reading Confucius as we worked on a problem. But the next term it was again Mr. Spencer who made math incomprehensible.

I was soon a favorite of the staff. Mr. Bam sent glowing reports home, and one day early on asked me to be a monitor responsible for keeping order on the stairs as we came to and from school, or went on trips. A bad word from me about some classmate's behavior meant a disciplinary note home to a parent. I accepted and was very good at this, and soon heartily disliked. For awhile I didn't care, but others saw the ostracism I earned, and when I offered to let someone else monitor, Mr. Bam was happy to take back my white stripes. Thereafter I was subjected routinely to the smirks, even contempt, of many of the students. I was not much of an athlete and shunned fights, which worsened their contempt. Given my home life enough was enough—better to turn my back on provocation and walk away. Wasn't I the boy found so inadequate by his father? I endured their torment in silence.

One day on a school trip my other side appeared. Suddenly any taunting was too much. I turned on several of my tormentors. The staff looked the other way. The taunting boys were at first shocked, and then no match for my anger as I struck out with fist and lunch pail. No one ever taunted me again.

Did I learn from this to keep up a normal, manly aggressiveness? No: this alternation of seeming cravenness followed by fierceness continued into high school before I finally overcame it. Did I learn from the dance fiasco? A year later I went to the same affair successfully, but only after my parents brought in a young dance instructress whose perfume and shapeliness went straight to my head so that for the only time in my life I danced the foxtrot, cha cha, rumba, samba, waltz or whatever else she demanded with conviction and, almost, flair—but only with her. I just got by at the dance, not without an obligatory step or two on the foot of my partner, who was not Rosemary. She sensibly arranged to be with someone else.

My years in Manhattan are larded with behavior swings of this kind.

One autumn Bud persuaded Mom to enroll me for riding lessons at the 96th Street Academy where he rode. I did well enough, even after one old nag abruptly bolted, jumping the rope separating my class from another and cantering through the startled riders before at length jumping back into our circle where he slid to a trembling halt. I was then seated on his neck. No one knew why he had suddenly bolted, and far from reproaching me admired me for keeping on.

The glow of this triumph soon faded. One day Bud took me out for a ride in Central Park. All went well, but eventually he told me to wait while he went off to have a good canter. Time passed and, bored, I dismounted against Bud's injunction to stay on. Immediately the horse reared, jerked its reins loose, and bolted off up 5th Avenue. Bud returned.... Mutely I pointed after the horse. He galloped off, amused drivers on 5th Avenue leaning out their windows to urge him after the fleeing horse. We didn't ride together again.

One child's mother in our building thought I and my best friend tickled his sister too intrusively. I treated another attractive girl obviously interested in me to silence for years when we ran into each other on the elevator ride to the ground floor in the morning on our way to school. She finally asked Mothie about me, and was mortified to find out she was several years older. I was a good-looking boy who seemed mature beyond my years, and exuded at unguarded moments a commanding air far from what I actually felt.

One moment I could play the best player in a chess tournament to a draw, the next be steeped in self-destructiveness, as when I crept up on Bud one evening in our living room and slugged him in the stomach. I thought this very funny until he caught up with me in fury and gave me a well deserved swat. How else could it be with a father who confided to his journal that an afternoon he found he had to spend with me left him with the sense of being "trapped?" Or with a beautiful mother inevitably seductive in the too long baths we took together for years after moving to Manhattan? Where was a child to find a middle ground in these circumstances?

Reading became a crucial avenue of escape from and then confrontation with reality. Gar thought I "was slow to discover books," but by the early 1950s they made up the longest part of my annual Christmas list, primarily history and biography. Popular novels, science fiction, and fantasy I supplied out of my allowance that grew to $1 a week by the time I was fourteen. Classic Comics were sprinkled in liberally at first, with other comics Gar disapproved of in principle, although these soon gave way to the fuller variety of alternate lives my book reading provided. I could be Lancelot for a time, or Tamerlane, or Lewis or Clark, or.... I devoured books like candy. My life took on focus through fictional or historical lives, their achievements became mine and, as adolescence came into view, their sexual adventures made up for the absence of my own.

Nothing satisfied me as much as science fiction and fantasy. It wasn't the absence of our daily, flawed realism that appealed but a story's denser alternate vision of reality. Even more important was the way these stories imaginatively and decisively engaged with fundamental issues of good and evil, truth and falsity, courage and deception, so unlike my reality.

These books at once evoked, confronted, and affirmed my own sense of moving constantly through alternate realities. There was how I behaved with Gar, how with Mom and Mothie, how with Bud, then Bud and Jill; and how all these differed from life at school, or with friends. Reality, I saw, contained many lives that in strict logic should cancel one another out but in fact simply constituted the richness of experience. The reality I grasped imaginatively in the pages I turned was layered, multifaceted, and held together only by my mysterious, abiding sense of self that felt fully real only in odd moments of heightened self-awareness, sometimes among others, more often when I was alone.

It is no accident the late Shakespeare likens life to a play, or Strindberg's deepest grappling with experience resulted in *A Dream Play*, or that Bergman in *Fanny & Alexandra* contrasts the world of the imagination so favorably with the insistence on bleak (and hypocritical) truth. We simplify reality to make it useable and comprehensible, yet it effortlessly contains our own and countless others' simplifications within a complex, existing, indefinable whole only metaphor begins to grasp. Our mythicizing simply provides us with a narrow path to follow through the forest of experience.

So I saw that George Washington had been real, and Benedict Arnold, while on the frontier Tecumseh lived in another sense of reality as equally true as theirs as he grew up hunting deer and taking scalps. Caesar conquered Gaul, St. Augustine dreamed of a heavenly city, and King Alfred fought off Danes; Robert E. Lee won battle after battle, Lincoln split logs, Mata Hari combined seduction with spying. How strange these lives appeared in their details and behavior to a boy in the 1950s. How had they all been part of the same world? How were so many different worlds possible? Tamerlane might just as well have lived on another planet with the exotic nature of his culture and activities. Then the insight hit me—if I had lived in one of those other times and read a story of our present lives, of my and Linda and Mom and Gar's lives, they would have seemed just as fantastic.

We live in fantasy.

Realism smirks at 'fantasy' although fantasy is far truer to experience.

Conventional reality paled before science fiction and fantasy for another reason: both so often turned into facts. Were spaceships imaginary? Weren't we steadily developing ever more powerful rockets, wasn't space travel only a matter of time, weren't men in orbit by the end of the 1950s? Were ray guns fanciful impossibilities? Weren't they in routine use almost as quickly as space-going rockets, as lasers? How long had it taken before Jules Verne's impossible Nautilus transformed into the U-Boats that provoked America into World War I and nearly starved England into submission in World War II? What were HG Wells' fantasies of Morlochs compared to guards throwing children alive into open fires in the Holocaust? J.R.R. Tolkien had already written *The Hobbit*: recently a hobbit-sized race of hominids has been added to our evolutionary tree. Apparently we cannot imagine what cannot be, a thought at once thrilling and chilling. Later I found in Freud the same complex sense of reality in his multiplicity of motive, dream, and drive, so much so I respect him still however much the field has outgrown some of his conclusions.

My father saw blocks of ice delivered for the family "Ice Box," a term I still use for my refrigerator. Once a call to a relative in a distant country was science fiction, then forbiddingly expensive: now we communicate, free, face to face on our computers and phones. We are always waiting, if we only knew, for the imagined future to turn into the ordinary present. We live in the dreams of our forbears, in this as in so many other ways, while simultaneously undergoing a steadily accelerating technological revolution unparalleled in history, one we have hardly come to grips with even now, a revolution that constantly transforms our inherited and current notion of 'reality.' As our physical and social realities go through these transformations, our most private selves change, not in our needs, but in what we imagine is necessary to satisfy those needs.

There is in short no Reality, only realities that proliferate, join, and divide. The world tolerates our variety, the fantasies we organize into 'lives' and 'societies' and 'cultures' and 'civilizations,' each one certain it is Real until in time, in history in case of extended time, the arbitrary nature of given arrangements become apparent. So I first sensed through my intense reading in these years, however outwardly conventional I remained. A real adjustment to reality means the ability to meet the constant variety of life creatively, and with a minimum of fear.

This sensibility did nothing to diminish my awkwardness. My peers almost all seemed a good deal more focused on their studies or sport or, increasingly, on girls. The gaps in my memory haunted me, creating the constant sense of an unknown history leading to the complexities in which I and Linda lived. Plumbing history in books took on the vicarious value of dispelling mystery.

I loved Westerns, too, with their quintessential pattern of the dude, or put upon good man, or self-restrained hero who finally, under duress, straps on his gun and goes out to overcome the ogre. I knew about ogres.

The same need for clarity and focus made me a lifelong Yankee fan because they beat the odds and kept winning improbably in the early '50s, taking five straight pennants and world championships as Stengelese became a national phenomenon. It's a wonder that with my intensity of imagination and emotional need I didn't become a good deal more confused than I was.

All in all I was always after 'the truth' that Gar extolled as the virtue above all others but which I felt so little of around me. I read for the truth, whether of this historical act or that, or of the nature of desire and sex, or of the nature of a man's true character, revealed most under pressure. Finding the 'truth' was an omnipresent need, and I searched through one byway or another until old enough to search for it directly in myself.

The result of all this is that I knew too much. You know the kind of boy, the one of whom others say, "He's mature beyond his years." That was routinely said of me, even while the opposite was also true. I turned a cool eye on others and became an apt judge between pretension and reality. I found the deception in both my parents ever more apparent. I was not always a likeable person to be around. Others sensed in me more good nature than I was aware of and far more, usually, than I was able to show. As, ironically, was true of my father.

Oscar

    One pleasant spring afternoon Mothie sits on a bench in Carl Schurz Park which borders the East River across the street from our apartment. Mothie's hair is up, wrapped around the bun she used to add body, her fine-featured face looking straight ahead. A man holding an open paper bag on his lap sits beside her; the woman on the other side holds a plant.

    Another woman walks down the path and stops, curious about the three figures on the bench.

    "What are you doing?" she asks the woman with the plant.

    "Airing my geranium," as if to say, 'of course!' The other woman stares. She turns to the man.

    "What's in your bag?"

    "Have a look," he smiles. She looks in and steps back with a little shriek.

    "My snake likes to be aired too," he says.

    The woman looks at Mothie, so proper, so normal.

    "You don't seem to be doing more than enjoying the air," she smiles, as if to say: 'You aren't crazy like these two.' Mothie looks at her, then pulls on a string the woman hadn't noticed tied to the bench. It takes some time to pull Oscar into view, a large box turtle we found in the country.

    "His name is Oscar," Mothie explains. "I'm taking him for a walk." She smiles. "He only eats raw meat."

    The woman gives a choked cry and walks away.

Linda, Memory, Destiny

Linda

Linda is four when Gar records a conversation in his journal.

Linda: I'd like more money.
Dad: I gave you your allowance, dear. Now, tell me, if you could have a quarter but had to cut my throat, would you do it?
Linda: No, daddy.
Dad: For a dollar?
Linda: No.
Dad: A million?
Linda: No, daddy.
Dad: All the money in the world?
Linda: Yes daddy.

It is typical of him to pose and push such a question to an extreme, then be amused. "It seems, therefore, that every girl has her price," he concludes. This is meant in good fun, but is not the sort of thing a girl or woman is apt to find amusing. "Good fun" is a special phrase here—once Nanny defended Gar's infidelities to my mother as "good fun." Mom recalls this lying in her nursing home as she reflects on her life half a century later. She still isn't amused.

What then of Linda in this new world of Manhattan where our parents simultaneously deepened their reconciliation, pursued their interlocking dreams that Linda and I were to exemplify, and started their process of polarization?

I remember Linda best on our walks on weekends with Mothie up East 86th Street on our way to the movies beyond 3rd Avenue, where the elevated 3rd Avenue El still ran. Linda always walked half a block ahead of us, unaffected by Mothie's demands to stay closer, constantly alarming her as we approached corners. Our first summer in Manhattan Linda was dismayed by my birthday. She insisted on an equal number of presents for herself. Her recourse with Mom and Mothie if thwarted was dramatic—she flung herself on her back, legs flailing, and howled in rage. Such fury was beyond anything in Mom or Mothie's experience, and always led to capitulation.

Promises made then might not be kept, but they bought time to negotiate, and an end to the tantrum. Promise making, inconsistently fulfilled, turned into a fixture of my mother's character. Later my children grew frustrated in turn with her unkept promises. She learned with Linda never to frustrate directly, and by the time my daughters Heather and Alyssa encountered her, Mom was a polished exciter and evader. They could take their mother Jeanne at her word, so couldn't understand Mom. They learned to live with her good intentions, and to take her promises with a grain of salt, but it was a hard lesson. That frustrating quality of hers became Linda's and my daily bread. Linda learned to insist and to continue insisting until the promise of the moment was kept.

In this it is easy to see a spoiled child, difficult at the time, amusing in retrospect—but if we are lucky, we have all been spoiled a little as children. Didn't I force them to react to grunts and gestures at home in place of talking until five? But with Linda in this and other behavior there was a deeper root.

Gar praised her as noted earlier if she was letter perfect in appearance and demeanor, but turned relentlessly critical if anything less, which meant most of the time. On many occasions he eyed her even if perfectly turned out. He'd begin,

"Dear, do you know...."

and pick at some trivial flaw until he drove Linda to tears. Tears reduced my father to a bemused confusion about what he had done to provoke them. Sometimes, however, Linda stormed off, behavior he tolerated in a daughter, lumping her with all irrational women.

His journal as it resumes in Manhattan is full of fond recalls that again force me to wonder how there can be such a reversal between his words and reality. On March 2, 1952 he wonders if

> …it were possible—(it is)—or practical to photograph and record one whole day—not this one in particular—tho through these pages I can treasure many moments of the past.

That evening he records one such treasure.

> …I crept between you two and Linda, you cradled my head between your arms, while you, Lance, flung your left arm over my side. Soon, Linda, you were snoring away, while Lance slept in his quiet sleep.

But a secret ruled Linda's life and gave a lie to this pretty picture, as well as made scenes of shared intimacy between Gar and Linda fleeting. One day when Mom came back from some errand she found Linda on Gar's lap on his 'throne.' He was caressing her in an intimate, inappropriate manner. "I never left her alone with him again" she told me years later: I never knew at the time.

As I think back I realize Linda never gave any sign of regret over diminished contact with Gar after Mom blocked further intimate contact. Gar became someone to see with other women around, an intruder into her feminine world, someone to put up with as well as love with a child's instinctive if, in her case, offended love. No wonder she was resistant to demands to 'behave,' and a desire to keep her distance on our walks: she wanted attention, she wanted fixing: besides, why should his impossible demand for perfection apply to her?

But this, I discovered was not the end of the story.

In a later conversation in the nursing home my mother mused, "I wonder sometimes if I was too hard on David," referring to not allowing Linda to be alone with him again.

"But you did see something that upset you?"

"Yes."

"Was he caressing her under her dress?"

"Yes."

"Was he invasive?" I asked bluntly.

"No."

"So it was just too intimate."

"Yes." A pause.... "You should hear Linda on the subject though." This wasn't reflective, but as much to say: 'You should hear her anger.'

For the truth is Gar's violations continued beyond the point Mom intervened to keep her from being alone with him. They continued in her presence, and Mothie's. Often as the four of them sat together watching a television show Gar's hand slipped down Linda's back under her skirt, then slipped under her panties to caress her bottom's cleavage. This went on until she was twelve in 1958, almost 8 years after Mom's initial discovery. One evening in Weston in his study as he and the three women sat together and again his hand slid down Linda's back Mothie said,

"David, that's not appropriate behavior at her age."

There was silence, except for the television. He withdrew his hand. No one said anything more. He never touched Linda again.

At his end when Gar faded by inches over two years at the Beverly Hills Rehabilitation Center Linda routinely visited him, usually with one of her dogs, which always made a welcome stir at the Center and intrigued and distracted Gar for an hour from his decline. One time he was on antidepressants, and as she walked into the room he broke into a wide smile.

"Dear, how nice to see you! How well you look!"

Linda turned to see who was behind her....

When Gar no longer needed antidepressants he reverted to kind, giving Linda his usual dour, critical look when she visited.

"I was relieved," she told me, after one visit. "I'm used to that dour look. That other man just wasn't my father." She's amused telling me this—but each time during those two years when she left the Center she wept throughout her hour drive home. That was the only way she could come to terms with her feelings over what he had done to her.

Gar's behavior with Linda is a darkness in an already troubled family dream, appalling however far it fell short of penetration. It's enough that Linda's sense of self was insulted. How much justice is there in claiming to any extent that his behavior was due to an ignorance of women? That he saw them as something to place on a pedestal—or demean? In his fiction the women characters are uniformly unbelievable.

Nanny may not have given him a basis on which to build a wholesome ability to relate to women, but he was always acutely aware of her feelings, her power over him, and the consequences of his behavior. He would have known with Linda that what he did could not be without effect and affect.

He would have known the same with my mother, and all the other women he idealized or exploited.

His behavior was a constant puzzle to me before I was old enough to reflect on our experience and try to put disparate insights together. Yes, Gar went emotionally where he shouldn't, invading others' senses of self, not so much maliciously as, strangely, in a perverse way, innocently: he was brought up that way. Not until one of us, primarily Mom, took him to task did that behavior become self-conscious, at first defended, then apologized for abjectly.

Nothing here is meant as an excuse, only as an attempt to understand how we continued to love him. In his moments of collapse and apology a different man emerged. Then he too sensed there was a better way for him to be, but he could only go there briefly under duress, and only as a tourist. He was not his own master, however he projected a contrary image. His fantastic journalistic transformation was the closest he could come to being a 'good' father.

This peculiar combination of behaviors faces a further complication. The sense of limit, of going so far but no farther, is one of the earliest things we learn as our childhood omnipotence gives way to reality. A child can have his mother entirely to himself in that phase, or seem to, but what a disaster if so early a child finds a competitor, and that his needs are not met first, for Charles was there, always more favored, 'the first son,' as opposed to just 'David.' How hungry it must have made my father for what he didn't have, a thread that later in life made him so ardent a pursuer of my mother, and later when it became possible, so ardent in pursuit of being first in the corporate entities where he worked as a substitute for being first among twins. He was fatally wounded in his amour proper.

It is no wonder we were inadequate: he saw in us his own failing to be good enough. The wonder is that there were not even more frequent explosions between he and my mother as she fought to maintain normalcy.

How suitable a profession he moved into, one structured to make money from transformative, reality altering acts of the imagination through a medium whose invasion of our homes we all aided and abetted eagerly. This 180 degree flip-flopping of reality was our crazy making childhood air.

Memory & Destiny

Consequently Mom and Mothie's greatest failure with Gar was that they couldn't say routinely, "No, this is not acceptable," or, "You must do this" or "You must not do that." Normally, Mom and Mothie tried to appease Gar so all could indulge their myth of the perfect family. Our dreaming blinds us to the life we do, in fact, live, and which seeing truthfully is all too often too painful. So we live *as if* in ideality. Only desperation alters this behavior, periodically, routinely, and all too briefly.

Every part of our experience was falsified in this manner. For example, one of Gar's journal entries in these years is about religion.

> You wondered today, Lance, why I don't go to Church, and I put off the answer, not because I don't have one, but because going to Church fairly regularly, as you do, is a nice habit, and I wouldn't want to disturb it. Church going is one thing, religion another.

The passage moves on into increasingly general remarks about whether "most men" are religious, or clear about their beliefs (they are not), before concluding that "the subject is so confused in their mind" and "set" by tradition and "tabu" that one can't be "dispassionate or rational about it."

Lost in that is how I was raised a WASP with a Jewish father because of his infidelities and the near collapse of his marriage, as well as because of his mother's extraordinarily vituperative behavior. Lost are my own feelings on the subject, that I did not enjoy being taken to Church "fairly often." I am not involved in his reflections as a person in his own right. Someone with an amorphous sense of boundaries cannot get past himself.

I wonder, now, what is memory when it can be so altered by inner necessity? What, in a family history, is recalled when we struggle to bring the past to life? Memory, reality, and our sense of self are inextricably bound, but what if, in this transient moment in which we live there is an abiding sense of things too dark, of realities too disturbing to endure, a suspicion the truth is other than we assert? Gar stared until a bright light obscured the darkness, as darkness does the sun if we stare into its face. So he writes,

You know, of course, that this is in no real sense a diary, which would have to chronicle daily events and daily thoughts [which is, in fact, exactly how he initially undertakes his diaries]. Thoughts are even more changeable than the events and experiences through life. *Real thoughts* [my italics] are in so many ways more alarming, more revealing than deeds—their very explosive nature is reason enough to keep them submerged. And, in a diary, a man could give to [sic] much currency to his thoughts and here, as in spoken words, it is best to remember Polonius' advice to his son Laertes which went something like, "To thine ear give many, to thine tongue, few...."

In the same speech Polonius does advise keeping your thoughts to yourself, and not giving "any unproportional thought his act." The speech famously climaxes.

...to thine own self be true,
and it must follow as night the day
thou canst not then be false to any man.[11]

If, I add, you are in touch with any part of your true self, one not bent or distorted by experience but still intact, then...Polonius' words represent a possible truth. Gar is 39 in 1952, facing thoughts so "explosive" he fears they could outweigh mere events, and need to be "submerged." This is the closest he ever comes to the dark side of his emotional life.

He succeeded in making Linda doubt herself too. In Linda he managed to create some of the same dark anger Nanny caused in him, just as he passed on to me his sense of inadequacy from the same source. Linda had no outlet for these feelings as I did partially in nature until a few years later she took to horses with a vengeance. In her fifties after raising her family she became a nationally ranked dressage rider.

As for Mom and Mothie's responsibility in what happened to Linda, their very myths forced them into compromises, silences, and tacit tolerations that guaranteed an ever deeper imperfection. So many mitigating circumstances could be brought up, like: he didn't, actually, do much, compared to all those who have suffered far worse; or Mom and

Mothie's upbringing worked against both confrontation, and even thinking such a problem could be one of their own. Their falsification of reality made them prey to Gar's...and so on.

Yet what they did was dreadfully wrong. Not least because it compromised memory, and so the self, in Linda and me. So again I wonder about the nature of this effort to reconstruct the past: what is made? What is its value? Something the late Freud pondered in *Constructions In Analysis* is relevant here, of how, in working with a patient, the past that after great effort is reconstructed often turns out to be at least partly an illusion. Freud wondered if that invalidated the construction, and concluded no, it didn't matter if the construction led to understanding and improvement.[12]

Shakespeare, Nietzsche, Freud: illusion makes life possible.

Waffles

Smokie, the black cocker who guarded my crib and was my companion through the Great Neck years finally had to be put down and was succeeded by Waffles, a spunky red cocker spaniel.

Gar hated all animals. Smokie he endured because he was there before him, belonged to Mothie, and came of course with Mothie when she stayed in our apartment in Manhattan. Perhaps he thought having his mother-in-law almost always present with her pet a small price to pay for the freedom gained by my mother to come with him on his social outings. Perhaps after the reconciliation in 1948 Smokie was one of many things he could say nothing about. But Mom's drive for a normal life meant pets: dogs, cats, lambs, fish, hamsters, stray turtles from the woods, and ultimately horses.

One evening as we watch television in the dining room Gar passes through to get something in the kitchen. He goes there so infrequently that he is gone before Mom or Mothie think to warn him Waffles the Puppy is now on the scene. We freeze. A moment passes, then he storms back from the kitchen through the swinging door.

"What is that monster doing in the kitchen!" he shouts. We're stunned. He doesn't think he is exaggerating.

"Oh, David," Mom says. "He's a puppy, Waffles, to replace Smokie for the children."

He storms down the hall and slams into his study with the maimed leather chair.

Jonah in Manhattan

There is a way to bring all these threads of experience and sensibility together, for however personal our lives seem, they are enmeshed in larger social and cultural realities that are inescapable in an urban setting. We may feel our choices are our own and yet discover these and our private actions are only echoes of a larger whole. How else could it be for my parents and for Linda and myself enmeshed as we were in the heart of New York City in Manhattan during these years? How unnatural, disorienting and strange such a setting and experience are we deliberately blind ourselves to through our presumed familiarity with the modern city and its glibly labeled 'urban lifestyle.'

To begin to understand a city's true reality, imagine layering one natural view above another like unmounted slides edge to edge vertically. A desert scene lies below a tropical rain forest canopy, while above that surf crashes along the shore, each view above another reflecting every possible scene. Assemble each vertical grouping beside one another into a building's façade, join them into three-dimensional apartments and skyscrapers, assemble these into blocks, blocks into boroughs, boroughs into cities.... Imagine further that when you turn the corner of one block a radically different set of views confronts you across the street on every facade. Some blocks you sense are unsafe, full of dark foregrounds and violent scenes that try unsuccessfully to hide their content. Others you walk down blithely, unconsciously aware you are among reassuring sights and signs. Still others have a grueling, relentless repetition that is soul-destroying.

Within each building elevators constantly take you from one slice of reality to another: on one floor brilliant parrots fly noisily across the sky, on the next crocodiles jostle under a blazing sun in a shrinking waterhole. Each floor in turn is divided into as many unrelated views as there are apartments.

You peer across the street through a window, and see a sandstorm rage, while one floor lower the sun throws swords of light through a redwood forest. Then you realize yours is just one of these scenes....

The idea is fantastic, the degree of disorientation staggering. Worse, if you are in something that holds all places, then you are in none in particular, while the only value each retains is that of a momentary, decorative variation of the whole. Poverty may reduce you to living in a 'desert,' wealth place you in a benign, temperate meadow. Money becomes the great arbiter, divider, and goal, empty of intrinsic value but in sufficient amounts vested with a power over circumstances. Money is a medium of power, not exchange. Imagine further one year it is fashionable to have a yurt in the Gobi, the next an Ark in a flood: each slice of nature, of life and lifestyle, becomes a constantly shifting variable also empty of intrinsic value.

I touch on this in a poem, where the city is a cornucopia to be devoured:

> In cities calligraphies of new plays envine marquees
> while paintings leaf from gallery walls
> and things and things and more
> pile up in windows where passersby
> and children press as though
> these were corn and wheat and round harvest
>   ripenesses.[13]

Most striking, of course, and what makes a city even more chilling, is the exclusion of actual nature. Nothing makes this more obvious than a visit to an Italian city with roots deep in the past. Tree-lined boulevards are rarities, expansive parks within the city walls rare as hens' teeth. What nature one finds there is carefully curtailed in the gardens of the rich. Outside the walls later civic gardens are carefully clipped and contained. 'Nature' is the primary creation of urban life, that which is outside, where all is consigned that is dangerous and threatens civic life.

Modern cities have grown so large they now incorporate natural stretches within city boundaries, areas where, as in Central Park in New York, or the Bois de Boulogne in Paris, or Hampstead Heath in London, you imagine yourself in nature as long as you keep your eyes down to avoid a horizon ringed with buildings, or those strolling about with eyes similarly downcast. You forget for a moment that your jogging or riding outfit or… are examples of current fashion. You are where a child on a path can be excited by a rare rabbit or a frequent squirrel, who have replaced the lurking danger, the jaguar among the trees. Cities contain any lurking danger or more exotic creature in their Zoos, only recently expanded outside city boundaries into Nature Parks where nature is reduced to a tourist attraction for those ensteeled within their cars or Zoo vehicles. Or the city itself becomes in a familiar phrase the reality it thought it could exclude—a concrete jungle where areas of predation vary and few feel entirely safe except in very narrow bounds….

A paradox: what better place than one of our cities to dream of the perfect family, or to write in one's journals of one's idyllic children, or be photographed showing just the right way to deal with social disharmony? Yet it is just such a place that generated books like David Riesman's famous *The Lonely Crowd* in the 1950s, or film classics like *Rear Window* that explored alienation, where one cannot rely on a strange face for help and unspeakable crimes are committed a floor above or below or in a neighboring building? We live in these cities still that grow steadily larger, their opportunities and dissociations, rewards and insecurities, their potential for despair and violence ever greater.

Czeslaw Milosz gets the 'city' just right in his *Legends of Modernity*.

> That is the terrain to be studied by the social naturalist, the zoo in which pairs of all species on earth are gathered. The observer requires a strictly defined field of observation in which processes take place intensely and can be grasped in quickened tempo. That is why the naturalist raises bacteria in a Petri dish.

He goes on:

> A great modern city, with its feverish activity…rejection of the brakes that men have no time for here, is a living specimen that simply begs for a microscope. The speeded-up tempo arises from the very fact of living in a throng: a month goes by, a year, and…I

am surrounded by new fames, new careers, new conquerors whom I encountered just yesterday in student dining halls.

and:

Where…new forces are forever swimming up from the depths [or] sink to the ranks of the proletariat; where…new faces and their images obscure the faces of friends, separating the friends seen today from those seen the day before yesterday—there the rush to transformism and the interest in transformism are understandable.[14]

My parents with their love of "café life," their incessant socializing, and Gar's career in advertising typified this constantly transforming existence. Each sponsor made possible an exercise of the imagination in the shows Young & Rubicam underwrote, often funny, always with familiar mores, and whose audience appeal made it possible to move their sponsors' commercial products. Or they did the same ad by ad in the print media to summon a need in order to satisfy it. Want this, buy that, and for a moment you imagine yourself on the crest of the urban, transforming wave. One year one sort of show might be 'in:' the next, another. Certain products might try to have staying power: Lipton Tea, Kent cigarettes—others, like the cereals constantly brought out by General Foods, are things of the moment. As the '50s wear on and 'planned obsolescence' became the watchword, the construction of cars began that soon fell apart and needed to be replaced—and so opened the door for Toyota and Honda and…to take an ever larger slice of the market. Linda and I grew up in this sea of empty change and took it for granted as 'the way things are.'

The speed with which Elizabethan drama went through some of its stages, high bombast to pastoral to antiquity to comedy to aristocratic comedy to domestic comedy to satire to comedies of manners to revenge plays to tragedies to…pales with the tidal, constant shifts in taste and need in the modern city measured not by years but months. Even a month is too long: think weeks, think 'one day' wonders. This urban experience is the antipodes of being in a wilderness, or even merely in real country, where an oak outlives generations in the house it shades. We do not study the clouds or stars in the city, but the momentary shifts of desire and mood in one another, while the buildings all but melt before our eyes in our haste to tear down and build ever more impressively.

To be modern is to ride this transforming crest and hope it never breaks. It is the body of the myth of human perfectibility, of the Golden Age to come, that underlies the myth of the perfect family. Recessions we can bear, barely: another Depression and we would despair as we came so very close to doing in the 'Great Recession.' Let there be a pandemic and we recoil from and tire of the restrictions necessary for health. Anti-vaxxers proclaim there is no need to be vaccinated, popular revulsion against masks leads to a 'mask mandate' being rescinded even as a new wave of illness crests among us. Perhaps the accumulating absurdities of this myth will finally bring it down—no one in the 1950s wanted to avoid Salk's polio vaccine and instead walk about crippled.

Milosz' language with its use of "the proletariat" sounds quaint to our ears with the collapse of communism. The modern city is quintessentially a function of the success of modern capitalism, of the modern industrial-technological heart of our civilization, of productive forces whose momentary effects Marx understood well but whose development he foresaw badly. Our constant proliferation of goods seen to be desirable whether they are or not, and consequently our confusion of necessity with passing desire, is at the heart of the economic success of our system and of our collapsing natural world. Dreams have price tags. There is always a reckoning.

A Robinson Crusoe on his island might make do with a savage helper and a slowly constructed, essentially static lifestyle that allows him to hold his own with unconstrained nature for years: a Robinson Crusoe in the city would soon require a staff to organize getaway tours to his magic island, a formula at the heart of more than one modern television show. To pull back deliberately, to stop, to consider, to judge beyond the quick flow of activity needed to keep this machine going is judged asocial, quixotic, threatening if done in fact, as opposed to celebrated in the imagination. We take Greenpeace to court, but revere Thoreau and *Walden*, reassured that if there are more important things than this transitory exploitation of our lives we do not have to take them to heart and change: instead we change Walden Pond into a public swimming hole crammed with summer bathers, surrounded by parking lots.

An urban man or woman feels with sufficient success there is no limit to their attainments: their wills can be satisfied in ways impossible on Crusoe's island or Thoreau's pond. Nature, by contrast, however tolerant of diversity, imposes necessity.

The modern city is a land of mirrors, as well: what good are these achievements if they are not made images for others to reflect? For men like my father creativity here meant inventive responses to this hopped-up urban existence where desire is the only necessity. We must continuously fool ourselves to remain productive, and so, happy—the oldest urban behavior. Yet under the surface is a sense of illusion and pointlessness, not of cultural fullness; of a missing, not overwhelming, plenty; of being in a rat race or on a treadmill, not living a free or happy life. Hence the intuition that perhaps a move to the 'country' to provide a more 'natural' or 'rooted' life for the children might be desirable, quite aside from such a move's symbolization of status and success. Our recent pandemic for a time reinforced this, but the rush out was soon counterbalanced by the rush back.

Yet even as the urban experience fuels desire and envy, it equally punctures illusion with an occasional savage thrust, as once when Mom and Mothie and I drove to the edge of Harlem to an antique dealer looking for a statuette of a Civil War New York Zouave to add to Gar's growing collection of soldiers he carefully repainted and turned into lamps.

Mom slammed on the brakes to stop for a light as a black woman stepped in front of us. The woman wore a cheap imitation of the suits my mother bought in Saks Fifth Avenue and Bonwit Teller, with a red hat. She stopped, startled, staring: I knew both Mom and Mothie avoided eye contact, exactly the wrong thing to do. They should have smiled, mouthed an "I'm sorry," and waved helplessly. Instead the woman came to the side of the car where my mother sat with her window half down.

"What's wrong with you!" she shouted. "Didn't you see me?" She cut off my mother's reply. "Do you think you can just do what you want? Do you think I'm not a person too?"

The woman pushed back the sleeves of her jacket and blouse.

"You think because I'm black I'm dirt?" she demanded. "My blood is the same color as yours. Red! Just like yours!"

The light turned green, cars moved ahead. Before she could say more, my mother drove off.

She and Mothie were indignant. How dare anyone talk to them this way! Hadn't they supported the New Deal? Wasn't that a stirring moment when Marian Anderson sang at the Lincoln Memorial? But they voted for Wendell Willkie.... Hadn't Truman desegregated the Army? But that was the Army.... Weren't they good, well-meaning citizens? Thank God the woman didn't know how as a girl my then sheltered and naive mother tried to scrub a black girl white in the tub!

The modern city draws all into its vortex—move accidentally from your own familiar scenes into the wrong area and your dream is mocked by poor imitations and a resentment at having to settle for second best by those who live there. These take the prevailing myths and dreams for their own even if doing so means depriving themselves of anything authentic, too, race and ethnicity augmenting the classic division between haves and have nots where that came into play as well. If the success we crave to free us from circumstance: racial, social, gender, economic, and educational remains elusive for many, it is felt to be just at the edge of our fingertips for families like my own—but those that find the dream out of reach fill with despair and anger. So the city too is where resentment flashes out in periodic spasms of violence.

The great irony of our middle-class myth of attaining the perfect, happy family is how it creates social division as it collides with reality.

And if success did lead to independence, what then? What else do we know but this ceaseless desiring that oils our political system, feeds our economy, and which our religion blesses? For the very rich can there ever be a large enough yacht, enough buildings or foundations with their name to permit something to trickle, if not down, at least out?

This is the "period when in human consciousness the legend of the monster collective arises, the monster organism in whose entrails, as in the entrails of a whale, contemporary Jonahs must live" adds Milosz, who experienced firsthand the collective life in conquered Poland, first Nazi, then Communist, then in chosen exile viewed the sprawl of development on either side of San Francisco Bay from his home in the Berkeley Hills.[15]

I was a boy who found his balance and saving grace in the turn to nature in Great Neck. No sooner was that found than the possibility of exercising it was removed in 1949. Yet it is this turn to nature that made me immune to the appeal of the modern city. That turn to nature opened me to the deprivations of city life, and made me hostile to the social and economic machinations that so benefit from the ways in which urban life isolates men and women from their roots and confuses them with its disposable cornucopias, as if nirvana was one shopping spree away.

Yet we can hardly live in nature in this world unless we choose some extremely distant place to live in as a hermit—and then face the chance of becoming a tourist destination, a fresh oddity to be consumed. Even now I live within the confines of Los Angeles, on the fringe of the Santa Monica Mountains by the Pacific Ocean in this most endless of cities, where I have played my part in saving mountain land from 'development' by transforming it into a 'park' to be consumed by tourists.

But in New York as I took the first steps towards poetry I was swallowed by the Whale Manhattan in whose belly phantasms exclaimed in mad pursuit of the unattainable how marvelous this life was, how brilliant, how all in all.

Shazzam

I stand behind a bus taking on passengers on the way to McBurney. I just missed my favorite bus whose driver sings from one stop to the next. I have been reading a comic book where the hero transforms into a superman by crying out "Shazzam!" I wonder if I breathe in the bus exhaust deeply enough as it envelops me in an otherworldly moment and cry out "Shazzam!" whether I will be transformed.

The bus starts, trailing a gray fume that surrounds me. I breathe in deeply.

"Shazzam!" I cry.

Nothing happens.

PART TWO:
MAKING THE DREAMS

So in a running stream one wave we see
After another roll incessantly,
…
The water still does into water go,
Still the same brook, but different waters flow.

   La Boete, quoted by Montaigne, *Experience*

THE LEVY MYTH

Waldorf Astoria

One day my father greets one of his professors at the University of Pennsylvania as he crosses the campus. When the professor gets to the other side my father greets him again.

"Levy, didn't I just see you heading the other way on the other side of the campus?"

Charles smiled.

"I changed my mind." Neither ever told the professor the truth. They were that alike. It used to make dates nervous, but unjustifiably so, as their rivalry never permitted them to share a girl.

Some years later Charles comes up from Philadelphia to meet my father for lunch at the Waldorf Astoria. Charles is often late for their meetings so my father expects to get there first. He enters the hotel, crosses the lobby, and heads up the grand stairs towards the restaurant. He is pleasantly surprised as he reaches the landing to see Charles coming towards him: how nice of him to be there early for a change! He returns smile for smile, reaches out for Charles' hand, and walks into the mirror.

Myth and Story

I've written interchangeably of our stories, dreams, myths. 'Story' I know we're comfortable with, while 'myth' has an aura we're uncertain about, and which we associate with ancient myths, not our present lives. My explanation in the beginning of how ordinary mythicizing shapes our experience into a whole doesn't seem to contradict our comfortable assertions. Few of us wish to believe elements like childhood experience are deterministic or that even ethnic or biological factors outweigh our freedom to choose our lives or sex.

But implying there are unconscious let alone inherited elements in our mythicizing, storytelling, and dreaming—that there are elements of who we think we are or of choices we think of as our own that are not but instead are predetermined, doesn't sit well with us. Never mind the spread of Freudian thought and its various derivatives that are everywhere, or Jung's insight that we elaborate our experience into certain given patterns, like the 'hero' pattern. Contemporary psychoanalysis is in one of its periodic cycles of disrepute, while Jung's archetypes are famously confusing. If we are aware of someone like Joseph Campbell it is largely because of his association with George Lucas and the original *Star Wars* films rather than from how Campbell's work in comparative mythology establishes prevailing patterns in myths across cultures.

Although we may include lies and illusions in our stories/myths/dreams that motivate, thrill or frustrate us and others, by and large we try to make the best sense of ourselves that we can. T.S. Eliot thought we could bear little of reality, but our stories/myths paradoxically make our lives bearable—and facilitate our approach to the truth, for which in the midst of our dreaming we hunger.

Inevitably our mythicizing begins in infancy, and as we settle into a recognizable personality with a recognizable outlook based on our and our families' objective situations and personal circumstances, it becomes extraordinarily difficult to change our self/story/myth however much of it actually is not uniquely our own. Nietzsche writes of how unlikely personal transformation is given how incredibly difficult we find it to deal with even simple change. Yet we aren't 'fixed' but in a constant three-way dialectic: with our parents and their world, the world beyond them, and with ourselves. Changes we make are necessarily spread over years, and even then, difficult: a little self-examination reveals our 'stories' to have links of iron, not silk.

A good deal of this was driven home to me when I turned to my parents' ancestors and childhoods. That revealed the formation and strengthening of a set of stories/dreams/myths ingrained in my parents from birth, as in theirs before them—how else could it be—and driven forward in turn by each generation. The past is a living not fixed entity subject to evolution and sparking fresh insights as our own experience and hunger for the truth accumulate. Add an 'r' before 'evolution' and you have always the potential for revolution to break out from the shadows when the dialectic becomes too rigidly constraining.

Thus, my parents' lives took enduring shape through their ancestors,' and were lived necessarily in an illusion of freedom and choice, just like yours and mine.

The Mouse

On one of the rare visits of Nanny and Poppy to Great Neck after Christmas, 1946, Poppy discovers I am going to be sent to Sunday School and raised an Episcopalian. He is furious and loudly berates my father, not at all his typical behavior.

There is nothing, really, my father can say.

Not, "Dad, they steamed open Mother's letters and found out how hate-filled they are. They're furious—" or "Dad, Lucille converted to Judaism but you and Mother wouldn't come to our wedding.

What did you expect?"

My father idealized his parents inversely to his distance from them: face to face he was helpless.

He stands wordless as his father climaxes, "What are you, a man or a mouse?"

The Descent from Garchmarski

We visited Poppy and Nanny in Philadelphia as a matter of course before that fatal Christmas of 1946. Poppy was a graying man who appeared to have an easy way with a boy, having already raised three sons. Later I knew he led a life of great regularity, rising over the decades in the Midvale Steel Co. to earn $50 a month at his apogee as a supervisor. He had a group of friends he went out to play poker with after work at least once a week. Even after he and Nanny were allowed to visit us only twice a year and Philadelphia became taboo, I anticipated seeing Poppy. But I hardly remember more, vaguely recalling only that he always wore a suit.

Certainly I was never put on my or his father's knees and told stories about his or Poppy's youth. My father's side of the family after Christmas 1946 was foreign territory. Tracing my father's ancestors, and how their inheritance affected myself and Linda, waited for me to begin this history.

My father's paternal grandparents, Louis and Lena Levy, were both born in Lithuania, he as a Garchmarski, she as a Goodman. For years Gar believed the family name was Gumbinsky until a more knowledgeable cousin set him straight: then he was struck by the accidental echo of the ancestral name with the one I invented for him. In early 1865 when Louis was twelve his father David Garchmarski, after whom my father was named, emigrated with his wife and family to America seeking a better life. At first they lived in New York, but their movements and history are largely lost, as well as his wife's name and character.

Louis tried to enlist in the Union army as a drummer boy in the Civil War, but the war ended that April. Boys his age had served in the Union and Confederate armies: some who could pass themselves off as older fought, and Civil War battles were prodigiously bloody, their aftermaths even worse given the medical resources of the day. Louis was spared a potentially grim maiming or death.

David Garchmarski was a tinker and traveled to sell his wares, a practice picked up by Louis who began by selling picture frames and anything else he could set his hands on. By the time he married Lena Goodman, a date that has not survived, Louis was a Levy, his father having changed the harsh Garchmarski to Levy sometime in Louis' youth. The family wanted to fit in. Lena's parents Jacob and Bertha remained in New York where they had emigrated from Lithuania, while she and Louis moved to South Bethlehem in 1887 or 1888 with a growing family, only the second Jewish couple in the community. There Louis rose steadily, telling his landlady that one day he would own the home where they rented a room. Eventually, he did: the home still exists, owned by the YMCA.

At one time Louis made loans to Lehigh University students with their clothes as collateral, but after varied undertakings opened a secondhand store with some new items, sometimes referred to as a pawnshop in the family literature. He and Lena and their growing family moved from one house which was near the river and periodically flooded to the home of their former landlady which in time became the patriarchal home at 430 Wyandotte St. My father visited there throughout his childhood when Poppy visited his parents. There they also celebrated Seders with Louis and Lena, the only reference to religious observance in all my father's journals and biographical fragments.

Nanny and Poppy celebrated Christmas, not Hanukkah. Religion faded in their lives: neither Charles, David, nor Abner had a bar mitzvah. When Abner married Margie she was shocked at his ignorance of Jewish rite and custom, and restored those for his family. This casualness about their own faith makes my father's desire to have my mother convert a pointless offering to those already indifferent to their own roots. Only once did my father observe anything from his Jewish past: one day in 1956, after his father's death, I found the Jewish prayers for the dead on his bureau. Gar duly recited them, but never in our hearing.

Louis had an identical twin, Abraham, in a family of four who slowly drifted to different parts of the country. A youthful picture shows a dapper, bearded man in top hat and overcoat, although it is not apparent he was only 5' 2," or Lena a mere 4' 10." He used a bamboo cane for effect, not from need, one my father eventually possessed, which is now mine. Louis must have been educated and bright enough to hold his own with Father McEmry and the Reverend Stirling (a high Episcopalian) with whom he often debated religion in the Wyandotte home in the evenings as they played cards, the root of his son Benjamin's later poker playing. Louis was especially good at pinochle.

He also frequently spoke at the YMCA, where he was popular because of his vivid speaking style.

Gar remembered his stocky figure, strong voice, hearty greeting of, "Well, boys!" when they visited. He recalled Louis walking home uphill with a large bag of coffee and another of doughnuts, or gathering eggs from the chickens in the backyard. Some eggs he punctured with a pin, then sucked dry to the boys' fascination. He gardened, pruned his fruit trees, and carried scuttles of coal from the basement to the coal-burning stove.

Their icebox used chunks of fifty pound ice delivered by an Ice Man, and was always full of birch beer, sarsaparilla, and cream soda. Two tables were placed in the large kitchen, the center of family life, one for the copious meals Lena cooked, one for card games later, or discussions with Father McEmry and the Reverend Stirling. Once his son Benjamin had his own family it would often be Louis and Lena with Poppy and Nanny and the three boys playing at that table. My cousin Myles, Charles' son, redid his kitchen so that it is now the center of family activities, one wall taken up by a large unit full of films and a very large television, with a large table around which family and friends gather to visit as well as eat. A smaller, second table occupies another part of the room, unconsciously echoing the same arrangement as Louis and Lena Levy.

Louis never used his front parlor or entered through the front entrance past the stairway with its mahogany banisters, but always came in through the rear. He was never seen in that parlor until after Lena died in 1929. Gar and Charles would find him there during later visits sitting in the twilight staring at a photo of Lena. He passed away six years later at 82.

All points to Louis being a genial man, a poor boy made good as a local burgher with an appealing personality that easily surmounted the very real ethnic and religious divides of the day. No hint of crisis in his life darkens my father's memory, no strife or strife's resolution. Hardly any mention is made of Louis' identical twin, Abraham: he is only named once in my father's recreations of his past, and only one unguarded phrase in a late biographical fragment mentions that Abraham at some point abandoned his wife, after which Louis never spoke to him again.

Who knows what cause Abraham had to act as he did? Even if he had little, for his action to be followed with no tolerance, no understanding, only a lifelong unyielding rejection, was a flash of light dispelling the golden haze surrounding this portrait of Louis, revealing a darker reality altogether, like Hans Castorp's vision of the dark rite underlying civilization itself in Mann's *The Magic Mountain*.

I thought of the difference between my father and Charles, my father always dour, Charles always chipper. I thought of their childhood pictures, Charles always smiling, Gar frowning. I thought of their identical genotype. I thought of how Nanny celebrated Charles as "my son," and Gar as "David." He might as well have been born years later. I thought of the tremendous insult of that treatment to his sense of self, fueling that lifelong need to be, impossibly, number one. I thought of my father's cryptic and regretful references to the strife surrounding his public marriage, and of the failure of his parents to come to their wedding despite his efforts and in fulfillment of his worst fears. I thought of how Gar always spoke of his parents with almost unbearable sentimentality, especially of Nanny, unless they were physically present. Then Nanny could reduce him to fuming discontent with a look, or drive him wild even when as an old woman she began in a high-pitched voice to recount how "Daayayavid" put her through severe birth pains.

"Oh, Mother! Not that!" he'd fume, without effect on her narration. I never heard her speak that way to Charles.

I realized, sobered, there were deep intolerances present in my father's family spread over generations, of adamant emotional decisions taken with harsh consequences, of unbending perseverance in strife. His golden recreation of this part of his past then is a mythicizing that cloaked his experience in a golden blur.

I knew my father wrote what he wished had happened in the 1944 journals onward that he kept up for myself and Linda, but was shocked, naively, I suppose, that this extended to his own past. Partly that was because the constant emphasis he placed in my childhood on telling the truth lingered on improbably in defiance of what I found to be his deceptiveness. It's taken me a lifetime to learn those who constantly stress this or that virtue invariably practice the opposite.

Louis and Lena, and Nanny and Poppy, preceded Gar in this constant rewriting of the meaning of events. Louis and Lena presented themselves as 'normal' to their children, jovial, maternal, respected, incapable of extreme or unbalanced behavior. Abraham was simply relegated to the void of the unmentionable.

My father's transmutation of a bitter past into its opposite allowed him to love the unendurable, and deny the existence of suffering. Charles took a different course, dismissing all with a shrug and a smile like the Cheshire Cat's in *Alice in Wonderland* whose smile hovers in the air after its body disappears.

The Descent from Levy

Benjamin Levy was born in 1882, one of Louis and Lena's six children, two of whom died in infancy. He grew up in South Bethlehem and revered his home: "Nothing could keep me away from home in South Bethlehem" he wrote even after he left.

He went through the Bethlehem school system, a bright young man Louis hoped would go on to college and become a civil engineer, the quintessential immigrant story. The first generation migrates to the promised land, suffers prejudice and hardship but survives, happier than where they came from. The second generation looks both ways but become Americanized and, with luck, prosper, usually in blue color work, sometimes becoming success stories like Louis Levy. The third generation is simply American, considers college and dreams of becoming lawyers or doctors or engineers. Their children become professors, executives, creative types. Or in the case of Abner, run their own large business, in his case commercial real estate.

In High School Ben was both head of the Shakespearean Society and played football, becoming the team captain. Happily my father reproduced a picture of Ben in his uniform with his team, and recounted his father's anecdotes of being injured and playing tough, biting through his tongue in one game then trying to get a helmet with a faceguard so he could return. Later Gar played tennis and participated in track in High School and then the University of Pennsylvania, taking part in that meet where he was the only one who showed up for the hurdles race which he ran alone against the clock. But at 30 he gave up all physical activity except for walking, for fear of the stress on his heart.

Ben was not an adventurous young man, as his sentiments about leaving home show. At first he helped in Louis' store, then as a junior draftsman in one of the steel factories in town. He endured a month of study at Lehigh before turning his back on college and Louis' dreams for him, content with a life echoing his father's. He might have gone on permanently like this except for his best friend taking a job in Tonopah, Nevada where, after much equivocation, Ben followed in 1906.

This was his great adventure, although only a clerk for the Tonopah and Goldfield Railroad Company. Tonopah was still a frontier town full of rough men, miners, railroad workers, a few cowboys, remnant Indians, saloons and saloon whores. The small businessmen tried to make Tonopah a respectable community. Their wives fought against drunkenness while the law tried to keep the lid on violence. The railroad men lorded it over everyone. It was colorful, dynamic, America in the making, the opposite of the family home in South Bethlehem, and for two years he loved it, going so far as to invest in gold stock that later turned "sour." But two years was enough and he returned home, took a sequence of jobs, then ended at the Midvale Steel Co. in 1909 where he remained until 1949.

Ben's brother Harry, who outlived him by five years, dying in 1961, was something of a black sheep in this solid, stolid family, and was a major influence on my father. Harry was a showman, starting at 11 as a dancer and precocious pianist in local shows. In these, even as a child, he was billed as Harry Lewis. A little older, he joined a variety of troupes that toured Pennsylvania, New York and New England, sometimes venturing into the Midwest, part of the thriving review and burlesque scene which was itself only part of the much larger little theatre scene that dominated the country until silent movies matured and radio, then television, reduced live theatre to secondary importance, and burlesque to television sitcoms with canned laughter.

But in 1916 Harry mysteriously lost his sight. For many years he continued to play the piano at silent films in movie houses in South Bethlehem, his wife beside him to describe the scenes so he knew what to play. He opened a cigar shop in 1921 which he ran until his death forty years later. Its walls were plastered with playbills and the photographs of actors and stars with whom he had worked. My father in due course followed his example into the entertainment world while Charles stayed in Philadelphia with the exception of his one adventurous fling in the Book of the Month Club in Boston, after which he became a professor of English and then Journalism at the University of Pennsylvania, rising to become the Vice

Dean (but to his disappointment, no more) of the Annenberg School. He was as fixed in his orbit as Ben.

But Ben's influence can't be evaluated apart his wife's, Lillian Potasch. He had known her as a child and then lost contact. Years later they met again at his Aunt's in Bayonne after his return from Tonopah. They married three years later in 1912 and were parents of twins in 1913 and of Abner in 1915.

The Potasch Addition

Lillian was born in 1894 and grew into an attractive young woman with masses of dark hair she was very proud of—it came as a shock to her children when she cut it one day for a shorter style. She was the daughter of Jacob and Millie Potasch, nee Goradensky or Goradetsky: history is confused on this point. Jacob was born in Russia in 1854; when or why his family migrated is lost. But the family prospered in New York, Jacob's father working in a yeast factory; Jacob eventually owned a factory making overalls.

Her mother Mildred (Millie) came from notable stock, meaning educated and prosperous, from Poland or Lithuania, depending in which country Vilna was at any given time. The Garchmarski/Levy strain had no claim to notable antecedents. But Lillian's paternal grandfather whose name they anglicized to Charles was a prominent rabbi in Kiev: Charles was named after him. When her mother's family came to New York is also unknown: Millie was born there in 1867, and outlasted Jacob by only three years, dying in 1928. She and Jacob married in the 1880s. Their lives are nearly forgotten in this sketchy description, their griefs and joys erased as if they never were, their faces removed even from the relative immortality of family memory.

How are families ever to break their repetitive inheritances that diminish and burden later lives if the past is forgotten? Churchill had History in mind, but it is as true to say we are doomed to repeat ourselves until knowledge of our own history offers us the chance to be free, a choice we then find hard to take.

Even in the 1880s New York was crowded in all but the elite areas, ethnic ghettos proliferating ever since the first great wave of Irish immigration in 1848. These were areas where people lived cheek by jowl, families crammed into tiny flats who suffered the endless unrecorded violence and disease endemic in such crowded neighborhoods. In the summer the air reeked with effluent and garbage. If there were no cars with their modern smog, the streets were filled with horses, horse manure, and the odors wafting from their stables. All the while those remaining islands of undeveloped land in the five boroughs went down under tides of fresh immigrants and crowded brownstones.

Jacob moved his young family to a country home with clean air in Bayonne, New Jersey, from where he commuted daily to the seasonally aromatic city. He and Millie eventually had eight children, although only three survived infancy, a familiar accounting in that age. The commonness of that shouldn't blind us to the grief of each child lost to each parent, or the terrible burden women labored through. In their lifetimes Jacob and Millie saw advances in health so that that taken-for-granted bearing of hostages to fate was transformed, a transition we have taken further without appreciating what a historical break that is with misery.

Jacob and Millie's children lived a sheltered life in Bayonne, Millie's life eased with maids, and gardeners for the grounds. Lillian adored her mother and the pleasant, farm-like environs of Bayonne, although neither softened her personality even as a child. She wrote of herself that from the beginning she "was always a crank and fussy." When a black gardener died and was laid out in the parlor Nanny couldn't understand why he wouldn't waken. She had never seen death before, she explained, although this hardly squares with her family's infant mortalities. But it is unlikely Gar could have become the practiced forgetter and transformer he was without a model to build on. Nanny went through the local schools where she excelled in drama, usually getting the lead. She writes how

> ...my poor mother had her hands full with me. I remember one play.... I had to have white satin slippers. Well, I got them.... Mother was always so proud of me. I always wanted to do things for myself—no one could suit me.

When she wanted a coat she saw one day when eight, she cried until her mother gave in and got it.

Peering out from between her lines is a strong-willed, demanding, emotionally blackmailing child and later young woman who wanted things her way—the seedling of the person who would refuse to accept her twins' marriages, who needed to be carried into Abner's, and who then tirelessly worked to destroy her sons' marriages.

Perhaps she would not have been so responsive to Ben who, comparatively, was far less well off, and who was never able to duplicate the lifestyle of her earlier years. But in 1894 in Grover Cleveland Alexander's second term Jacob lost almost everything through one of the periodic 'bust' cycles of 19th Century capitalism. Thereafter they were no better off than Louis and Lena.

Ben with his love and steadiness, perhaps even with a frisson of romanticism for having lived for a time adventurously in the West, seemed just right to her when they met again in 1909. There was never a mention of any difficulty when they began courting. After marriage their lives followed a predictable path, Nanny holding sway at home with the children, Ben enjoying his freedom at work or evenings out playing poker with his cronies. Nanny, however, lost no children, and was content with her three boys.

My father remembered how Nanny saved $5 a week for years until she had $2000 for her astonished husband, enabling him to purchase a home for the family. In his retelling the five dollars shrank to twenty-five cents secreted from a weekly allowance of two dollars. But he mentioned no other memories of Nanny alone: most are devoted to his father.

> Images of father—his pulling me in a wagon along Stenton Ave…going sleigh riding in Fernhill Park, with Mother flopping on top of him in the 1920s!…His listening to his first radio around 1925, marking down the call letters of stations from all over the U.S.… Listening to the Dempsey-Tunney fight (it was raining and we listened with earphones)….

In a similar vein he runs through a long list of memories down to Poppy's carrying a clipping of the newspaper notice of my father becoming a Vice President at Young & Rubicam in 1950.

Not mentioned is how Lillian dismissed my father as an equal to his twin, and how Charles was given all the traditional weight of the firstborn. We do not hear how Charles in turn was challenged to match David despite being her firstborn, adding fuel to their lifelong, nonstop competitiveness.

He doesn't mention how Abner had the twins held over his head. "She just went on getting worse," my mother said, thinking of this: "it was crazy."

Gar never explains the feelings behind the dour expressions in his youthful photographs, or his twin's relentless smile. He never explores where his drive to succeed, to be number one, to win at all costs, to make enemies of friends who could then be surmounted, came from. There is no exploration, even, of why he remembered sleigh riding with pleasure, or listening to the Dempsey-Tunney fight, when in reality he despised boxers, and would not have been caught dead on a sleigh with Linda or myself, while if I try to conjure a picture of my mother flopping on him on a sled, it refuses to form. He would have been dismayed, not amused or erotically aroused.

Once my mother shamed him into playing catch with me. We stood in the driveway in front of our house in Connecticut, I with a glove, he pitching. I was fourteen, fully aware this was a unique, onetime occasion plucked out of improbability by my mother. I was so tense I was unable to move quickly as Gar reared back, then released the ball as hard as he could. I missed the catch, and ran up the driveway as the ball skittered on the gravel. I was shamefaced when I lobbed it back to him—surely the fault must be mine for forcing him to do this, then failing half the time to catch his throws. Our contact had to be intellectual, aggression ritualized.

There is no explanation, either, in my father's memories for his repugnance at his physical nature, or of how he came to confuse our excretory and sex organs. Ben must have explained sex to him in the same manner, passing on his own confusion to his son. Given the prevailing sexual ignorance and repression of the era, such confusion is not surprising. Vistas of sexual confusion open in all directions, reaching into the modern era as if Freud, or sex education, never existed. That was one of the reasons, I think, Gar doused himself in cologne. Nor is there ever a mention of "strife contend weep," which was the order of his homelife.

Only intimated is how poor they were. At first Poppy and Nanny lived in a crowded neighborhood of small apartments in South Philadelphia until Nanny did succeed in saving a down payment from their minimal funds for the home they purchased in the mid 1920s.

It was in those earlier, crowded circumstances she bore the twins and Abner. Having identical twins gave her a certain cachet, and she made a point of making sure her neighbors knew. These were the circumstances and neighborhood the boys knew until their early teens. Louis and Lena's home in South Bethlehem must have seemed palatial.

One consequence of those years was that Gar stayed poor in his mind no matter how his circumstances altered. Giving financial help to others was almost beyond him. Perhaps in this he echoed Grandfathers Louis and Jacob: the former apparently gave Ben little help to live better, but left him to make his own way. The latter did the same with his daughter Lillian.

This offers a historical root to Gar's nightly ritual examination of his bankbooks: they represented a superiority to circumstances that needed constant affirmation.

For myself, Nanny was always pleasant to me, but even as a child I was uncomfortable with her. Children are hardly savants or always truthful, but in their singleness of focus on the adults around them there are few nuances they miss.

The Affair

Early in her marriage my mother visits Philadelphia with my father. The entire family gathers in the Levy living room after dinner to listen as a singer begins on the radio.

"Daayayavid," says Nanny, "Isn't that Betty George?" I'm not sure I have the name right.

"Yes, Mother."

"My, she's awfully good, isn't she Chararles?"

"Yes, Mother."

"What do you think, Abner?"

"She's awfully good, Mother."

"Mother, be quiet, or we'll miss her," my father insists, desperate to silence her.

"There I was," my mother told me later, "newly married, and she carried on about that woman everyone in the room knew your father was having an affair with, even then, including Abner and Margie who weren't yet married. No one said anything to me, or ever apologized afterwards. Including Margie."

The insult still smarted in her eighties.

Abner

Uncle Abner struck me like a younger, more vigorous and genial version of Poppy. His laughter filled the room, and he amused me with his tricks. He was an exotic, something from my father's side that was fun. I remember him leaning against the mantel in Great Neck and making spoons ring for my amusement. He dressed well, a clothes horse in his son Bob's memory. All the brothers dressed well, but Abner even better than Charles or my father. Somehow it mattered more to him, I suspect, for if my father could never be "my son" and first, Abner, as Bob pointed out to him, could never be one of the twins. Like Uncle Charles, he stayed in Philadelphia where, like his brothers, he too was in daily communication with his mother. Unlike them he went into Philadelphia commercial real estate and throve, living happily with Margie all his life, personally stable as the twins were not.

Many years later when Bob and I tried to understand how Nanny could have such a grip on three such able men, and I said a few nice things about Poppy, Bob corrected me.

"They were the same," Bob said. "One made the bullets, the other fired the gun."

Abner neither made nor fired bullets. He benefited by having the twins as a buffer between himself and his parents—it must have been clear early that he was not going to shine intellectually like they did. Envy them he may have, resent them, certainly, love them—and treasure his moments of successful rivalry, like once meeting them for lunch with a blonde on his arm neither of the twins had succeeded in dating.

"We wondered afterward how he had done that," Gar said.

But Abner was seen only infrequently, not tied to Gar and Charles as they were umbilically to each other. Once my mother banned Philadelphia and limited Nanny and Poppy's visits, the occasions to see Abner diminished. A later photo shows he and Margie at our summer cottage in Westhampton in the 1950s, but I have no memory of that trip.

He alone of the brothers had an air of 'normalcy' about him, despite Nanny's lifelong grip on his attention.

A Trip to Philadelphia

Without direct evidence it is hard to grasp just how badly Gar and Charles were warped as children, or how potent was their parents' malign, continuing influence in their adult lives. But two late events bring that vividly to life.

In 1982 when I turned 40 I thought it a good idea to do something with my father and so after 36 years had passed since I was last in Philadelphia I accompanied him on a visit to see Uncle Charles. Charles was retired, aside from one radio station for which he still wrote reviews, the tail end of his long domination of the Philadelphia cultural scene. His apartment drowned in books piled on the floor, stacked in closets and in the kitchen cabinets, even stuffed into the oven. He still received review copies of books he gave as gifts to family and friends. His own books are anthologies he put together in earlier years, and seven page chapbooks of short, witty poetry he sent out at Christmas.

He also painted, largely small, primitive, Roualtish figures of clowns, turning only occasionally to other subjects. Sometimes wealthy friends arranged local exhibitions. A number of these friends had dropped him by the time of this visit.

"He's a skinflint," my father explained to me. "He never offers to pick up the bill at lunch or dinner. People, including wealthy ones who expect to do so, are annoyed by that sort of thing. He never saw how they came to resent being taken for granted." I took this in the context of their constant rivalry, but it has a certain truth to it. The greater truth was that Charles never had the sort of money possessed by my father. When he died there was nothing but books and paintings for his widow.

At 69 Charles was still unusually good-looking in contrast to his twin whom age differentiated ever more sharply from Charles. Charles' hair was white but full, with a youthful wave. He walked without a stoop, always with that ready smile, and a good color, as if a much younger man. Gar's hair was flat and thin, he rarely smiled, and steadily developed a stoop. It is worth repeating they were genetically identical. Their competitiveness never compromised their closeness or daily contact with one another, often several times a day by phone as well as by letter. They were closer by far than either ever was to his wives or children. They were each other's true intimates.

Only Nanny matched this intimacy. So I was not surprised to hear the phone ring in the morning after we arrived.

"Hello?" Charles answered. "Oh, hello mother.... I thought the doctor was sensible.... Yes, you should take the medicines.... No, mother, I don't think you need to see him right away, the medicines— .... Yes, mother.... No, I'm sure he is right!"

His voice rises. I am in his study, and do my best to look elsewhere.

"Mother, you know you need to take your medicines.... No, you'll end up in the hospital if you don't! What?.... Yes, I'm coming over.... No, not now—.... Because I have to finish my review, mother.... The review I do every day, that you know I do every day!"

There is a screech in his voice. I am astonished.

"I'll be over when I finish my review, mother, with David and Lance," he continues. "About noon, mother.... No, I can't come before that mother, there's no need to—.... There's nothing wrong with your medicines— ...."

Before my eyes the accomplished man melted into a thirteen year old.

"No mother I'm not coming now I have to finish my review and yes about noon then Lance and David and—.... Jeez! Your medicines—.... OH Mother! I'll Call You Later!"

He slammed down the phone. I drifted out quietly and examined the omnipresent piles of books. Fifteen minutes later she called again. The same distinguished professor again melted into a 13 year old screech by the call's repetitive climax. Nanny called every fifteen minutes for an hour-and-a-half until we left. I said nothing, but reflected on how ingrained such a pattern must be for Uncle Charles to take it as a normal part of the day. All through this my father was conspicuously busy elsewhere in the apartment.

Gar walks in with a cheery greeting at Nanny's where her three sons maintain her with around the clock care, but as she replies and stares at him I watch his shoulders sag and head lower and hear the almost immediately false note in his voice. His words are like rain, but they cannot drown out her presence. It is Sunday, but Nanny declares she would like a Reuben for lunch. In 1982 Philadelphia was still mostly shut down on Sundays. Although Charles protests that none of the delis are open, she is insistent. Her voice, always nasal with a note of complaint in it, whines with a sharp edge. She sees poorly without glasses, and her eyes float behind thick lenses as she takes in her boys and stares appraisingly at me.

I greet her pleasantly. I can all but see the strings in her hands rooted in Charles and Gar's chests, and can tell from her gaze she is puzzled that none lead to me. I am a stranger from a strange land.

"There must be someone open," she says to Charles, determined on her sandwich. Helplessly he begins calling delis, and at length finds one open with a kosher Reuben. It will take 45 minutes to get there, he tells his mother, no longer the professor, plaintive.

"I'll wait," she says. She smiles. Charles sighs, I steal a glance at my father's face, and turn to Charles.

"I'll come along." Gar visibly wilts. He will have to spend an hour-and-a-half with his mother, alone. There is nothing he can say. Only his mouth smiles as I follow Charles out. Charles recovers in the car, and we brightly chatter while he points out interesting landmarks. He is himself again as we stride into the apartment nearly two hours later brandishing the sandwich in triumph. Her attention shifts from my father who is exhausted and angry.

"Here you are mother," he smiles. He puts his trophy on the TV table before her.

I wonder how often as boys he or Gar or Abner strode proudly into her presence with some sports or academic token of success and later, some professional accomplishment, hoping to bask in the sun of her approval.

Now she smiles and unwraps the sandwich with great deliberation. Her sons watch her hands, hanging on each movement. At length the precious sandwich lies revealed. She pauses. She looks up at Charles, her eyes swimming behind the lenses.

"But there's no pi-i-i-ck-ckle, Chararles." Her nasal voice is full of disappointment. She has heroically waited well past her normal lunchtime for Charles to meet her desire, old and needy as she may be, and what has he done? Brought her something thrown together in haste, something not special, something not even ordinary but sub par, without even a conventional condiment. What kind of place has he gone to? Who does he think she is to be so cavalierly treated? The strings jerk in her hands. Charles and Gar are speechless. She begins to rewrap the sandwich.

"Mother," Charles begs, instantly reduced to 13, voice high-pitched, incredulous: "aren't you even going to try it?"

It's all in their performance. None of their words are extraordinary in themselves. But the emotional transformations were. She looked up at her gray, distinguished 13 year old children. She smiled.

"I'll try half." She lifts a half and takes a bite, my father and uncle rooted in place watching the sandwich rise to her mouth, waiting to see if the taste will please her.

My God, what she must have put them all through.

Disowned

A second piece of direct evidence surfaced in 2003 when Charles' widow Ruth sent three letters from 1952 she found in his files to his son, Myles, who shared them with me. As I read them I thought of my cousin Bob's remark regarding Poppy and Nanny, "One made the bullets, the other fired the gun."

Charles parents' hostility to his first marriage was unrelenting after he and Erma eloped in 1940, but as he declares in a 1952 letter his intention to marry Judy Kellem (a Catholic divorcee with four children), Poppy executes a 180 degree turn and castigates him. He begins by reminding Charles how he was

> …raised properly, and had the love of the best mothers any boy could have…decent, not because of your own self but from good training and there are many who know this decency and this training. You came through all childhood sicknesses and turmoils, not through your own efforts but because of a good mother's work & efforts; you received education better than the average—not because you made it yourself, but because your mother willed it—wanted it & deprived herself of many things so you were able go and be somebody—and not all mothers are like that especially in the financial situation we were in.

Everything is due to his parents, especially to his mother. Charles' subsequent maturation has "brought you nothing of value," Poppy adds, "nothing that shows the good breeding and upbringing that you had." Poppy concedes Charles "knows many things—things you like to show off," but that is nothing to be proud of, for

> ...you are all mixed up—mixed up in life, in general. Your mind is wandering; you are running around in circles and have no pleasure in all this "know all." You never will!

Charles has lived a life of "lies" with Erma, Poppy claims, telling him a few weeks after marrying Erma that he, Charles didn't love her. Is such a life "the way of a good man?" Worse,

> ...many times you hurt your own mother by injustices just to have her suffer, no doubt, but still clinging to the wife whom you say you did not love in all those years.

On top of this, Judy is

> ...one who crept (slyly) into your home and between you two, you find something—a feeling—an intense feeling of sexual love(?). And this degrading <u>love</u> carried on in secret for a few years. My god! What about your growing son and daughter?

So Charles perpetuated a lying marriage, lied again to hide his infidelity with a 'sly' woman on the make who inserted herself into his "home" as if between the marital sheets, governed by blind lust. This sounds as though Charles is still married to Erma, at last determined to divorce her after years of deception, but Charles is already divorced, as is Judy. They marry five months later. But Judy is the least of it.

> What about your mother. She is closer to the end than you know—<u>much</u> <u>closer</u> and if anything happens to her through this terrible ordeal—through this sexual disturbance you will regret all through the rest of your life—through your momentary Bliss(?) more than anything in this world. If that is love, God help you.

Charles now is endangering *Nanny's* life for low, sexual pleasure. "All of this will kill—maybe not as a murder, but worse than one."

Don't send doctors to your mother. She is sane—too sane and too loving. She needs help and help from those she loves. You are callous—through and through and time will tell. At 39 or 40 or 50 you still are not a man.... You are a coward—a cur—who will learn, maybe too late. I pity you—not as a human, but as a human to a poor beast (and you don't deserve even that name).

Charles in 1952 is 39, a popular reviewer of film and literature in print, radio, and television in Philadelphia, a tenured associate professor at Penn, the firstborn, always favored son. Poppy isn't done with Judy. She

> is worse than a w------- should hang her head in shame although I know she is shameless and so are you. For your mother's sake for your <u>own</u> children's sake (and not for your own selfish pleasure—sexual or others) I pray that you think—think and think again before you kill those you once loved and held dear. Sex and sexual pleasures are not a decent end to a good life. Others may do these things—<u>don't</u> <u>do</u> <u>what</u> <u>others</u> <u>do</u>.... I hope and pray you will see this the way a good father and son should. I could have been <u>bad</u> myself I was strong enough to know right from wrong and never disgraced anyone.
>
> As for me, I never care to hear from you or see you again.

He signs it, "Benjamin Levy."

Now the story of how Nanny was carried into Abner's wedding reveals itself as the final act of a failed attempt at extreme emotional blackmail that must have been extraordinarily hard for Abner and his brothers to live through, to say nothing of Margie and her family. When my father sought to have his parents come to their public wedding in Great Neck in 1942 this was the extreme intemperance and emotional blackmail he faced. Such intemperance lends force to my mother's words that "he was afraid to death of his mother."

Poppy's obvious contempt for sex and physical pleasure is also plain, echoed and reechoed in my father's contempt for the lack of cleanliness of sex even as he serially indulged in affairs.

Charles' reply affects an above-it-all air in a ten page, typed, single-spaced reply, managing repeatedly to hit the wrong note, as if out to confirm his father's charge he is a "know-all." Charles starts by noting the virtues of:

> love: nations that respect one another...live in peace together; families that regard the privileges and privacies and aspirations of their members with equal tolerance, affection and good humor also live together in mutual respect and love; individuals who compose their desires and their capabilities and who try...to do the right...achieve a poise...that permits them to function.... Mercy is a greater word than justice, and harder to practice; love is a greater word than mercy, and still harder to practice. And if you are going to toss commandments around, the greatest of all is the eleventh—namely, the injunction thou shalt love.

He is a professor instructing a student, an older man enlightening a troubled younger, a 'father' patiently trying to make a recalcitrant 'son' see the light. Charles adds there is no argument about his gratitude for all Poppy and his mother have done for him.

> I am and always will be grateful for everything done me by my parents, but I have never believed that the proper expression of that gratitude is uncritical and unmanly obeisance.

It is easy enough to guess from these lines that gratitude was often extorted from Charles and his brothers, explicitly demeaning. Poppy speaks of Charles' instinctive and moral ignorance; Charles argues his education has not been taken far enough! Poppy must be quarreling with Charles for his having an "independent mind," instead. This is ludicrously far from Poppy's charges, as is Charles' casuistic attempt to say the charge he is all mixed up or "wandering" is tantamount to thinking of him as insane, and would you be cruel to someone in such a state? No, what is needed, again, is that "hard word," "love."

The same academic tone continues as Charles turns to Erma. He denies having fallen out of love with Erma as soon as a few weeks after they were married. But, as a man can discover he is in love, "A man also discovers that he is not in love...."

It doesn't help to point out that they came "to a mutually satisfactory decision" to divorce. Charles does "not blame, I try to understand." He avoids the accusation it was Judy's presence in his life that caused him to discover "he is not in love" with Erma any more.

He at last becomes more direct against the charge he hurt his mother "just to see her suffer."

> ...you say I did injustices to Mother "just to see her suffer" on the several occasions I defended Erma from what I thought unreasonable treatment. I will not go into causes though I know you know that *intemperateness of language* [my italics] is not uncommon in our family, but I did not defend Erma in order to injure Mother, I defended her as I would defend anyone unjustly treated. Unfortunately, Mother has long had notions that if you are not on her side, you are against her....

This in reference to a woman who from childhood carried on until she got what she wanted, and evidently found a soul mate in Poppy. Her relentless emotional blackmail, blindly supported by Poppy, remained unbroken towards my father and Charles. Gar's transformations of experience pale before his mother's distortion of reality to make herself the fount of all good and her boys of all evil. All that was 'true' in their home were Nanny's emotions, however illogical or incredible.

Charles piles on words and sentences and reflections in his letter as though the sheer weight of verbiage will carry the day. Judy's divorce had nothing to do with him, he adds, or his with her; she was anything but a "w-------." He turns to Nanny, again.

> You say her health is being affected. How is it being affected? Can you really believe that your attitude, never mind mine for the moment, is helping her? Isn't there such a thing as aiding and abetting morbidity? Isn't there at least the shadow of truth in the notion she nurses her griefs?

A picture clearly emerges of a mother prepared to go to emotional and verbal extremes, who nursed griefs, and who slipped into a melodramatic questioning of life itself in the face of her children persisting in behavior she found offensive. An adult may see through such manipulations: a child is laid under an appalling burden, and the child in us remains so. That "morbidity" was a sword hanging over them to enforce their acquiescence to what she desired.

Finally Charles appeals to his father to constrain his mother if only to establish a "truce in relationships," and reminds Poppy,

> Once Mother asked me, long ago a plain question: to wit, would you be happy with Judy? I said yes. There was no uproar at the answer, though the matter was not further discussed.

The truth is Charles and Judy's families had socialized for years, even on occasion with Poppy and Nanny. Charles and Judy's growing attraction would have been apparent, however that grew step by step, immersed in the difficulties and ambivalences of failing marriages. That is not a perspective open to the black and white world of Poppy and Nanny.

Poppy apparently referred to Charles' endless letter derogatively as a "book" and dismissed Charles' arguments. Exasperated, Charles at last wrote:

> There is insincerity here and a history of prejudice I would not so often revive: one doesn't mention rope in a house where there has been a hanging.

Gar and Charles would have debated Charles' divorce and remarriage repeatedly, but in no journal or in any of his later memorabilia did Gar refer to these events. There was only the kind, hard-working father and devoted, self-sacrificing mother.

There were so many reasons my home was divided into opposing camps, but none stands closer to being the root cause than a mother and father who ascribed all virtue to themselves and relentlessly berated the failures of their unworthy children.

If we are reluctant to admit how this external shaping in our childhood becomes part and parcel of our innate sense of self, in Gar and his brothers that shaping resulted in their virtually instinctive sense of being maimed and inadequate. The 'sins of the fathers' descend down the generations as each individual in turn creates a life that *feels familiar* to their early wounded selves, perpetuating their *emotional* inheritance. That in turn engenders the same reproaches in *their* children towards them and their own inner selves which they, their parents, first felt in relation to themselves and their own parents.

So each wounding drives each of us to formulate a sense of ourselves in a story at its root comfortable with this primary wounding, which in turn drives us to transform experience into something else to make it endurable—a method apparent in Gar and Charles. That is how both 'the sins of the father' and their mythicizing move on, one wave rolling into the next, each wave different, but always the same water.

Poppy never did speak to Charles again during the last four years of his life.

Nanny, however, demanded and received unbroken her daily calls and letters.

The Myth of a Golden Age

I thought my mother was the greater fantasist with her memories of Daddy Wilds, just as I thought it was her swings in weight I blindly emulate. Now I realize my weight swings were modeled on my father's, who complained of his own swings in his post 1944 journals or letters to my mother after her first flight, while his rewriting of experience dwarfed her own.

Gar drew a golden, sentimental haze over his grandparents and his own childhood and youth, and then drew that same haze over his marriage and character with the 1944 journals and the later biographical fragments, to say nothing of his conscious memories. In these he was a beloved son, then a doting father and husband, his parents genial presences wishing all well. There were no steamed letters, no parental viciousness, no wedding difficulties. His ambivalence over my name is not expressed until his 60s. My attending Sunday School is never remarked on at the time, nor his father's mocking taunt. That his father could mock or be angry, let alone disown a son was unimaginable. That was the world my father sought to convince me as a child was the actual world. His reconstruction of reality was a continual moment to moment process with himself as a first step.

There is though a wistfulness about it all, as in this letter Gar wrote for his mother's 50th birthday in 1944.

> Dear Folks,
> Greetings to the mater and pater—and a hope that they have shaken off the bug.
>
> I've enclosed a small check for you mother—and tho I know you've had bills—I hope you can use this birthday gift for

something personal. Why not indulge in something you've always wanted like a bottle of Chanel or whatever you'd like. I'd thought of sending you a gift—but I'm doing that at Xmas and finally concluded you might enjoy a bit of shopping for yourself.

Say this means you're fifty! First it's Dad who goes into a new decade—then Charles and I into our thirties—now you—and in a little while Ab will leave these wonderful twenties and cross the bridge into the maturing thirties.

I suppose when you reach 50 you begin to think of all the people you remember who were 50 when you were 20—and you wonder—am I like that! Well even when you're 30 why you think about the people who turned 30 when you were 20. Actually I find that I'm the same in many respects as I was at 20—slowed down a bit—and a little more used to the world—but actually barely changed. I think—if a person stays mentally alert—he never cares a hoot about physical age. You certainly don't show it. That may be because your family is still about you—and growing. Five years ago you had no Myles or Gail or Lance. Now isn't it fun to think of them growing into "people"—little personalities—a whole new world ahead of them? You'll doubtless relive your own early parental days as they go to school—as you see <u>them</u> graduate as you saw us. Yes on your 50th birthday you have the greatest gift of all in yourself—and the challenge that lies ahead—in the helping to further mold a little bit of you——for these youngsters are in part you—and together there is a great deal of real joy and full happiness to look ahead to. Their future is yours—
love
David

This 'mater and pater' tone is one my father used with no one else, full of 'spontaneous' expressions like, "Say this means your fifty!" or "he never cares a hoot." He manages to be the dutiful son and virtually a parent chiding a child about how much she has to be grateful about. It is barely two years since the marital confusions of 1942, and he writes knowing full well the degree of hostility emanating from Philadelphia. So he works through the birthday to the imagined perspectives of different ages until he can get to the heart of it all, the reminder of the joy to take in grandchildren in the future who "are in part you"—Nanny's various suicide threats or insults consigned to limbo.

Our mythicizing is an ineradicable process in our very core not just to make sense of ourselves, but to make that sense bearable, so this family history will be misunderstood if taken simply as an expose or condemnation. We live in hope, in the effort to make out of unsatisfactory experience something cleaner, happier, more elevated, and meaningful. We live in these illusions unless driven to extremes, like my family's, they finally collapse around us.

The Mustache

When Ben and Lillian first marry he has a mustache.

He is proud of it, and though Nanny hates it, Ben refuses to shave it off in a rare instance of his defying his wife.

Nanny stews as the weeks then months go by.

One day she has a brainstorm, and begins chewing gum a little before he comes home. When he walks in the door she embraces and kisses him—and pushes the gum up into the hated mustache. Try as he does Ben can't get the gum out, and at last has to shave off his mustache.

He does not try to grow another.

THE WILDS MYTH

Bananas

Daddy Wilds was down to a few small coins on his travels in Central America as a young man and did not eat for several days before he came across some men loading bananas on a wagon. He liked bananas, and one bunch was ripe enough to eat. He had just enough pocket change to buy it—bananas were cheap in the Banana Republics.

Feeling like a king he sat by the side of the road and set to heartily. He ate even after hunger was sated, and finished off the bunch. Then a wave of revulsion hit him, and he never ate a banana again. Years later, in college, I decided to make a dinner out of turnips. I was short of money and turnips were cheap. I mashed a plateful and ate after hunger was sated, determined to clean my plate—until a wave of revulsion rolled over me. I have never eaten a turnip again.

But all my life I have had an almost insatiable hunger for bananas.

Where Do We Experience Experience?

What a strange question! you may well think. It is all very well to talk of family inheritances, mythicizing, parental or cultural influences on children, or the 'sins of the fathers' being handed on generation by generation but: where does this happen? If you are part of the same culture as I am, rooted in Cartesian dualism where 'I' and 'You' do not overlap, how does such transmission cross the gulf between us? The English psychoanalyst Winnicott had the genius to ask just that question of where shared experience—play, and later adult shared creative or any other shared activity—exists.

Poets, dramatists and screenwriters know instinctively an either/or dichotomy of selves cannot explain our imaginative power to make leaps of identity between viewer and created work, be that with a Hamlet or a Dr. Strange. Winnicott acknowledges there is indeed a private realm of what he calls the true self, my 'I,' and your separate 'I.' But he saw there is also an area of overlap where 'I' and 'You' blur and blend in all those activities that make up the world of shared experience and which constitutes so much of our lives, an 'I-Us-You' division of experience whose boundaries fluidly overlap, one so obvious I wonder why it is so hard for us to take it in.

He calls this area the transitional space.[16]

In that space we interact with others, first in the world of childhood play, then in that of adult shared activity. It is there that the infant, then child, encounters his parents, and they him. It is there that the dialectic of our myths, our stories, takes place, outwardly between the family and its members with the surrounding social/cultural/historical world, inwardly between family members down to its youngest member.

This tripartite view of reality implies our 'I' contains elements of the supposedly absolutely-divided-from-us 'Other.' Some part of the 'Other'—

you, for example, becomes an intrinsic part of 'me.' Worse, an abusive 'Other' in childhood takes up residence in our own 'I,' our supposedly private sense of self, so that we will abuse ourselves even after the original abuser is gone.

Understandably, we struggle with this.

Ours is a transformative age, and dualism a view we are moving from into something new and still largely inarticulate and undefined. The day is slowly coming when we will realize if we misuse another, we directly misuse ourselves.

Our 'I' in its greatest privacy is always something of a crowd, of our family and equally of our inescapable strangers.

The Woman Who Knows

Mothie was no ancestor but as contemporary and nearly as important as Mom in my experience, although she trailed a long, complex inheritance. Mothie, too, was in the ascendant when Mom and Gar moved to Great Neck after Daddy Wilds' death. There as my mother grew up under the pressure of her relationship with my father she reversed Mothie's ascendancy until Mothie became her accessory, her role then to free her daughter to accompany my father on his social whirl, give my mother moral and conventional direction and, while she could, financial aid.

As we saw Mothie nursed Linda and I if we were sick with a frozen cloth for a feverish brow, or hot, fried rags for a congested chest before a doctor was called. Mom might be desired at night if I woke from nightmare, but Mothie provided the solace even after Bud's interdiction. Mothie provided the performance I required to eat, and potty-trained us as she did years later my daughter, Heather. Crucially, Mothie knew when Mom went too far and drew the line, swift to support Mom's anger if Gar misbehaved, then quick to urge reconciliation if he caved. It was Mothie who was our pillar of normalcy and conventional standards in a family increasingly at sea. She and Mom were a match for the intimacy between Gar and Charles although, like them, as often irritable with each other as not.

Linda and I thought Mothie was Prussian in background, as did her own children: Prussia seemed the right source for her authoritarian character. Years passed before we learned she was also English, and later was actually from Bavaria, which is at least as much Catholic as Protestant, and where the good life wasn't equated with Prussian discipline.

Her steel was a self-manufactured element of character, her youth its forge, the finished pillar of society a willed self-transformation.

Femme Fatale

There may have been Dutch blood in her too, for her mother's great grandfather was one Harold C von (van) Wart. Whether he was German born in Holland, or Dutch, isn't known. He became a protestant minister and spent his life as a pastor in Belgium and then the Alsace, that region along with Lorraine perpetually contested by Germany and France until now, eerily, one freely drives back and forth between the massive, deserted custom complexes that litter their modern border.

Three generations pass before sure knowledge is available, and Harold's great granddaughter Charlotte is born German, a Do(e)bler in Kirckheim unter Teck in the then Duchy of Wurttemberg in Bavaria. Charlotte received Harold's Bible from her mother, who had received it from hers down the generations, and in turn passed it on to Mothie. It is a pity no one in the sequence of generations kept a record of births, marriages and deaths on a front or back leaf, as with so many other family Bibles. Perhaps Mothie's hostility to records and dates was not unique but a peculiar family trait.

Mothie was born Emma Emsley in 1894: her English father William died two months before she was born, only twenty-eight. How Lotte met William, whether in Kirckheim unter Teck, England, or America, is lost. Lotte was in New York at William's death and returned to Kirckheim unter Teck to her family with her three young daughters under the shock of that loss. Kirckheim unter Teck is a prosperous, small city only fifty miles from Nuremberg, twenty minutes from Stuttgart. The name in part comes from the Dukes of Teck, one of the key ancestral lineages for the Dukes of Wurttemberg.

There the star-crossed Lotte remarried again, only to lose this unknown second husband shortly after their marriage for unknown reasons. Now, mysteriously, Lotte returned to New York on her own, leaving Mothie behind with her older sister Minnie and a third sister who died during Lotte's absence. I don't know which family relatives the children were left with during the next four years without their mother, only that the family was successful, and counted among its cousins the Lord High Mayor of Nuremberg. There is nothing like the information on my Levy ancestors available for the Wilds or Doblers.

In New York Lotte married a third time, to Adam Baehr. She bore him six more children. Once settled she sent for Mothie and Minnie, now proper little German girls who had to relearn English and American ways. Worse, Mothie had to leave behind whoever from her infancy filled the roles of parents for her, and start over with a mother Mothie at least would not have remembered.

We know today how traumatic it is to uproot and confuse these early childhood relationships. There is often a fundamental insult to one's narcissism and an accompanying anger, a self-assertive drive to control events, and paradoxical self-depreciation. We can only guess how these elements affected Minnie and little Emma as first their mother left them, and then they were taken from those who filled in for her.

What came next in New York with Lotte and Adam complicated matters further. Adam was fond of Mothie, but not Minnie. Minnie was always a stocky, stalwart figure as well as stolid in personality, growing heavier as she aged, a frequent figure in my childhood, as she remained Mothie's favorite sister. She was not always unattractive, drawing in time the impassioned ardor of Fred Buehler, whom she married. He wrote her in 1902:

> It is only since I know you that I have really begun to live. Life seems more beautiful, the skies of a more lovely view, the odors of the flowers more fragrant.

Eventually Aunt Minnie had rolls of flesh under her arms that shook when she laughed or let me jiggle them, while Uncle Fred became a quiet gentleman with a cigar always waving in his mouth that Minnie paid particular attention to when they drove anywhere. If it stopped moving, she jabbed him.

"Wake up, Fred! Keep your eyes on the road."

The cigar began to move again, and Minnie, for a time, to relax.

Mothie was a pretty child who promised beauty, so much so Adam showed her off to his friends, even taking her into the saloons where they drank. She was apparently a confident character, not shy or easily intimidated despite the upheavals in her childhood or Adam's behavior. As she put it, "I was socially aggressive." But something went wrong in the Baehr home because of Adam's attentiveness to young Emma. Adam was an awning maker, and well off, so the pressure of children in an age of large families was unlikely to be the reason why at ten years of age Mothie found herself ejected from her mother's family and her sister Minnie's companionship and sent to live on City Island with her Aunt Sophie Gauss and her husband, Frederick, with their four children. Frederick was a successful inn and apartment builder, including the Noble Apartments on Manhattan's east side, prosperous enough to own a large sailing yacht he raced with others from City Island Yacht Club when City Island was one of the places to be. One of the few pieces of memorabilia Mothie preserved was a clipping of Fred and Sophie's 50th anniversary at the City Island Yacht Club, two happy faces behind a large, white cake.

Again Mothie had to form a new set of attachments, a third sense of family. The relations between herself as a teen with a mother who was not there and an Aunt who was now in effect her mother must have been complex. As Emma turned into a young woman she turned to Aunt Sophie for counsel and as an example crucial to her shaping, not to her mother. Her own growing forcefulness of character as she matured must have added a great deal of teenage stress to the process, however better behaved on the surface a teenager might then have been. Yet at 16, after six years, Mothie was ejected from the Gauss household too and sent to live with her Aunt Lena Rapp in Manhattan, where she had an apartment at 72nd and Madison.

Again the reason is mysterious, for among their own children, Fred Jr., Arthur, Phillip, and Mildred, Mothie should have seemed just another sibling after six years. Even odder, Mothie did not return home to Lotte and Adam Baehr. Mothie never lived with Lotte again. Throughout her later life she preserved almost no memorabilia of Lotte: two pictures, a newspaper clipping that shows Mothie, Mom, and Lotte together, and two obituary notices. In her declining years Lotte lived with a daughter by Adam, Tillie, in Greenwich, Connecticut.

Aunt Lena had one daughter, Gertrude, and between the two of them Mothie felt ill-treated. She once described herself to me as now being a beautiful young woman, and I remember her description of herself as "socially aggressive." Trouble followed her, although the upheavals she went through did not lessen her self-confidence. She was popular at school, with a crew of admirers, but felt Aunt Lena and Gertrude envied her instead of being solicitous of a displaced young woman! Perhaps they did. Perhaps they also found her headstrong and too overwhelming a rival for Gertrude. Perhaps by now even well-meant charity seemed instead just another insult to Emma's self-esteem.

So by her own decision Mothie left Aunt Lena to live with her cousin Emily, who was married and had a family. By now she seems to have moved into a phase of permanent crisis, ever more distant from her family. For her life with Emily proved short-lived, too. Within half a year of leaving Aunt Lena Mothie found herself sharing an apartment with an unrelated girl with whom she worked in a millinery shop. She had dropped out of high school, begun to take night classes, and now needed to support herself.

Why was she cut off from her family, first by Adam and Lotte, then Aunt Sophie in City Island, Aunt Lena in Manhattan, and Cousin Emily, to find herself now on her own? How aggressive could she have been? How disturbing could her beauty have been? How daring her morals? This wasn't an age when prosperous families abandoned daughters to their fate. That would be rare at any time except in desperate circumstances. The strongest reason implied is inappropriate behavior and feelings by Adam Baehr. Good girls, let alone children, were not trotted out to saloons to be admired. That Mothie was sent away and not invited back later points to feelings alarming to Lotte in Adam—or in Mothie towards her husband. Yet there was never a hint of impropriety about Mothie then or later from anyone, except Nanny in her scurrilous Christmas 1946 letter who knew nothing of Mothie's youth and was only slightly acquainted with her as a widow.

Nor was Mothie so angered by her treatment that she forbade mention of Baehr later: Bud even used "Emzley-Bhaer" as one of his middle names when he joined Phi Sigma Kappa in 1939 at the University of Alabama.

But Mothie was not invited back after she left the Gauss home, either. Was there too much rivalry between Mothie and Mildred? Or did she become too attractive to Fred, Arthur, or Phillip? That seems suggested by her belief Aunt Lena and Gertrude felt jealous of her, despite her situation, for what was there to envy in a girl cut loose at sixteen now from two families?

Nowhere, in all this, was there a 'mother' for Emma, if we mean by that a caring presence who saw her through to adulthood and marriage. If Mothie came to embody the role of reigning matriarch in our family she created that role out of a desire to transform her circumstances into their opposite, an idealized but actual behavior contrasted to Gar's idealized version of himself and his family which did not accord with reality.

Just two months after taking an apartment with her coworker in the millinery shop Mothie came home to find the girl's father had come for his daughter and removed everything else in the apartment, too. It was yet another abandonment. Desperate yet buoyant, Mothie now stayed with her Spanish-American neighbors, paying $18/week for a room while she continued to work and go to school at night, although that figure seems high for the times. At least in Mothie's case, we are sure of the power of her youthful allure and self-confidence, for the son of the family she rented her room from fell in love with her, and she was sent packing after only eight weeks.

Briefly Mothie returned to Aunt Lena. Things had reached a crisis: there was no one she could be with, and she was too young to be left wholly on her own. Fred and Sophie Gauss came to her rescue: she was put in one of Fred's empty apartments. She would be supported there by the Gausses, not by Adam and Lotte. She would live by herself. There she stayed and finished high school, and for two years attended classes at Adelphi University.

While at Adelphi Emma became a Gibson Girl. The "Gibson Girl" ideal was created by Charles Dana Gibson in the late 19th Century, who drew satirical sketches of society figures, and created an image of the ideal young woman that became definitive for fashion in the 1890s and 1900s as Mothie grew up. Such a girl had to be beautiful, athletic, and at least outwardly modest. The hairstyle and clothing Dana imagined became de rigueur for aspiring young beauties.

It is not clear whether Mothie modeled herself on this idealization, or became a model for one of its late incarnations, or even whether in looking back long after these events she confused the two together. There is no history of her having actually worked as a model, no preserved clippings or pictures (with dates removed), no appearances in magazines. Instead the image of a lovely, assured if modest, athletic, impeccably dressed and coiffed young woman, poised, at home in all situations, became the first of her self-remodelings from which the woman, wife, mother, and matron she was to become could emerge, the pillar I knew in childhood on whom her daughter increasingly leaned.

At least now, cared for but on her own, neither her beauty, social aggressiveness, nor the unwanted advances of others were a threat, however many suitors she may have had. She proved quite capable of managing on her own in this fashion, and the years following her installation in Gauss's apartment pass without further upheaval.

Two pictures survive of the Emma of this period. She sits without a smile, serious, her dark hair framing a piquant face of striking attractiveness. She seems to be in her Gibson Girl mode, a broad brimmed hat held casually in one picture. It is not hard to animate her face, to picture that slender beauty in motion, vivacious and self-confident, or to imagine her startling those around her with her strange laughter, in later years unexpectedly close to neighing, that counterbalanced the image of perfect poise. But that laugh only came among intimates, and when startled. The face she offers the world in these pictures is serious, composed, and in control.

Nothing changes in her late teens until one day she goes to the beach, either to Jones Beach in Long Island, or to one closer to the city. She is not alone: as usual, as she remembered it, a cloud of beaux surround her, vying for her favor. But someone else notices her that day, an older man with the features of a refined boxer, exuding confidence and some extra element of personality that dominates anyone close to him. He walks up to Mothie and asks her, "Why are you with all of these when you could be with me?"

The man is Leonard Wilds, and by 1914 they are married.

Matron

What emerges from this blend of fact and conjecture is Mothie's resilience. Some might have been traumatized by such difficulties: Mothie flourished, whether with a flounce or a grim determination I don't know but, apparently, with a good deal of the former. The impropriety of so much of the way she was treated left her strengthened, her confidence proven under fire. After we moved from Great Neck to New York in 1949 and Mothie lived for a time in her own apartment she astonished my mother by working in a department store. Mothie didn't need the money. She wanted the involvement with others and the sense of self-sufficiency.

Once married Mothie insisted on the proprieties missing in her own youth, and was relentless in her drive for stability, material success, social acceptance, and as privileged a life for her children as possible. The middle-class, affluent, proper lifestyle she erected was not to be upset however little outer and inner realities agreed. Not even my mother's Jewish conversion or marriage was allowed to upset this aura of propriety, however outside its canons, at the time: as long as Gar made a good living and the proprieties at home were observed, the outward appearance of middle-class propriety was sufficient. Besides, he could be absorbed. It was as an image of the Victorian family myth within which she and her family lived and were perceived to do so by others that was not to be questioned.

This construction of herself and family extended to her name. She replaced Emsley with Wilds: by 1920 "Alma" supplanted "Emma." No reason was ever given nor were my mother or Bud aware of this until I researched Mothie's story. Names are as much a problem on her side of the family as my father's. Emma became Alma; was it Lucile, or Lucille? Baehr became Bhaer; Emsley became Emzley, Aynslie, and Ainslie, implying an association with an English porcelain ancestor. Wilds itself may have been Wiles, or Wildes.

I think "Alma" appealed to Emma because there was no precedent for such a name change or that particular name in her family annals. "Alma" and the middle-class propriety she insisted on were complimentary self-creations, things "Emma" caught only glimpses of in her own upbringing. As late as 1916 Minnie still wrote to her as "Dear Emma," but thereafter Mothie is Alma. What Daddy Wilds thought of this is entirely unknown.

There were strange gaps in the perfect family façade she elaborated over the years. Most noticeable was her wholesale antipathy to the past. This may have had a strong family root, as we saw, but she took it to an extreme. Dates were systematically eliminated from any record she kept, as though time itself was not to interfere with her family's self-perfection. Newspaper clippings of school events with her children, as well as all the modeling mementos she kept for my mother, had their dates removed. Nor did she keep carefully dated photo albums of her family for herself or future generations. She was uninterested in family trees. She kept no dateable keepsakes, no mementos, no heirlooms. Everything erected with Daddy Wilds was new, untrammeled by the past or allowed to show the passage of time.

What wasn't hers could be appropriated—items from hotels, plants from others' gardens, names on paintings. Reality was hers to reshape. She passed these traits on to my mother, who later accompanied Mothie on their larcenous gardening expeditions in the country. She replaced the names of artists on paintings she acquired with her own. In Junior High I won a copy of Webster's *New Collegiate Dictionary*, suitably inscribed to me in honor of my writing. It disappeared. After Mothie's death I found it again: she had erased my name and written in her own.

"We were an odd family," Bud told me once. "Everyone had their own friends. There was no mixing."

"You mean Mothie and Daddy Wilds?"

"Yes. Everyone." Their circles didn't mix, mother and father's, sister or brother's. Everyone went their own way. More surprising,

"We never celebrated birthdays either."

I sat back, startled. If anything is a feature of our middle-class life it is our overkill when it comes to celebrating such days. Not for Mothie. Her family might age, but that would not be acknowledged, only defied. So what if feelings were hurt—as they were. My mother substituted the cornucopias surrounding Linda and my birthdays for her own lost celebrations. Gar was not just assimilated to Christmas, but required to provide yearly those tidal waves of birthday as well as Christmas gifts, ever larger, as were our Christmas trees, on one occasion reaching two stories.

These are only hints, yet they point to an unusual childhood for my mother and uncle. Did Mothie ignore celebrations because these were confused or omitted in her youth? Propriety was flouted then, too, yet she created its perfect image later—why not in these respects, too? She caught up her family in a dream at once ultraconventional and surreal.

I only once heard Mothie celebrate time—on her 88th birthday. She was impressed with that number as she had not been with 87, or 85, or 65, or.... On that day she openly admitted it with her high laugh, a day when she seemed fully to recover herself near the end of her late, long decline.

Only Daddy Wilds overawed Mothie; only my mother's success as a model, who in fulfillment of the Mothie's earlier Gibson Girl identification, actually became the template of beauty in her youth for the country, led to any inconsistency in Mothie's edifice.

A Welsh Lord

In the early 1930s Daddy Wilds inherits a title and estate in Wales, his family's original home. The terms of inheritance require him to take up residence there. He, however, a successful American stockbroker, has no interest, although for a time my mother and Mothie call each other 'Lady Lucille' and 'Lady Alma,' and my uncle is intrigued. But Daddy Wilds is adamant. He spurns the inheritance.

So goes the myth

Actually he visited the property in Wales, and was so enthused he wanted to accept the baronetcy and accompanying pile, but Mothie would have none of it. She had spent their married years building a life of stability and order, and was not about to begin over, land and title notwithstanding. Daddy Wilds continued to live in Great Neck, his noble heritage receding into a romantic 'might have been.'

My mother believed the heroic remains of one Wilds ancestor laid within a stone sarcophagus in Salisbury Cathedral under his knightly effigy, although far from Wales. I have seen him there; the thought we might be related is as strange as learning a distant cousin came from the dark side of the moon.

I am still trying to find out the nature of the inheritance, but Mothie's hostility to time has left little to go on with Daddy Wilds: three pictures, a few scraps of memorabilia she missed destroying, a few pieces of furniture, a death certificate, and a few rugs. Only Daddy Wilds' overarching myth survived her erasures.

A Man Larger Than Life

Leonard (Daddy) Wilds' family came to America about 1870, settling at Pensacola or Jacksonville in Florida. Originally Welsh or Anglo-Welsh aristocrats, the family moved to Jamaica in the earlier part of the 19th Century when they ran afoul of the royal family in the years before Victoria became Queen. They supported Victoria's accession warmly, but remained in Jamaica where now they were entrenched landowners, until Daddy Wilds' parents moved to Florida decades later. What caused that move is unknown, or what happened to their Jamaican landholdings. The nature of the original dispute with the monarchy in England is similarly unknown. When Bud tracked down and visited this Jamaican plantation he found a black Wilds on hand or in possession.

Once in Florida, Samuel Wilds, Daddy Wilds' father, is said to have been among the founders of the Florida Republican Party. This would have become a frustrating experience after the end of Reconstruction in 1876 and the eclipse of the Republicans for more than a century thereafter as the old Confederacy turned Democratic with a vengeance and segregated and repressed the black population so briefly liberated during Reconstruction. There are shadowy stories of Bud and Mom visiting grandparents in the Pensacola or Jacksonville areas—but almost nothing of these Florida roots escaped Mothie's ruthless suppression of the past

One shadowy story has Samuel's family with commercial, hence political interests in Central America, including gunrunning as one family activity. This at least lends some rationale for the young Daddy Wilds finding himself momentarily strapped for cash in one of the Banana Republics and buying that bunch of bananas with his remaining change.

Samuel married a Floridian, Clara Garnes, and Leonard Samuel Wilds, Daddy Wilds, was born November 19, 1882, the eldest of six siblings who made it to adulthood. My mother's memory was faulty here, believing her father came to this country at the turn of the 20th Century with his parents, already 20 or 21. Maybe she told it that way to magnify how Americanized and how successful a stockbroker he became to underscore the size of his rejection of the Welsh baronetcy in the 1930s. Nothing of his childhood is known, or why he moved to New York in the early 1900s. His brother Lindsay also moved into the same area. In the family myth Daddy Wilds was an increasingly successful stockbroker by the time Mothie met him, as well as a man so sure and settled in himself he was proof to Mothie's aggressiveness, dominating her instead for decades.

Daddy Wilds himself when he joined the Masons in 1922 listed his occupation as a broker. Part of the myth was that he was so successful on Wall St. the family was able to move into ever more impressive lodgings culminating in a mansion in Kenilworth on Long Island's fashionable North Shore. He was hurt by the Great Crash of 1929, yet still was able to provide a good home and comfortable life in Great Neck where he indulged his passions for large cars and his children.

Unsurprisingly the truth is different.

Daddy Wilds went into construction and became an expert in flooring, the occupation he listed in the 1920 Census. If he flirted with stocks, or even became a stockbroker, that was a way station to becoming a fraud specialist for Hartford Indemnity, his profession by 1930 and thereafter. Perhaps by "broker" he meant insurance broker.

Lost in this confusion is an apparent decline in the family from aristocratic, landed wealth in Wales and Jamaica, together with a loss of their aristocratic identity and memory, so that the offer of a title in the 1930s came as a surprise to all. Perhaps Samuel Wilds was a junior son, and the main line of inheritance died out in the early 1930s. At any rate Daddy Wilds' story is more conventionally American: hard work from modest beginnings leading to an ever better material lifestyle, in his case diminished only from wealth to affluence by the Great Depression.

Lucille Wilds was born in 1915 one year after Mothie and Daddy Wilds married, and in 1919 her brother Leonard Samuel Wilds, Jr. (Lenny as a youth, Bud later) arrived. In between there may have been a lost son Charles, but his arrival and loss are even more shadowy than other parts of the tale.

Large age differences between couples were not unusual then: there is still something of that model extant in Europe. Early marriages were hardly unusual for women, either, although at twenty Mothie was not a child while at thirty-two Daddy Wilds was not twenty years older as family tradition held. Bud echoed his father's behavior, marrying my Aunt Jill with the same age difference.

The Wilds name went through vicissitudes and confusions, as touched on. Variously Daddy Wilds is said to have changed that from Wiles or Willis or Wildes to Wilds. One variant is that his favorite brother Lindsay defaulted on his debts in the 1920s, and Daddy Wilds added a 'D' to 'Wiles' to differentiate himself from his improvident brother. But he was already Wilds on the 1920 Census, and the individual Bud met many years later on the old plantation in Jamaica was a Wilds, also.

On the face of it nothing seems to provide a basis for the overwhelming potency accorded him in myth and by his family. That grew less from his achievements than from a larger-than-life personality that provoked the lifelong adulation of his children. This kind of personal mystique is lost in a recitation of fact, like the mysterious qualities of more famous men whom we are told overawed their contemporaries in themselves as well as beyond whatever they might do. We turn to anecdotes to humanize and dramatize the unique personal impact of such men.

For example, Mothie was proud of her Persian rugs—no doubt a successful man in the flooring business knew how to find good ones. One splendid blue and white rug still survives in use with myself. Mothie was so careful of these rugs that as soon as Daddy Wilds left home in the morning she went from room to room to roll up their edges to protect them from wear and tear. Once Daddy Wilds came home early and discovered the rugs rolled up and made his displeasure known. Mothie hurriedly unrolled them. This did not stop her from rolling them up again when he left the next morning—but from that day on she hovered about as the afternoons wore on to avoid surprises so she could unroll the rugs before he walked in.

That moment of homecoming also brought Daddy Wilds' Scotty to the front door. He was his master's dog only, despite Mothie and her children's affection for dogs. He retreated under the master bed when Daddy Wilds left in the morning and growled at Mothie if she tried to lure him out. Only when Daddy Wilds' footsteps sounded in an apartment corridor or his Lincoln turned into the driveway at Kenilworth, then

Great Neck, would he emerge while Mothie raced room to room unrolling the carpets.

Cars for Lenny once he was old enough to drive form the basis for a number revealing stories. Daddy Wilds got him a car as soon as he could drive legally, and not some safe heap but a racy convertible with a rumble seat in back. Mothie must have worried, for Lenny was a wild driver who raced from township to township in the days when police could not pursue across town lines. He was a daredevil, often steering and shifting with his knees in front of his friends and girlfriends as he left fuming police in his wake. He remained proud of these driving skills after he had his own family.

"Watch this," he said one day while out driving with his son, Brad: he leaned back, dropped his hands, and steered and shifted with his knees. Brad was duly impressed.

"Don't tell anyone!" Bud said when they finally turned into their driveway. But Brad immediately blurted it out to his mother. Aunt Jill is not a duplicate of Mothie, but actually something of her opposite, but her reaction is easy to imagine. "Why'd you tell her?" Bud reproached Brad, later.

Needless to say Lenny crashed cars with a frequency magnified in the myth. Each time he and his companions walked away unscathed. Each time he totaled the car. Each time Daddy Wilds quickly found a replacement, assuring Mothie he had made a deal.

"I found it at a good price," he would say about the latest new racy convertible. "These two old ladies had it in their garage, and weren't using it." He had to explain the car's newness somehow. "I think they were maiden aunts." He must have known what Mothie really thought, but she could do nothing but simmer and accept, disciplinarian that she was.

Not that it was always easy for Lenny: if Daddy Wilds was generous and understanding to a fault with him and my mother, he could nonetheless turn overwhelming. One stormy night while Lenny was in High School there was a fierce argument between Daddy Wilds and Mothie: at the climax, Daddy Wilds slammed out of the house.

"Coming?" he challenged his teenage son, and obediently Lenny followed him and climbed into Daddy Wilds' Lincoln. They backed out of the garage and Daddy Wilds gunned down the street through the rain, easing the car onto the Long Island Expressway which then had no speed limit.

"Let's go to Florida, Lenny," he said. The rain beat against the windshield, made worse by the windshield wipers of those days. The Expressway was unlit. The speedometer needle hovered around 100.

I try to imagine the teenage Lenny, doted on by his father, reciprocating his father's feelings, bold, fearless all his life, the man who not so very far off in World War Two served under Patton and one day in France stayed on the field of battle, guiding his tanks to victory in battle while seriously wounded. He received both the Purple Heart and Distinguished Service Cross. I remember in the 1950s how when he lost his job he went out every day month after month without telling anyone what had happened, not even his wife Jill, until he found a new job against the odds at NBC where my hostile father also worked. He was tough, self-reliant, certain, private.

But this particular night Lenny can barely see the road. His father is silent. His mother and sister are receding, without knowing where they are going.

"Dad, we didn't pack any clothes," he finally gets out.

"We'll buy whatever we need."

The motor hums, rain slathers the windshield, near blinding.

"Dad, don't you think we should tell Mom where we're going?"

Daddy Wilds looks at his son, his speed never slackening.

"So you don't want to come with me."

There is no time for Lenny to reply, for Daddy Wilds slews the wheel around without slowing. The big car spins on the road. The weak wipers clear momentary visions of the drops twisting in the headlights, so many pearls smashed into the car or crushed under the tires. Time enters a new phase, instantaneous and eternal at once. I wonder if Lenny thought the car was still, and the world whirling. I wonder if he had time to think he could die, his all important sense of self be blotted out as some tree rushed forward to bend the car in half or stop it with a tall exclamation. When the world is still again they are heading home on the Expressway at the same speed, time passing normally once more. No one says anything. For once in his life Lenny is too afraid to utter a sound.

When my mother began to model not Mothie but Daddy Wilds made the time to accompany her. No one was going to take advantage of his daughter: no one did. Lost in this is how early her career began—in the early 1930s—and by their midpoint she was functioning with spectacular success on her own, traveling widely with other models, with her parents left behind in Great Neck. Yet Great Neck remained her home, and any beau who wished to take her out had to pass Daddy Wilds' sizing up. No matter what she got up to she knew Daddy Wilds was there to pick her up and bring her home, her refuge, where he reigned.

Revealing as these anecdotes are, Daddy Wilds' activity as a mason from 1922 until ill health forced him to stop in 1939 casts another light on him. A participation in Freemasonry was a fitting association for someone in construction; however changed, Freemasonry derived from the medieval guild tradition, specifically from the stonemason and cathedral builder guilds, broadening its intellectual and social concerns in the 17th and 18th centuries. He did not just attend Howard Lodge 35 in Brooklyn, now the Lodge of Antiquity 11, but rose steadily through the various Masonic degrees to become a Grand Master.

Masonry is organized in lodges, and its secretive practices retain the trappings of chivalric and medieval religious orders. It is not a religious organization per se, although it requires a belief in a supreme being and the immortality of the soul. Masonic work is often charitable, and socially offers a link between leading individuals in a community, at least of the traditional, shrinking WASP governing class. Being a member was not without controversy, as masons in the past have been charged with antisemitism, anti-Catholicism, and racism. Both here and in Great Britain its male only members were usually Protestants, and masons still tend to be pillars of establishment society, although in Latin countries there is a freethinking, radical element.

Presumably any male can become a mason, and despite a period of persecution in the 1840s in America, Freemasonry has flourished here. Benjamin Franklin was a mason and published the first Masonic text in America. A surprising number of the founding fathers were masons, including George Washington. The most recent mason in the presidency was Gerald Ford.

Here Daddy Wilds found a congenial group of men and activities and private practices whose terminology was at odds with the outer, commercial world, devoting time and effort to Masonic meetings and enterprises. The rituals of Freemasonry are kept secret, so we must picture him in the heart of his family or among his associates at work with an aura around him of a private and important realm of knowledge and practice from which they were excluded. The very world Mothie dreamed into existence and Daddy Wilds made materially possible he simultaneously cordoned off from important parts of his life. Oddly enough, the same was to be true of my father's entertainment world, although his cordoning too often broke down.

Daddy Wilds' mastery was unquestioned and even, in the masonic realm, literally confirmed.

GRANDFATHER DADDY WILDS

Two images haunt me: Daddy Wilds
willfully slewing his Lincoln around
at a hundred miles an hour in the rain,
sure he would spin the right way home:
and, his face battered as a refined
boxer's, shambling from his room
at the end, though warned
any motion would burst his heart.

He was the wild free father brimming
with gifts: cars replacing those
his son smashed, always found unused
in some maiden aunt's garage; money
he went on making as a stockbroker,
after the '29 crash; adoration
of my mother he kept company
as she modeled, outfacing
all the young men until too sick
to face my father down; the castle
and title he spurned because
they weren't good enough:

and he was the man whose mastery
grandmother punished for ten years
with no sex,
who laid in his deathbed while
his son went on smashing things
for someone else to make good, and
his daughter brushed leadpaint and

turpentine around, as if no one was there:
the man who got up and broke
the only heart he knew he could.

I

Some nights I hear him hum
like an engine under the dry
white rain of stars we spin beneath
and I grow dizzy looking for true home
and lie there, short-breathed,
my jaw set like a boxer's against
the pain in my side, weighing
what fuels our pride,
our bribery of love,
our final love of death.[17]   1985

II

Or so my father whispered
when I was young. Older,
the truth is precious as breath.
Grandfather smelled no paint
where he lay on the far side
of his home, while all his son smashed
were Germans in North Africa,
then came home with a Purple Heart:
and grandfather died in bed
in my mother's arms, who was
heavy with me—his death
a shockwave to us both.

Some nights I hear him hum
like an engine under the dry
white rain of stars we spin beneath
and I grow dizzy looking for true home

and lie there, short-breathed,
my jaw set like a boxer's against
the pain in my side, weighing
what fuels our pride,
our bribery of love,
our final temptation to love our end—
or if, as he clove to her ripe body
he knew too
life is more pure more adamant
than death.[18]   2017

Many years after writing this poem in 1985 I had learned enough to know its ending was not true, at least to fact, and had to be revised. But both versions were true to the time written…. So 'I' is the original ending, 'II' the revised ending 32 years later when myth was replaced by something closer to reality.

Despite Clay Feet

Daddy Wilds' death was a recurring subject in the constant revisiting of family history during my teens and twenties, the lost family savior. My father claimed Daddy Wilds liked him, which fits his modus operandi. He must have been aware of Daddy Wilds' untouchable eminence for my mother and Bud; once when I was older he told me Mothie and Mom far from revering Daddy Wilds killed him by painting the room next to his. The smell of the fresh, lead-impregnated paint tormented him in bed where he lay with a heart whose walls had become paper thin. He called out for relief, was ignored, and finally in desperation forced himself up and staggered out to the hall to cry for help. There he collapsed and died in my mother's arms. That story was the source of the first version of "Grandfather Daddy Wilds."

My mother was incandescent when I repeated this story many years later.

"That's a terrible thing for him to say! My poor father! If he had been well he'd have gotten rid of your father! No one was painting near his room—Mothie happened to be painting, but it was outside, on the kitchen stoop, downstairs and on the other side of the house! And I heard him call and went to him: he needed the pill to put under his tongue for his heart condition. There weren't any left on the table beside him, so I hurried to bathroom to get one, but by the time I got back he was gone."

So, I thought, Daddy Wilds didn't die in her arms on the upstairs landing, but she was still eight months pregnant; I was still all but there as the impact of that moment ran through her body and the attendant chemical changes rolled though mine....

Daddy Wilds' feelings were in fact unfriendly towards Gar after the 1941 elopement and the folly of the 1942 public marriage, and from his parents' treatment of his beloved daughter. What a weak man my father must have seemed to Daddy Wilds!

Yet he proved to have clay feet.

One day at Mothie's house in Weston, Connecticut in the late 1950s we gathered for a birthday party for Bud. Gar stayed in New York that weekend, and without his presence we were all relaxed. A fire warmed the living room as gifts were given. By accident a gift check went into the flames with some wrappings, and mild reproaches built to a fiery exchange between Bud and Mothie that climaxed when he reproached Mothie for denying sex to Daddy Wilds for the last ten years of his life. Her denials were explosive, the afternoon ruined though we soldiered on through a taut meal. I was the one who got slapped by Mothie for tasting some whipped cream set aside for dessert.

1932-1942.... Sexless.... From his 50th and her 38th years!

It was a bolt of lightning at a time I was trying to understand family history as a teenager, so at odds with anything I'd heard.

What could have gone wrong? Was it some act of infidelity once discovered never excused? Was it the steady accumulation of one act of resented mastery after another until finally Mothie's character reasserted itself in anger, and struck back in the most telling way possible? Remarkably the same pattern asserted itself in Bud's marriage, a period of mastery followed by an even longer period of sexlessness, as well as reappearing in another variant in my mother's. She, year by year, resentments controlled but increasing, reached a point of repeated sexual denial too, choosing her moments well.

Quintessentially, as my father told the story, on the first night of their first trip to Venice he was full of "amatory interest" but left to his own devices as my mother pleaded a headache and turned a cold shoulder. Their difficulties would not have been helped by Gar's confusion of the sexual and excretory organs. Worse, my mother, Mothie, and Gar had the same opinion of sex.

So I accept Bud's reproach that afternoon as a truthful repetition of a complaint he must have heard once from his father, in no small part because of this generational repetition. And yet...no other details ever emerged as to what Daddy Wilds had done to so provoke his wife, or even whether or not Bud's charge was true. We have only the strange family divisions into separate, largely unmixing groups of friends, the erasure of time from all documents, and the destruction of nearly all mementos. Adding to the mystery, if that is what it is, is the unquestioned continuing dominance of Daddy Wilds over his fractured-in-fact but publicly idealized family, a potency that grew larger after his death.

A different picture emerges then for Daddy Wilds. Dominant he may have been, yet from 1932 he was excluded from conjugal relations, as seems likely, whatever the cause. How he might have consoled himself out of the home is unknown. Not a whisper of unfaithfulness ever attached to him: there is only the unknown transgression, and the rigid punishment. Carpets may have been unrolled before he stepped in the door, modeling and beaux monitored for my mother, cars provided for my uncle, but the separate worlds of his parents Bud noticed must have increased decisively through these years, the outer sign of the inner split. A façade of normalcy prevailed over a reality profoundly at odds with appearance. Omnipotence warred with weakness, obedience with rejection. A dream of middle-class perfection was insisted on, a golden haze to obscure the cliff off which they had already fallen. Here my father's golden recounting of the past and the Wilds' myth uncannily coincide.

Another private, magic mountain opens, and at its heart is the sacrifice of love. If Mothie continued to advise my mother against divorce throughout my mother's later arguments with Gar, because appearance mattered, we can understand now the full, personal cost of that stance. Besides, what more could be asked from such a flawed, dirty creature as a man beyond this attention to appearance and provision of a decent living for the women?

Even now armed with knowledge of Daddy Wilds' clay feet I cannot stop contemplating buying a Lincoln, while it is Daddy Wilds' dresser that has become my own. I should honor my father's creative drive, his twin's intellect and culture, or my great uncle Harry Lewis/Levy's involvement in theatre instead. I became a playwright and teacher, then a poet and occasional essayist, writer on film, and novelist, none of which have any roots in Daddy Wilds' world. Revealingly, at one time the painter Max Ernst lived near Daddy Wilds and Mothie in Great Neck. He was enduring hard times, and they helped him in one crisis; in gratitude he offered them a painting. They found his surreal style unbearable and politely declined, not even willing to store it away in the attic.

Yet the deepest revelation from Mothie's treatment of Daddy Wilds' transgression shows how the Wilds myth of the perfect middle-class family was in some ways the least of it. What Alma-transformed-from-Emma insisted on was that this appearance be real. Mom, Bud, Daddy Wilds and herself had to be perfected figures, not just be seen to be. Incredibly, they did their best to be so. The emotional violence turned against Daddy Wilds lets us see that breaking the reality insisted on by the linking of our own with the surrounding collective myth provokes not just resistance but a traumatic reckoning.

Keeping appearances up as Alma insisted after 1932 possessed an inherent hollowness, one my mother would have witnessed without fully understanding. She would have felt a better reality opening before her by my father's ardent pursuit unclouded by the ambivalence that only emerged after marriage. Her realization this was not so during her first flight in 1943 after she saw my father's actual nature gave an extra edge to her bitterness. She had wanted to escape and married an ardent man outside her 'normal' circle, only to find his ardor was conditional and strategic, and her life what she had wanted to flee.

Aftermath

Mothie was deeply depressed at Daddy Wilds' death despite the arid life she imposed on their last ten years, so much so that as time passed Bud and Mom took counsel, and sent her on a cruise, although neither was clear where this could have been in 1942. Actually, this happened years later, and not in connection with Daddy Wilds' death, although when Mothie came home she was better, with many photos, all of which turned out to be of cemeteries.

Only as I grew did any of these ancestral facts come into view: as a child I lived inside the Levy and Wilds myths where Daddy Wilds, disembodied, hovered over all, especially after Bud returned from military service at the end of World War II, heroic and decorated, and we all lived together ever more unhappily in Great Neck.

I sensed that my father was there by the skin of his teeth, a stranger in a strange land, a Levy among the Wilds, a Jew in a lion's den of WASPS, the exotic in the conventional, genteel and gentile world of my mother, the man whose children carried other names than his own.

Yet Daddy Wilds was not physically a big man. One of the three surviving photos shows him leaning on one of his Lincolns, his head hardly reaching the great car's roof with his hat on. When the Welsh inheritance arrived Daddy Wilds and Mothie were already locked in combat, and any kind of bending on her part was out of the question. But Mothie's revenge had to stay private—there was no public substitute for that short, dominant man. No public shadow could fall on him, for that would have destroyed Mothie's perfected family.

An even more important consequence of his myth is its power to make anyone in Daddy Wilds' orbit larger than life, too. Here indeed is a seduction, a man with the power to undo life's damages, erase its mistakes, mock fate with generosity, and protect his family even as a penumbral presence, proof against life's degradations, a private Arthur waiting to be reborn in one of his descendants to show with what gusto life should be lived. Not for him a stunt like the *We The People* segment Mothie and Mom duped my father into broadcasting—he was the master of the real. His was an idealization my father could never match.

I am the transitional figure, the man still touched by this myth, yet seeing how it fades in the family's latest descendants towards the time it will be forgotten.

Gown

My uncle at 14 reluctantly accompanies my mother as she goes shopping. She is looking for a gown for her senior prom in High School. She drags him through several stores, but can't find the right dress, except for one in the last store that is simply too expensive. With a sigh she leaves the store, glancing briefly at a few items on her way out. Bud catches up with her on the street.

"I thought you liked that dress, Sis," he says.

"Which one?"

"You know, the one you didn't get."

She's not in mood to talk with him, and shrugs her shoulders.

"You know which one, Sis. This one."

He pulls the dress out from under his shirt as she stands rooted in place on the sidewalk. Horrified, she hides it under her coat, and they hurry away.

She shakes her head as she tells me the story.

"Did you wear it to the prom?" I ask.

"Of course not," she laughs.

PART THREE:
SURVIVAL & REBELLION

Authenticity

as being true in substance
as being genuine
as being real, actual

The Oxford Universal Dictionary, 3rd edition

SURVIVAL, WESTHAMPTON

A Dinner in Westhampton Village

An almost apocryphal story....

One September night in 1938 a couple drive down Dune Road across the bridge into the small village of Westhampton for dinner. Dune Road is the narrow, two lane road that runs the length of the barrier beach along this part of Long Island's south shore from Westhampton north and east past Quogue, and south towards Fire Island. The barrier island, hardly a hundred yards across in places, faces the Atlantic on its exposed side, and before Westhampton, Moriches Bay on its inner, and after Westhampton, Shinnecock Bay. The Hamptons are already a summer escape from the crowded environs of New York, although there are no direct roads, and the nearest railroad station is some distance away in Riverhead.

Dune Road has no lighting, so on the way home after a pleasant evening the couple miss their beach home and for a moment are lost. But when they backtrack, they discover their home is gone....

All the homes are gone.

While they dined the great Long Island Express hurricane of 1938 had struck.

One Spring Day in 1950

The Long Island Express got its name fairly.

That storm hesitated early in the 1938 autumn off Cape Hatteras, then picked up speed over open water, ultimately racing north at 96 mph. No storm has ever been that quick since. What's more, given the primitive forecasting of the day, only one junior weatherman saw it coming, a Mr. Pierce who understood the storm was being squeezed between two other fronts and funneled north directly to Long Island and New England. His superiors overruled his analysis. No warning was issued.

Worse, it struck September 21st, the autumn equinox, meaning there would already be an unusually high tide. Only at 2 pm, an hour before the storm struck, were schools told to send their charges home. At 3 pm The Express hit Long Island's south shore with gusts up to 186 mph as it pushed a surge of water fifteen feet high on top of the equinoctial high tide onshore. It sped across Long Island and struck New Haven at 4 pm, undiminished in power, then slammed north into New England.

Nearly 9,000 homes were obliterated, with almost 700 fatalities. Westhampton Village had a population barely in excess of 1,000 people: 29 of these were killed. Overall the storm did more than $5 billion in damage in today's values. Westhampton's barrier beach was permanently altered: a new inlet to the south, Moriches Bay Inlet, was punched into Moriches Bay, and another to the north, Shinnecock Inlet, into Shinnecock Bay. The ocean surge altered the southern shoreline on the 'mainland' part of Long Island: Moriches Bay itself was deepened.

Only after the war and the newly prosperous middle class's demands for summer homes did development start again in earnest. Daniel Bohan seized his chance and became part of our lives. For our first summer of 1949 in Manhattan with its heat, humidity, and sweaty dirt rings on my neck from every outing provoked Mom and Mothie to a second radical decision on top of forcing Gar and Bud into their own apartments, and Mothie, by choice, into hers. As that summer wore on or later in the fall they contacted Bohan in Westhampton Village, a two and a half hour drive away, and arranged for him to build Mothie a beach cottage at the southern end of Dune Road along the Atlantic beach where the third of his 'Bohan Developments' was taking shape.

A Bohan beach house had the advantage of being, relatively, cheap: Bohan was selling them for $5,000 each along that narrow barrier, and making money. He was thought something of a visionary for buying, let alone building, on Dune Road after The Express, given the lingering dread it gave to the 'hurricane season.' But in his modest way, for his three developments were nothing like the massive 'Levittowns' rising in postwar, prosperous America, Bohan grabbed the chance and started building beach houses for those newly affluent middle-class families looking for an escape from postwar New York's summer.

Here Linda and I drove with Mom and Mothie one spring weekend in 1950 to Mothie's almost finished beach house snug against the dunes, overlooking an endless, broad, sandy white beach pounded by Atlantic breakers.

I was entranced. I'd stepped out of a nightmare of stone, strangeness, impersonality, strife, deceit bordering on weirdness, and alienations into a sunny reality. The unmistakable tang of salt was in the air. The city's humidity and dirt rings around my neck were banished. There was hardly anyone around. The beach was empty. Across the street spread green stretches of land overgrown with bulrushes with hidden openings into marshy meadows I would explore that bordered Moriches Bay. Not even Great Neck had felt so real, so in touch with nature. From now until a last visit in 1958 Westhampton held my heart and gave my head its balance: my turn to nature in Great Neck for solace was not, after all, to be cut off. Each summer I came here with enormous relief. I dreaded the coming of the cold weather that made even weekend visits impossible, for none of the Bohan cottages were winterized. Even so over the years I drove the family into coming ever earlier and staying ever later until the Westhampton season stretched from late April to early November. Only during the four months in Manhattan unrelieved by its presence was I in danger of being swallowed by the whale.

Police Chase

One Saturday Gar joins us at Mothie's beach house. As he settles in the workers hammer the last horizontal slats over the outer supports to the deck to hide the foundation. He puts up with that for a few hours, explodes, and drives off in a rage.

We sigh and go in. A few minutes later we hear a police siren grow steadily louder. Intrigued, we all return to the front of the porch and look up Dune Road. There is Gar racing back to Mothie's with a police car hot on his trail that follows him into Mothie's driveway. Gar steps out to meet the policeman.

Why hadn't he stopped?
How could he not hear the siren?
Why was he speeding?
Why had he turned around to come here?
Why hadn't he stopped!

Mom goes down to help him. The workmen stop hammering to watch. I don't know whether she dazzles the policeman with a blend of beauty and hopelessly confusing explanations, excuses it all as a family misunderstanding, or…but after a stiff 'talking to' to my father, the officer drives off without writing a ticket.

Gar is here for the weekend.
The hammering resumes.

An Ocean House

To get to Westhampton we first took the Long Island Expressway, but that only went halfway, then. Thereafter we drove local roads that cut across Long Island towards Patchogue, then brought us to Riverhead, and at last let us turn towards Westhampton Village. There we drove through the Village and down Jessup Road across the bridge to the barrier beach where Moriches Bay narrowed to a channel, then headed southwest towards its end to Mothie's cottage. It took 2 ½ hours in good weather without traffic. Riverhead was close enough for an occasional movie as an alternative to the local cinema, but too distant for a daily commute to Manhattan from Dune Road.

Part of our route was a narrow, unlit, overgrown shortcut we took with a sense of dread. At night it was a challenge to an adult. Some local wit put up a sign, "This Is It." We thought he had got it right and we entered reluctantly during those spring and fall visits when darkness came early. There during our second year driving to Mothie's cottage we saw in the twilight a shape on the road, stopped, and discovered the great box turtle Oscar whom we kept through the winter before releasing him the following spring where we found him.

Gar came only occasionally on weekends, except for two weeks of summer vacation. The rest of the time it was Linda and I, and Mom, unless she was in Manhattan to keep Gar company, and, always, Mothie. Sometimes Bud visited, sometimes with a girlfriend, though by late 1950 he was dating Jill Squires, his future wife. Once when Gar was in residence his parents visited, as they had at Mothie's in Great Neck. There are pictures of Linda and I with Nanny and Poppy on the beach in front of the house. Linda was only four in 1950, and I eight, so though I would soon roam freely usually Mothie had be with us if we wanted to go swimming. Linda rushed about happily in the waves' shoreward seethings; I quickly raised alarms by trying to use the breakers to bodysurf. I got very good at that.

The Atlantic was cold in the spring and early summer, though by late August the waters near shore warmed, and its almost constant turmoil calmed during the August 'dog days.' Some August days it was calm as a lake. The seafloor must rise about 100 yards offshore because the waves break there before resuming their surge towards the beach over the shallow, sandy bottom. My repugnance for Gar's cologne overdose carried over to any body scent, even sunscreens, and sunburn became a routine feature of my first days there each summer.

The freshness of the air had such an impact when we first arrived each season like creatures emerging from hibernation that we'd all be in bed by eight until we acclimated. Because there was only the fireplace for heat, a chore I happily accepted was to roam the shoreline in search of driftwood. There was always more than we needed. Picture us in the small but comfortable living room on the couch against the wall across from the fireplace, or in chairs either side, or curled up in front of the fire, watching with increasingly heavy heads the deep blue flickers, reds, oranges, and brilliant yellows caused by the minerals in the driftwood. The room grew so warm we barely roused ourselves to stagger into bed, pulling the covers up to our chins in the colder bedrooms, asleep before we could think or even, with Mothie, say our nightly prayers.

In summer's high tide all the windows were open for the sea breeze to cool the house from its midday heat although even then there were nights cold enough to light the driftwood in the fireplace.

There was no television: just a radio, and in the evening, family games with myself and Linda, and later, whatever we happened to be reading. The silence at night was absolute, even though the ground shook from the surf, and the waves' roll and crash and sucking withdrawals filled the night. Yet that was part of the natural order: the silence remained absolute where manmade sounds were concerned, the complete opposite of Manhattan. If I lingered awake in the darkness or escaped even then to the beach, on clear nights the Milky Way poured across the night sky undimmed by city lights and pollution.

I sensed myself in touch with wordless immensities, and far from the fear I recorded in the poem I wrote evoking early life in my parents' room in Great Neck as my eyes panned up to an empty sky, I felt at once a peace and a solace here. The small, warm space of the beach house felt precious within the embrace of that milky, embracing immensity. All our insistent family discords shriveled under that night sky.

We built an enclosure for Oscar in the living room. We weren't sure what to feed him, but between lettuce and hamburger he apparently thrived until the day we let him go. There is no mention of the turtle in Gar's journal either: it is easy to imagine what he thought given his animosity to all our pets.

As you entered Mothie's cottage you faced a long, narrow kitchen divided from the living room by the counter at which we ate. Just past the counter, past the living room, there was a small hallway: to the left was the bathroom, straight ahead a small bedroom, and to the right behind the living room a larger bedroom. There were two twin beds in the smaller bedroom, and double bunks in the larger for Linda and myself, and Mothie, when Gar was in residence. Otherwise Mothie and Mom shared the small bedroom. When Nanny and Poppy or other guests were there we were truly full up.

The stairs up from the driveway led to a porch that wrapped itself around two sides of the house. The part of the porch fronting the larger bedroom on its ocean facing side was screened in. Because of the breezes and closeness to the ocean mosquitoes, though present, weren't as omnipresent as they were inland, and that screened porch allowed us to escape those that were about. Perhaps, once summer was fully in swing, it was possible to sleep there.

Facing the counter was the living room, with a picture window over the deck with a view over the dunes to the beach and ocean. The house was filled with light, including the reflected light of the sea. The fireplace was on the wall against the deck as you entered. There was room enough for stools for the counter, a space to walk to the bedrooms, and for the living room to contain a couch and assorted chairs. Everything was intimate, yet, although our being children no doubt influenced this, nothing felt crammed.

There was only one lack Mothie and Mom encountered here so far as Linda and I were concerned: there weren't any other families with children of a similar age nearby, while they could see in Bohan's second development just back up the road past the public beach on the ocean side and what we called Big Dock on the bay that there were always children about. This didn't matter to me, but they felt the lack, and perhaps the relief of our having others to interact with than themselves. Perhaps the day they saw me walking home with a girl I'd met at the Big Dock influenced them. The closer I came, the more uncomfortable I grew until I finally mumbled something about 'another time,' and Betsy headed back up Dune Road.

"Why didn't you bring your friend home, Lance?" Mom asked. I had swung as I approached them from the self-sufficient, confident child with multiple mothers to the inadequate, insecure child rejected by his father. There was no way to explain that to them or myself, then. Westhampton might be a solace and escape from New York, but the family drama was within me and needed little to constellate its contradictions.

Nonetheless even by the first autumn when Westhampton was reduced to weekend visits I begged them to stay longer into the fall, defying the cold. The idea of returning to Manhattan grew so repugnant I was soon able to make myself physically ill as we crossed the Triborough Bridge homeward. Crossing the same bridge towards Westhampton was a delight, underscored by the presence of a Wonder Bread factory just across. Worthless as that bread may have been, the aroma from the factory was heavenly.

Daluanda

Two summers of Gar using Mothie's beach house possessively while contributing nothing was enough for Mom and Mothie. He would not have appreciated having Bud in such close quarters, or having to alternate weekends with him. During that time they had hosted his parents, very likely with the same mistaken generosity as in Great Neck. What was said on phone calls after that between Gar and his impossible mother is unknown; whatever she wrote to him would have been steamed open, read, digested, then resealed. His parents weren't invited a second time.

So after those first two summers Mom and Mothie decided Mom should have her own beach house closer to the children they'd seen on Big Dock, setting Mothie free to use her house as she chose, including renting it for income. What was clear to me and Linda was that in the spring of 1952 we moved into what had been Bohan's model home on the bay side of Dune Road in the middle of his second development up the road from Mothie's. That house had a deck that wrapped around the front to the back on three sides, unlike Mothie's where the deck ran only on two. Otherwise the houses' layouts were identical, like all Bohan homes.

Later I learned Gar, always poor in his mind, would not advance the money for a beach house of their own. So Mom borrowed it from Ginny Meade, his superior's wife, and informed my father he owed the Meades $5,000. That was a debt he couldn't avoid paying. It may be Mothie first put up the money, and was repaid with the loan from Ginny. But then Mom demanded an additional $5,000. The first $5,000 may have repaid Ginny, but did not take into account all my mother's expenses, or her embarrassment at having to ask Ginny; or perhaps she felt the first $5000 dealt with Mothie and Ginny, and now she was entitled to it on her own account. Or was it she told him she'd paid off a separate debt to Mothie, and now Ginny had to be repaid? It proved impossible to disentangle these possibilities, but Gar insisted he paid for the house twice.

He was further informed he had to pay rent when he used the beach house for a weekend or his summer vacation. Bad behavior now came with a price, aside from the embarrassment of Ginny being involved. Grumbling, he paid. Perhaps he knew he was only paying the beach house's expenses after refusing to have anything to do with it, after all. He made use of it occasionally on weekends and for the next few years took his vacations there too, on occasion inviting family members from Philadelphia, though not his parents.

The tale is not finished. Mom redid the interior of the new beach house herself, and after a year enclosed the deck running down one side of the beach house along the back of the living room, dividing it into a small bedroom for me and a bathroom. She did all but the plumbing and electricity herself, electric saw, hammer, and paint brush in hand. So now one entered "Daluanda" Beach House, "Da" for David, "lu" for herself, "an" for me, and "da" for Linda, by walking down a long boardwalk from the parking area along Dune Road, climbing up four or five steps to the front deck, and entering through the new entrance at the far end she had enclosed. Since the fireplace backed onto my room it was always warm at bedtime in the cool stretches on either side of the summer. There was no screened porch.

The rear deck faced Moriches Bay, a short walk through the dune grass and reeds to a cove where one day Bud built a dock where an older neighborhood boy was allowed to keep his small motorboat. Across Dune Road on the ocean side were a string of beach houses identical to Mothie's. There were beach houses on either side of us, and further up the road after another break the first Bohan 'development.' Between ours and that development were more expanses of bulrushes and marshes with hidden clearings. Mothie and Mom were happy to see there was an assortment of children for Linda and myself in those neighboring homes. We soon had two societies: our friends in Manhattan, and those in Westhampton.

None of our family arguments and financial maneuverings appear in Gar's journals for these years, or the move from one beach house to another. Linda and I felt the tension in the air, which we took for granted, until we saw how it disappeared in Westhampton in Gar's absence. It was muted somewhat when he was there, too, as he liked going to the beach and sunning, little as he wanted to credit how it came about. No one remarked on how extraordinary our underlying realities had become. We were on a course of polarization as Mom asserted 'normalcy' with a vengeance with Friedberg's concurrence. Although Gar was able to resume his journal in 1951 because things had settled into this new pattern of Manhattan and Westhampton imposed by Mothie and Mom after the 1948 upheaval, the consequences of that upheaval never stopped growing.

Master Builder

Our first Sunday as a family in Mom's new beach house Gar tries to leave early.

"We'll go when I'm ready, David," Mom announces, exasperated by his attitude.

"What's keeping us?"

She looks at him, then around the living room: her gaze stops on the wall behind the couch facing the fireplace painted a dark brown spattered with white dots.

"That wall has be replaced."

"Jeez!"

"Get the hammer, Lance," she orders. I do as told. She is in her version of work clothes, a bandana like one of Mothie's wrapped around her forehead. We pry off the ugly sheets of spattered plywood and nail in unpainted ones. The ceiling is pitched, which means using the ladder to rip out the upper panels to use as patterns on fresh sheets of plywood she cuts with her power saw, then hands up the ladder for me to nail into place.

The hours wear on.

Once the new wall is in place we mask the seams between the plywood sheets with a narrow trim.

Done, Mom showers and changes, then brightly announces, transformed into a New York sophisticate in an equally transformed room, that it is time to go.

She chatters brightly on the way home, undeterred by Gar's silence.

Idylls

The sun is up, and I am out unsupervised. All the neighbors feel equally secure—there is no crime, no strangers, no jostling crowds, no reason children can't run free, here. One of our neighbors teaches me how to clam after watching me tug a rake under the shallow bay water. His technique is so much simpler—"just heel and toe" he says, and backs away slowly, his weight on his heels. When he feels the recognizable edge of a clam, he leans down and picks it up. I master the technique swiftly. I won't eat clams or crabs and detest fish, and survive on a diet of hamburgers, potatoes, corn on the cob, and chicken noodle soup, varied with macaroni and cheese. But Mom and Mothie love seafood, and so as the morning light lays lightly on the clear waters I heel and toe backward where I know there is a clam bed, bucket in hand, picking up the medium for eating, and a few of the very large Quahogs to cut up for soup.

You need a certain fortitude to clam this way. At times my heel crushes a fiddler crab hidden in the sand, or a baby flounder spurts underfoot to safety. Other crabs I don't need to worry about, especially the spectacular, beautiful Blue Claws who are large enough to intimidate but are far more frightened of me as they scuttle off. They too are fair game, net in hand, safe to lift from the net firmly held from behind in the middle, and dropped into the waiting bucket. If I look for them in the right season they are glorious as ever but soft-shelled. Those Mothie and Mom fry as they are, with no shell to pick off once cooked.

Or perhaps this morning Eddie is going fishing. He's the older neighborhood boy allowed to keep his boat in our cove so long as sometimes he takes me out fishing. Out we motor slowly into Moriches Bay until the water deepens, then cut south towards Big Dock to follow the channel, then west around an island just beyond Big Dock into deep water. Perhaps today my line tangles, and I'm too embarrassed to say anything until Eddie notices it and with a shake of his head helps me straighten it out. Perhaps it's the day I hook something large and mysterious that bends my rod in half and snaps my line. We stare at each other in surprise. Or maybe I succeed in catching a flounder or two, the most common catch, and arrive home in triumph.

There Mothie drops them one by one into the kitchen sink to dress. Once as a stream of cold water hit a flounder it flipped a good yard high before flopping back into the sink. Mothie screamed. They aren't good dealing with live creatures. Another day we drive to Shinnecock Inlet where there is a lobster outlet. They pick out two. Once home, the big pot of water boiling, they can't bring themselves to put the lobsters in. I'm recruited to tilt the bag over the boiling water. To this day I remember the lobsters scrabbling to stay in the bag, and their thin, high-pitched screams as they fell in.

If not clamming, or crabbing or fishing I meet up with Guy and Buddy and John whom Eddie replaces after the first year. Perhaps Buddy's sister Phyllis, or Ellen, or Patricia, or Alice join us. We make a group full of gender-based teasing as we change from kids to preteens to teens. Sometimes we split along gender lines, sometimes all together we head to the ocean to tease and swim. Often we walk up to Big Dock where Davy is waiting, another older boy with a larger boat than Eddie's with a powerful 25 horsepower motor. He likes to take us waterskiing. Even I, with my omnipresent sense of awkwardness before others, manage to get up and ski well enough one day to tempt Davy to cut ever tighter turns until I can't swing wide enough to keep going, and sink down.

Lunch is always something grabbed quickly before returning outdoors.

Then I go off alone to explore the marshes between our development and the next up Dune Road. I learn the paths through these and where the tall bulrushes open on secret marshy meadows. Here and there are foundation remnants of homes from another time, mementos of The Express. Their lost life fascinates me, while aside from natural sounds the marsh is silent, always amazing to me in contrast to the city.

Or Buddy and Guy are with me as we use our slingshots to hunt frogs, as at other times we gather and starve spiders in enclosed jars before putting them together to watch the lethal results. It's not that boys are cruel, it just takes so long for too many of us to move out of our insecurities or, paradoxically, our youthful certainties, into empathy for others, let alone that redemptive empathy for life itself, however odd its forms.

Some days we go up Dune Road almost to the bridge to Westhampton Village to The Swordfish Club, a beach resort with a pool with a daily fee, with an allowance for drinks and snacks before being picked up. Often enough I'm with Alice, a wash of freckles across her cheeks and nose, the girl I fall in love with every summer. Her older brother Bob, older than Eddie and Davy, goes off on his own, not even a peripheral part of our group. Her sister Nancy is Linda's summer best friend. They are inseparable. Nancy is convinced her waist is several inches higher than it is and pulls all her shorts and pants high.

At first Alice and I are children, and if we begin a summer holding hands the mockery of the others soon drives us back into the normal boy boy girl girl groups. Then we are preteen, then teens, and sometimes manage to bear the teasing through most of the summer, even at times keeping in contact into the winter before we lose touch. At first sight the next spring we resume. In the evenings she and I or some version of a grouping hang out at one house or another, or walk along the ocean, or it may be go into town to see a movie, where more than once Bob takes Alice and myself.

My day isn't done though after the others go in. At night there are family games and a fire going if cold. Soon I'm allowed to take walks alone in the dark along the ocean. Whatever else I did that day, whomever else I was with, however intensely remembered, it is those walks along the wave-shaken shore that sink into me deepest, the waves white bursts picked out in moonlight, the solitary beach stretching endlessly, the Milky Way a bucket of milk splattered against a dark wall the stars are so thick in that clear air. There I know I am in an indescribably larger world ordered by its own rhythms, naked here however veiled in the city, a reality in which we all of necessity live, aware or not. I know Westhampton is an idyll each night I walk under these stars, beside this ocean, know how hard to retain its freedom it will be in New York, yet feel all the tensions and conflicts I am subject too shrink to the manageable.

Once touched by these immensities I turn home, and small as it seems as I pull the covers up in my little room, am comforted.

Not every day is brilliant, and for two weeks of the summer Gar is there insisting on his primacy and control, even if more lightly than in the winter. Already anyone visiting us sees how different we all are when he is absent. One summer after the usual instant attraction with Alice something goes wrong and suddenly I and Patricia are madly in love, ignore all teasing and carry on after the Westhampton summer. She comes for a visit to our apartment, and we go to a Fair where I win an assortment of stuffed animals I give to her. I am startled by Mom's jealous reaction, and understand for the first time the goddesses as well as the gods in my life are jealous. When Patty goes I weep over the piano alone in the living room.

The winter drags on.

The following April in Westhampton I can't remember what that was all about as Alice and I hold hands on our first walk of the season along the beach.

Other times the tail end of a hurricanes brushes us strongly enough to madden the waves under a low, gray sky. To speak of an ocean roar then is an understatement as the constant inrush of towering waves breaks first on the distant bar, rushes forward and reforms, only to break on their neighbors in their haste to crash on the shore where they drive curling bands of heavy foam along the tide lines up and down the great beach to the foot of the dunes. I shout to be heard by John or Buddy or Guy or Eddie. Convinced I am immortal I dive into the bellies of the onrushing waves and work my way past the surf line until I breast their crests. That is like a ride up a swift elevator. At the top the crest slaps my face with cold water, then abruptly drops me into the trough before the next wave that towers over me. Improbably I rise to its crest, too. I am mad with exhilaration.

Maddest is coming ashore, the waves far too steep to bodysurf without being hammered senseless into the sandy bottom, as happens to me more than once, a great surge spinning me helplessly along, then pulling me back into the belly of the next monster. I flail and stagger forward through each crash, am pulled under, stagger up again, breathless, straining forward, until free of a wave's sucking power I heave myself out of its grasp, shaking thick foam from my feet as I go, unaware I am lucky to live, triumphant, laughing with my friends.

One late summer day we pack hurriedly, nail protective sheets of plywood over the windows as well as we can, and drive into town to find safer quarters for the full hurricane scheduled to arrive later that day. A great maple stands outside my room. By nightfall wind whips its branches, but the full storm is yet to hit as I fall asleep. The torrents of rain against my window and the full force of the hurricane winds fail to waken me. By the morning the storm has passed; a quiet, bright day dawns. Astonished, I see the great maple uprooted and lying on its side.

One day I hang a set of fish hooks on the wall just as you enter Daluanda and swing into the kitchen. Next to them is a small Indian with a motto:

Apron pink, weather stink;
Apron blue, sky is too.

I forget about the hooks until one day I swing around the entrance into the kitchen, my hand brushing the wall where they hang. I hook one finger. Mom and Mothie are horrified as I hold my hooked finger helplessly. We drive to the Village emergency room where a surgeon cuts it out after doing what he can to numb my finger, then stitches me up and enforces two weeks of idleness so far as swimming is concerned before the stitches, though not the bandaging, can be removed....

I never have a boat of my own. There are Eddie and Davy's, and for a time an old flat-bottomed wreck of a rowboat I and Buddy and Guy fix well enough to use on rowing expeditions along the bay shore, or out to the island beyond Big Dock. There we find the remnant foundations of what must have been another large house swept into oblivion by The Express. The hint of another, lost life again teases my imagination.

Once Mothie and Mom take me to see a boat they propose to buy for me. It is smaller than Eddie's, with only a five horsepower engine. I am horrified. I'm sure they are as startled by my reaction as I am now, looking back, but at the time I feel as though they are offering me something inferior. My fundamental awkwardness and insecurity and rebellion are never far from the surface, my root anger at being fobbed off as my mother goes out yet again with Gar never forgotten, my anger at being offered something else than what I wanted. And what was that but an ideally transformed father, not judgmental or rejecting or self-absorbed, and a mother who glorious as she appears at any given moment is not leaving me behind. I refuse the boat....

Our wounds never go away, our irrationalities, our childhood, our childishness. Fortunately, at least in these Westhampton ever-extended summers I have a communion with something incommensurate and am able for long stretches to balance resentment and anger and grief.

ESCAPE

Manhattan's summer evenings
steamed rings of dirt around my neck....
We found a beach flung between sea and bay,
a house hung on the dunes,

one nestled later in bayside rushes
that shook their silks in the dark like girls
    when embraced.
Light blazed from sky and sea and land
and burned me blond,

sand in my hair, my pockets, between
    my toes:
mornings I netted blue claws, hard or soft,
and burrowing fiddlers always freed,
or heel-and-toed for clams, young flounders
    underfoot,

milky light leaning on the bay.
John and Buddy, Guy and Eddie,
Phyllis and freckled Alice,
the girl I loved each summer,

tried to teach and tame me
but I loved nature more, happiest
alone by the ocean at night,
stars, long lunar sands, waves weaving

great distances into me until I learned
to know myself the part of these grown
    self-aware.
That night sea beats in me still—
all comes, all comes, all comes

those waves drum,
words that give and take my peace
now as when despite all I felt alone
and made solitude my friend.[19]

Unk & Jill

One afternoon in the late spring of 1952 there is a reception in our New York apartment for Jill Squires who will marry Bud in October (Bud is called Unk in this section). Jill's mother, Agnes Mary Egger came from London to attend. Agnes was a forbidding Englishwoman to a ten year old like myself, turned out impeccably. Jill was another matter, a warm, blond, peaches and cream all-American girl of twenty-two, outgoing and warm though overawed by her mother. The age difference between Unk and Jill is virtually the same as between his father and Mothie when they married and, in fact, Unk met Jill when she was twenty, Mothie's age at her marriage. Their marriage counted as heavily in my 'survival' as Westhampton, and for many years our relationship was centered there.

I hero-worshipped Unk, though he had limited time for a young nephew. We interacted enough that I always wanted more, but our time together was always limited, whether accompanying him to Jones Beach, staging that abortive battle with my soldiers in Manhattan, or actually riding together. He was a young man about town in Manhattan, and our most successful times together were an occasional weekend afternoon playing cutthroat games of Canasta together he taught me when (rarely) he had nothing better to do. He watched what went on in 'Sis's' marriage with a shrug, talked in a familiar way to Gar without a tinge of the respect and/or awe which Gar expected which he found intolerable but I delightful. Unk was a realist, like Mothie, albeit entirely within the Wilds myth as its ideal scion, which I took in instinctively as part of the 'air' I breathed. I appreciated most that he suffered from no internal warfare as did my father. After he settled into his marriage Mom offered he and Jill the use of the beach house on the condition they take me along too.

Jill possessed a broad naïve streak that continues in her nineties, and was easily alarmed. She'd had a difficult childhood with her sister Patty, two years younger. Her mother did the usual English thing typical of the more affluent English, and as soon as she could had them in boarding schools, and if home, with a governess. Agnes' first marriage ended in divorce: Jill remembers herself at 10 with Patty being accompanied by a guardian on the Duchess of Bedford that wallowed across the Atlantic in 1940, afraid of being sunk by U-Boats, and so unsteady no one was allowed on deck in a storm. Once in the US she found Agnes married to Irving 'Clip' Squires, who adopted and naturalized the girls and swiftly relegated them to new governesses so he and Agnes could party and travel at will. Clip was affluent, with a mansion on four acres in Quogue some miles farther out than Westhampton from New York, and an apartment in New York. Jill remembers in particular one governess called M.C., Clip's shorthand for Mildred C Meredith who was so cautious he dubbed her Mildred Cautious. But this wasn't enough for Agnes.

Unk told me how one day in 1947 on the night she returned from a trip to England Agnes ardently made love with Clip.

"How was that, darling?" she asked after.

"Wonderful," said Clip.

"It's the last time," she said. "I want a divorce." On her trip she'd met an old flame and decided to have him now, instead. She left the girls behind when she went back to England. They were Squires now, and thought of Clip as Daddy. He, to his credit, brought them up and stood by them. When he met Bud they hit it off, to Jill's relief. Agnes only returned for the shower and the wedding: an alcoholic, she died at 62 Jill thought from some careless combination of drink and sleeping pills.

Our lives open out in steadily wider overlapping circles, yet so much is lost for all our biographies and autobiographies, which are not even the tip of a pin on the tip of an iceberg of the vast flow of human interaction, influence, transformation, happiness, and tragedy. We live in small circles of light, astonished when something of the surrounding darkness is lit to discover familiar strangers....

But from now on in the spring of 1953 if neither Mom nor Mothie wanted to be in Westhampton on a weekend off I would go with Unk and Jill. I was less of a burden than might have been imagined—my meals were painfully simple, and I was eager to be off to the ocean or the bay alone or with friends, and made little demand on their time. The truth was we liked each other, and in these years Unk and Jill made a handsome, happy couple.

If in the evening we turned to games, that worked as well for Unk as for me: we both had a competitive streak, though mine only came out in games. Often we played a fast rough and tumble series of chess games. He had no patience for long, thoughtful pauses, or carefully plotted long-range moves: it was all dash and attack and constant improvisation. It actually made me a very good player, if unconventional to an extreme. Or we might all play monopoly, and later, Oklahoma Gin with ten cards each and three scoring columns which Unk and I played with an unforgiving ruthlessness as our scores marched across those columns while the fire cast shadows across the ceiling, and the stars came out over the ocean.

Sometimes our time together in Westhampton would last for weeks at a time. Linda on those occasions usually preferred to be with Mom and Mothie in Manhattan, love Westhampton as she did.

With Unk and Jill the air was clear of tension, ambiguities were banished, and increasingly difficult relationships laid aside. I was much less that boy 'who knew too much,' alternately shy and confident. Jill was youthful and full of fun, although she found Unk's quick temper and loud voice when he got angry startling in "the wonderful man" she thought she had married. "He wasn't the same after the war," Jill said Mothie told her once after she mentioned this to her. Unk hid that side of his personality during their courtship.

Still, easy as it proved for us to be together, I was the 'third' through stretches of their early years. But our relationship continued after the Westhampton season through the winters in Manhattan with many a Saturday or Sunday spent with them in their apartment on East 72nd Street away from the crosscurrents at home.

Unk and I developed a unique relationship. He was one part father, one part older brother, one part something that didn't fit categories. In later years his own children remembered his quick temper, or a swat to the head if they displeased him, even a kick in a moment of rage. Love him as they did, he could be a harsh taskmaster. His daughter Jillian spent her childhood in fear of him, although of his three children she is the most like him.

He drove Jill to tears with his inability to speak about intimate or emotional things. Once she tried writing letters she'd leave on his bureau, only to hear he was sick and tired of her complaints as he tore up the letters, refusing to talk. She ultimately had as mixed feelings about him as Mom had about Gar.

Unk was a bright, able man, not bound up in a continuous revision of reality like Gar. What you thought you saw was what you actually did get with him. After his years in the Army in WWII he made his way through a series of jobs, most notably with David Susskind's Talent Associates before NBC hired him in 1960 as a unit manager. The Army had wanted him to stay in 1946, but he'd had enough. Paradoxically, at NBC he was akin to a field general, managing production specials and major events as if marshalling a campaign. He was, if you will, a 'man's man,' and suffered from the traditional limitations of such men in dealing with emotions, women, or introspection. What was remarkable between he and I was that his quick temper almost never surfaced with me, let alone a swat or a kick. We shared a private wavelength despite the difference in age and character, so much so Jill once said to me, "He was wonderful with you," and it was true.

Westhampton....
Unk....
Jill....
They held the whale at bay.

A Spring Day in 1958

Mom and Mothie and I drive to Westhampton one spring day in 1958, first crossing the Long Island Sound in the ferry from Bridgeport to Port Jefferson. We live in Weston now, in Connecticut, and coming to Westhampton whether by ferry or now an even longer drive into New York and then the greater part of Long Island is harder to do. The previous summer I spent perhaps a month in Westhampton, torn between there and our new home in the woods and new friends. Yet the attraction still holds, and they bend to my will again, long disciplined to think of going to Westhampton as unchallengeable. I'm unsure how much time I will spend there this summer with them or Unk and Jill, who now have a family and live just down the road from us in Stamford. The attraction of nearby Long Island Sound, or their own large lot backing onto a river, has also made long journeys to escape the city seem irrelevant.

I feel a sigh of relief as we park before Daluanda. Yes, I will have to help repair the boardwalk to the house, repaint the slats around its base, for it is raised off the ground too, though not as high as the ocean-side homes. My spirits lift further as I see Alice is there with her family. She has become an indispensable part of Westhampton, even if always seasonal, although now, in our mid-teens, we are not as tongue-tied and hapless as before.

As soon as I can I go see her. It's just the two of us—her parents are off somewhere. They too have enclosed one side of their deck, as Mom had done with ours, and now Alice resumes ironing there after I come in. We're awkward, but no more than usual at our first, renewed contact, and ease slowly to an exchange of news. She's a pretty teenager, freckles and all, dark hair, lively expressions, and there is still something I find instinctively attractive. I sense she's reacting the same way to me from her nervousness.

But as we talk the exchange morphs increasingly into a chattering monologue on her part, and our nerves never settle: something is wrong. She's gotten into riding this past year, though I'd given it up, and had a fall during the winter and hurt herself, but is okay now.

That isn't it....

The family seems much the same, Bob out of university, Nancy growing up: that isn't it....

Then it comes out: "I have a boyfriend now too," she adds brightly, and launches into his description. It's all sunshine and light. She's not ironing anymore, and I'm very aware of how driven her chatter has become and how nervous her gestures and discomfort. He's a good guy, I'll like him. He's coming out to Westhampton too, maybe I'll see them sometimes.

I wonder to myself why I would want to see her with her boyfriend. She wonders aloud how much time I'll spend in Westhampton now we're living in Connecticut. I don't know. The conversation starts to come in fits and starts: neither of us really knows what to say, and finally I sense it is time to go.

I pause for a moment outside on her steps down to the sand. I don't know why it should finally turn on her, or if this is just the fated moment for a change to become obvious and a decision to be made, but I know Westhampton is done.

I never see her again.

I am in my 40s when I next drive down Dune Road.

I wonder if I'll recognize Daluanda or Alice's house or if Big Dock has survived the intervening storms. The landscape has changed. Dunes have been washed away, and in one place water foams under an ocean house on bare stilts. In our old development some of the lots now have two houses, and many of the houses have been altered. Big Dock is still there, unchanged, but it takes time standing on it to determine which house was once mine, which once hers. I am a stranger in a familiar land at odds with memory.

ON THE BEACH

   Westhampton, 1950 -1958

The girl I love each summer
is beside me on the beach
so close I smell her skin
with its wash of freckles
across her cheeks and nose.
We never say 'I love you,'
everything about us is too fresh.
A light breeze ripples the
summer Atlantic, puffs a few
grains of sand in the air
as I soak in the sun, the heat,
her smell, my salted flesh aglow.
The seagrass sparkles green,
the scent of sand mingles
with salt as soft waves roll in,
the memory of winter gone
as if winter itself is gone,
when winter is coming.
I feel complete: what do we
have to do with time and tide?
We are in flood, and ebb
seems outside belief—except
as the constant self sees
one image follow another
in the mirror as though in a
slide show, as I do daily now,
thinking these cannot all be me,
then that 'I am' is an illusion,

but not unreal, for these
dreams are my realities.

One spring day after we
have been apart all winter
her laughs go up in the air,
startled birds: she is ironing
and speaks of a boyfriend
who will be here soon—
and I understand, so heavy-
hearted, so innocent, he
will walk beside her on the beach.
Older, we live more distant,
unguessed others tug us away,
coming here is harder—
already our past becomes
images of summer idylls
swept free of shadows
where I am uniquely happy
and she less herself than
those idylls' symbol,
magnet, earth, although
it was the beach, the crab
and clam rich bay, the sea,
the stars I lay beneath alone,
the ocean's counsel in a
treasured solitude
that drew me and
consoled all troubles.
The flutter of those wings
deafens.... I step outside
for the first time old enough
to feel how our lives are
passages and forsakings.
We never meet again.
But even now there are times
when we walk hand in hand
down the shore, inchoate

with longing, stealing looks
at each other, everything flesh
and fresh as the beach
stretching ahead of us without end.[20]

REBELLION, WESTON PRELUDE

Washington vs. Weston

Gar was unintentionally prescient when he wondered in his diary in 1951 whether Linda and I wouldn't have a better life in the country. The 1950s became the quintessential Age of the Suburb where a family could escape increasing city congestion, expense and violence and show off their new home as a solution and a status symbol. I doubt Gar ever expected his musing about a house in the country to be taken seriously given his love of city life and hatred of moving once settled, while Linda and I were largely sheltered from all this in school, and then through the summers in Westhampton.

Nevertheless sometime in 1955 Mom and Mothie came to the decision that just such a country life would indeed be better. This time Mom brought Gar into in the decision. A Peter Lamazo was engaged to build their new home largely designed by my mother on two acres fronting the Saugatuck River in Weston, Connecticut. Next door was Westport with its convenient train station for Gar to commute to Manhattan. When we left Westhampton September 1956 for the start of the school year, it was to Weston's then Hurlbutt Jr. High for myself, the local elementary for Linda.

Mothie built her own home on an adjoining two acres fronting the river: beyond was a nature reserve of several hundred acres. Weston remains a beautiful place thanks to its strict zoning controls where most lots are two acres except those near the town or dating back to its earlier years. The woods are dense, the town alternating hills and dales and granite, Connecticut cliffs. Mom and Mothie had found a Mrs. Newman who owned much of the land along Fern Valley Road not far from Lyons Plains Road and bought their acreage from her, and over the years added twelve more acres. I remember a figure of something like $3,000 mentioned for the cost of a two acre parcel, then.

Mrs. Newman lived on her own, her greatest claim to fame in Linda and my eyes a partly tamed black snake who lived somewhere in her foundation for whom Mrs. Newman routinely left a bowl of milk. She claimed the snake was better than a cat at going after the wild mice that tried to nest in her foundation or walls. We were truly moving into the woods.

But more important than this for Gar was the 1956 election with which he and Y&R were deeply involved on behalf of the Eisenhower campaign. He left the supervision of building and furnishing the new home in Weston largely to Mom, who was no doubt happier to have this in her own hands. Gar's time instead over the summer was absorbed by preparations to put on a variety of campaign broadcasts in the autumn as writer and producer with the participation of Y&R top brass and a variety of Eisenhower Era figures, like James Hagerty, Eisenhower's Press Secretary, sometimes VP Nixon, and President Eisenhower himself. On September 20th he records in his diary:

> Yesterday I spent 40 minutes with President Eisenhower in his office in the White House discussing TV plans for the coming election campaign—specifically 10 five minute programs and a half hour on Oct. 12th. Mr. Larmon, Mr. Hardwick of Y&R were present, and Tom Stephens, an adviser to Ike—former Appointments Secretary. I spoke about eight or nine minutes outlining the half hour. The President liked it. ...I said we'd have a girl from Macy's say she thought he looked better than on TV. I suggested that he reply, "And tell them my eyes are blue." He laughed and liked the human touch which I elaborated on.

He is thrilled to be a player in significant events in the White House itself, just as he was earlier in 1944 for two years at the Treasury with Morgenthau.

He describes meetings and working lunches with a cast that reads like his entertainment Who's Who from his 1944 journal, except now filled with leading political figures.

He records on October 14th:

I went to Washington on October 10 to prepare the TV program "The People Ask the President" which was broadcast on Friday, Oct. 12, from the Sheraton Park Hotel.... I reviewed the program with James Hagerty, Press Secretary. He insisted on having the President select the people questioning him at random, which I opposed. The next day we visited the President's Press Conference, held in the Treaty Room of the old State Dept. building.

This goes well, including mentioning Eisenhower's response to one question that "McCarthy and Jenner weren't the kind of men who fitted into the new Republican Party." McCarthy's heyday had passed, and Eisenhower could be dismissive.

Gar is back in Washington October 31st, first visiting the Octagon House which for a time served as the White House in 1814. He tours through the White House East Room taking in the statues, and ends in the Cabinet Room with Tom Stephens, Y&R's Sig Larmon, and Tim Lapham. He describes Eisenhower's dress and posture approvingly, and how Eisenhower bursts out with: "I don't understand the British doing this. I've always been fair to them."

Eisenhower referred to the British veto of our effort to settle the sudden Israeli troop entry into Egypt via the UN as Britain and France instead launched an invasion force to retake the Suez Canal from Egypt. He was quietly angry, then settled down to listen to Larmon talk in general about the closing program of the campaign on Nov. 5th from Boston.

This goes through several iterations with the White House replacing Boston because of the ongoing Suez Canal crisis. Gar did the script revisions in the White House, and managed also to light the exterior of the White House for the broadcast and when all was ready,

Mrs. Eisenhower came into our "control" room at 8:45 to watch the President in a five minute special telecast to Boston.... Her mother was with her. I saw Nixon & his wife enter from the South Portico, ground floor, and later saw him and Ike in the long corridor and in the Library. Ike looked fit and fine—waved a cheery farewell to our crew after the show.... Nixon looked slick—smooth—more like a movie villain than a hero. I have only neutral feelings towards him.

He notes the cables had to go through the ladies room for the broadcast, then adds,

> I was in the White House from 10 am to 12:30 the next morning—and five to noon the ground floor—inspecting the China Room, sitting on Buchanan's settee, and sitting in other rooms as well. Thus ends another political experience—capped by my production of "Four More Years" on three TV networks and two radio Networks—and featuring Ike and Nixon, my third TV show for the President.

Who could deny him his pleasure and satisfaction at being caught up in real and important events instead of the ephemeral advertising world he held such doubts about?

He spent his lifetime reaching out to the politically powerful to advise them on media presentations and delighting in their letters to him, writing to Nixon to console him on Eisenhower's death, once applying for a post in the later Nixon administration, staying in touch with James Hagerty after he moved to ABC, advising Alexander Haig, Reagan's Secretary of State for a time, on a possible Presidential run, and proposing a Reagan documentary to Reagan's appointments and scheduling secretary, among many other Washington contacts. So how annoying in the summer and autumn of 1956 to have to talk about bathroom fixtures, window sizes, heating systems, or new furnishings for the Weston house! Not once in his 1955 and 1956 journal entries does he mention Weston or his actual fury over building, packing, moving, unpacking, or finding schools among the countless details involved in a transition to a new home, community, and routine.

There is no mention of his fury at me.

That September as we moved into our new home finishing touches continued which Gar could bear none of, as with Mothie's beach house when he first visited that in 1950. He complained about the inevitable extra expenses, the noise, disruption, and hated the new routine of being driven early by Mom to the railroad station in Westport to catch the commuter train to Manhattan. Equally he hated the reverse trip home. Family dinners became an agony of insults as first he picked on Mom:

"Don't slouch! Don't chew your nails!"

then on me,

"Lance, go clean your nails!"

or turned a gimlet stare on Linda, who froze, impeccably turned out. Our new schools were never discussed. Mothie hurried to her house before he returned each evening to avoid this barrage of criticism and unhappiness. He hated, too, that Mothie had her own house and visitors he couldn't control. He stood on our front patio to keep track of whoever drove by to see her, and complained to Mom this was all an invasion of his privacy. Mothie finally built a separate extension of Fern Valley Road to her home he couldn't monitor.

Bud and Jill often appeared for a Sunday meal, Bud with a cheery, deliberately inflammatory,

"Hiya Pops! How're'ya doing?"

Gar knew I hero-worshipped him, and resented that too, while Jill, against whom he said nothing, remembered how thick the atmosphere became when he appeared. But she was spared his criticism because he found her young and beautiful.

This behavior went on week after week.

Mom and Mothie had clearly driven the move, and knowing that, were prepared to endure his misbehavior until the work was done and he settled down into these new circumstances he would in turn hate to have disrupted. Instead it was I at 14 whose forbearance snapped in the middle of another tense dinner.

I defied his right to talk to Linda and myself or Mom so meanly. He was astounded. In the dead silence that followed he ordered me into his fine new study with its walls paneled in pine and lined with bookcases. A fireplace faced the doorway, and his desk to one side of that had a sweeping view from a picture window over the property down to the river. He sat in his red leather, Siamese-scratched chair, fixed me with an angry stare, and launched into how I had no right to speak to him like that.

I knew he intended to wear me down verbally until I apologized and asked for forgiveness, head hanging. His aura of withheld violence weighed on me. Normally my offenses were typical of my age and I would cave, to shorten his long-winded reproaches.

"I know this is all done with your money," I burst out instead in the middle of his lecture, and then was silent. He eyed me.

"Well?"

"I don't want to say," I said, "you'll just punish me."

"I never punish the truth. You can speak freely."

"Then why are you behaving this way?" I demanded. "You make everyone afraid to see you. We all want to hide. You attack Mom, you make Linda cry, and Mothie even runs home to avoid you because she can't bear the way you go on. You criticize me all the time." He is lost in astonishment. "I know you don't like the work still being done, but none of that gives you the right to make all of us miserable too!"

He is furious. I am told I am grounded, and without allowance for two weeks. I storm down the hall as he banishes me to my room:

"So much for your word! You said I could speak freely!"

That night there is at last an explosion between he and Mom, followed inevitably by his backing down before her rage and thereafter, if not behaving well, behaving better until Christmas overtook events.

Nothing would ever be the same for me, however.

I had defied his aura of omnipotence and taken a step past childish endurance. I had been the one to speak the truth others had been afraid to utter. Implausibly, I had been the adult in the room.

I sensed something decisive had happened despite my age and that there was no going back.

The Closet

One day Mothie is in the front hall as Gar arrives home early by taxi. Panicked, she goes into the hall closet and pulls the door shut as the front door opens. Gar enters, takes off his hat and shrugs off his overcoat, then opens the closet door.

She stands motionless behind a paper she has opened.
"Alma?"
Silence. He shuts the door.
"Lucille?" he calls.... "Lucille?"
"In the living room, David." Its wide entrance opens at the end of the hall facing his study. He steps in holding his hat and overcoat.
"Do you know your mother is reading the paper in the hall closet?"
"That's ridiculous, David!"
Quickly she goes to the hall closet and throws open its door, and beckons Gar. It is empty. Mothie had slipped out quietly when he went into the living room.
"Really David," she says as she walks away....

Going to Extremes

Mom took in my rebelliousness, combined with Mothie's final demand one night that Gar stop fondling Linda, and arranged for my sister to board thereafter at an exclusive school in St. James on the north shore of Long Island. To console Linda she was allowed to take her horse, General Grant. Although my riding flagged after a couple of years in Manhattan, Linda insisted on lessons too and took to riding with passion. Mom was in the full swing of her drive for 'normalcy' and soon Linda owned General Grant. When Gar heard he bit through his lip as his fist crashed down on top of the dining room table, a wrought iron affair with a thick glass top that broke at his blow.

He hadn't been consulted. His expected 'no' was judged irrelevant.

I was then offered a choice of going to a private school too. I flatly refused. I would not be dismissed or be sent away. Gar wasn't as insistent as he might have been: he didn't want to pay for two private schools.

At Weston's Horace C Hurlbutt Junior High School I was a stranger among others who had largely known each other all their lives. The Weston schools, like those in neighboring Westport, were first class New England public schools, with the graduates of Westport's Staples High School I would attend the following year going on to an array of fine, often Ivy League, colleges and universities.

I swiftly fell into the pattern I had lived through at McBurney, someone who seemed at once a boy others might turn to, and one also oddly vulnerable and noncombative. All through the year at Hurlbutt I was subjected to the same mockery I'd gone through at McBurney. Those who became friends didn't understand my aversion to conflict or my insecurity. Sometimes they slipped into the same mockery. Towards the end of the year I'd suddenly had enough, as had happened finally at McBurney, too. The news ran through the school, and after class I confronted my tormentors who backed down, or slipped away and couldn't be found.

Perhaps I had finally learned not to turn the other cheek. In High School there was no repeat.

At Staples High School I continued on the periphery. I excelled in what interested me, got by in what didn't. I drudged along in math until one term I walked into a class where a small man eyed us in silence, then launched into an increasingly fiery diatribe against those who didn't appreciate him. He carried a log on his shoulder. My classmates were intimidated; I was fascinated, paid attention to his lessons between his tirades, and aced trigonometry. But the parents in Weston and Westport Town Meetings were firmly in control of their local schools: he didn't last the semester, and I reverted to boredom. I was so bored I simply stopped going to school. For weeks I made my way to the Town Library in Westport to study on my own. I was convinced if I could learn enough history, psychology, and economics I could predict the future.

Inevitably the school caught up with me. A startled Principal realized when the librarians confirmed my story that I hadn't ditched studying, only Staples. He acted with much better grace than he needed to with my parents, who were flummoxed by my behavior. He reminded me I really didn't have the grades to get away with a stunt like that, but was sufficiently impressed by my seriousness he let me drop Chemistry over the teacher's protests and develop an independent study course in the areas I had been studying at the library with Mr. Allen, my History teacher.

Mr. Allen was my favorite, given my interest in history and biography, and I excelled in his classes through Social Studies, American, and World History. Nothing came of the course of independent study, although I did especially well on economic issues in class. I did prep myself and then excel on the AP advanced test on American History by absorbing the two volume Michigan history of the US by Kraus and Dulles.[21, 22]

There was also Ms. Higgins with an exaggerated Boston accent in English whom I liked—although I fell asleep in her class one winter day from the light hitting me in her warm room. She was mortified. It didn't help when she marked a paper down, not liking my style, which the class then liked when she read from it disapprovingly.

A football coach, Mr. Chappa, taught the athletic department's academic sop, Civics. One day a girl criticized me for writing an essay repeating what she said I'd heard in Mr. Myer's English class. I was incensed, and did the research to prove my point independently. Mr. Chappa was pleased at my combativeness as well as at how definitive a paper I turned in.

A French teacher sensed my intimidation, and like one of my old tormentors picked on me: when I switched to Spanish, I was confronted by an enthusiastic woman who so interested me with her passion that I wrote Spanish poetry by the end of the year. Thankfully, none has survived.

Then there was Mr. Myers, not yet jaded by too many years teaching know-it-alls or dealing with school bureaucracies, even on the limited small town New England scale. His enthusiasm was infectious, and while I can remember other classes in which great literature died a painful death in High School, in his it sprang to life. It didn't matter whether we dealt with a play, a novel, or what is worst in High School, poetry: with him even that took on force and relevance.

I began to write poetry under his influence, short, long, very long, deeply unfocussed, all happily lost, too. I even enjoyed his parsing grammar although that never stuck. Even that early I was struck by a simple thought: the English language was mine, therefore I could use it as I liked. It would be years before I wrote anything original, and then as a playwright in college and after. I didn't turn primarily to poetry until I was forty, but Mr. Myers planted the seed.

Increasingly I marched to an inner sense of direction, however incipient or confused, which moved step-by-step with my rebellion at home.

I made the football team my first year at Staples. Bud was pleased, and taught me the moves and stances from his glory days as a halfback on Long Island, then at Alabama. But Gar contemptuously reproached me every night for indulging in such dumb physical activity. Never mind he admired his father's heroism on the football field in his journals: I didn't know that until years later. I was failing French, intimidated by that mean little man. Then I had to sit on the bench once practices in pads started because they didn't have helmets for everyone. I was third string. A wave of self-consciousness and insecurity broke over me reminiscent of that time years ago in Great Neck when inexplicable pains made me sit and watch the other children at play in the schoolyard in what seemed to me increasingly absurd games, overcome with an intense sense of lonely uniqueness. I quit.

Had I stayed I would have become first string as the two fullbacks ahead of me went out with injuries. Gar was pleased. Bud shook his head but said nothing. The relentless evening derision stopped.

After my outburst at Gar's behavior in the fall of 1956 my discontent was ever more apparent as I watched he and my mother drive each other to extremes. In the interludes of peace Mom was the perfect hostess for an afternoon cocktail party for associates and superiors from Y&R in our vaulted living room overlooking the woods to the Saugatuck River through great picture windows, or provided a fine meal in our dining room with a view across the patio to her rock garden, and more woods.

Uncle Charles came for occasional weekends with dates who were always a present or recent graduate student after his short-lived marriage with Judy and her tragic early death. Gar's friend Vic Mizzy was there other times, ebullient, full of music, his future collaborator on *The Addams Family* with its famous introductory tune. Vic was soon with young women on his arm too after his long marriage with Mary Small collapsed.

Anything asked of me was met with a resistance rooted beyond the present in my disenchantment with our lives and a flat refusal to be 'used' or present some sort of proper 'front' or 'demeanor' which gave my typical teenage posturing an unsettling edge. If Gar demanded I stay home to help park cars for what I thought of as one of his meaningless parties with pretentious people in tweed jackets smoking pipes, I simply disappeared. If other chores were demanded in no way remarkable in themselves, I would do nothing on someone else's schedule. If left to myself, however inconvenient my timing might be, I would get things done.

Later I could never lecture from a prepared text in my professional university years—all material had to be studied, reflected on, but structured and delivered spontaneously. I hate making plans, though naturally have to as a necessary part of life. I cannot exercise unless I am moved to it. I floundered within their turmoils, emergent, but far from emerged.

My parents and I were not the only ones going to extremes.

It was now as we gathered for Bud's birthday and looked forward to Mothie's famous meatloaf and apple pie that the fiery argument between Bud and Mothie broke out that climaxed with his accusation she had denied sex to Daddy Wilds the last ten years of his life. Gar, had he been a fly on the wall, would have been nodding his head as if to say, 'See, I told you they weren't perfect!' Among other things that infuriated him was that I had rejected my given middle name, Millard, using Wilds now instead.

And, finally, there was: money.

Gar was now the family's sole provider. Mom continued to model for "The Correct Thing," but there were no more major jobs, so her income was token. He continued to give Mom a generous allowance on the face of it but which, as in New York, had to cover everything and anything. Mothie increasingly depended on her, which added even greater expenses. Yet to ask Gar for money triggered a humiliating sequence of asking, rejection, begging, rejection, insistence and only sometimes, acquiescence. He made it impossible for himself to gain any credit after such a process even if finally he turned generous. So Mom continued to go into debt in Weston too. Towards the end of the year her debtors showed up at the door, as in New York, and Gar finally had to pay. As in New York, each Christmas climaxed with a treasure hunt to find the extra money he hid that allowed Mom to catch up with some of these debts for leading the 'normal' life she insisted on and, perhaps, briefly draw ahead.

One Christmas there was the usual cornucopia of gifts, the usual sea of torn wrappings, and the climactic treasure hunt with alternating gales of laughter and comments about how ridiculous this was, followed by the next clue and discovery. Our long central hallway culminated in a set of picture windows rising two stories, in front of which a staircase went up to the master suite on the second floor, where a balcony lined the short walk to the attic. At the end of the treasure hunt Gar stood there, leaning over, grinning at the others below.

"Would you like some more?" he asked when they were done. Mom and Linda laughingly nodded yes. "Well then, bark!"

"Oh David, don't be silly!" He pulled out a wad of money and peeled off a large note and held it above them.

"See? Now bark!" He let the large bill flutter down to eager hands. He held out another. "Now, bark!"

"Woof! Woof!" Mom barked, half-heartedly, but snatched a large bill from the air. I watched from the entry to the living room.

"Really, David!" she laughed, the silliness catching on as he held out another.

"Come on," he said, " both of you bark like dogs!" He let the bill go. "Bark! On your knees!" Another bill fluttered down. She and Linda sank to their knees, laughing.

"Woof woof!"

Mom snatched more bills from the air. Then Linda. He held out more and waited.

"Woof! Woof!"

A green rain of bills fluttered down to increasing excitement.

"Woof! Woof!"

I retreated into the living room and sat on the piano stool to one side of the entrance hidden from view, nauseated.

"Again!"

"Woof woof!"

King

Just as we move to Weston my piano teacher gives us a German shepherd she rescues from Manhattan streets. Mom and Mothie think he will be good to have in the country. It doesn't matter King chases and bites a pair of sheep Linda has for a time: what King needs after the streets is love....

He is kept at Mothie's weekends when Gar is home.

One Saturday from Mothie's house King sees Gar step out our front door and stand on the edge of the patio to survey Fern Valley Road for unwanted visitors. King breaks loose from the rope restraining him and bounds from Mothie's onto Fern Valley Road towards him, baying. Gar sees him, freezes, then lunges for the front door he slams shut a split second before King hurls himself against it in full stride.

King remains....

Once he growls at me and without thinking I whack his snout. He yelps, but never growls at me again. But he has to be kept from all strangers or he will bite them. In the end he bites 34 people. I have no idea how no action is taken against us. One day I come home and am told Bud took him to a farm in the country where he could run free and not be a problem to anyone.

Bud put him down. Bud wept.

I loved King.

Weston Idylls

Despite all these upheavals Weston became my youthful 'home.' My turn to nature that started in Great Neck and continued in Westhampton now continued in Weston. Again, it was sufficient for the woods to be there to walk into, enough to attune myself to natural rhythms and events in an impulse at once Wordsworthian or Jeffersian, though I knew neither, then. Natural imagery and rhythms became the root of the poetry I wrote with increasing knowledge and skill down the years. I was immersed in my surroundings at the same time I realized I could write as I wished because the language belonged to me.

Thanks to Westhampton I looked forward to summer for escape and relief, though summers in Weston were warm and humid, and the nearest beach miles away on Long Island Sound, far from the Atlantic. The consolation of the woods and cliffs I explored replaced that of marsh and shore in Westhampton, something that grew in 1957 and completely supplanted Westhampton in 1958. The great surprise though in Weston was the autumn, and even more, the winter.

Autumn in New York was a dingy dimming of the light with a touch of color in the parks, and in Westhampton a paling of summer's green reeds and marsh grass in cooling nights. In Weston it was an oceanic wave of reds, red golds, golds, bright yellows, and last the Indian reds and russets of the oaks, unbroken in the hundreds of acres in the nature reserve past Mothie's, overwhelming the town's woods-engulfed homes. The last leaves lingered until Thanksgiving. Then the bare woods with their thousandfold spindly arms dominated except where the firs and hollies held their greens, the latter clustered with red berries.

A few hardy birds stayed the season, the most amazing the common red cardinal, so hard to see normally, so startling in a stripped forest, even more so in one covered with snow. Its flight laced arteries between the trees' bare bones. Death dominated in one sense. In another a brooding in the root and a regathering of strength filled the woods that only slept to dream of surging energy and sudden outburst. It was a brooding at once latent and potent. As the first snow threatened before Christmas there would be that eerie sense of the air thickening, of being able to smell the snow before it came, as in Great Neck. Then a flake appeared as though condensed out of the air itself, something lacily white that melted on my outstretched hand.

Better than snowfalls, hotly anticipated because they brought a 'snow day' off at school, were the rarer ice storms. A sensible person trying to go from one ice-slicked location to another in the morning hated these. Movement was impossible on a side road that went unsanded like Fern Valley Road. But it was miraculous to wake up after such a storm and walk out into the woods in the early sun. A forest where every limb and twig is sheathed in ice as the light hits it is a miracle of flashing prisms. How far from New York's gray, slush-covered streets this was! Seeing all stripped to its bare essentials yet aglow, exhilarated me. That childhood sense of wonder at the simplest things I had found outside continued unabated.

It didn't hurt, either, that there was so much work to do outside with our new homes. Mothie's front was overgrown with trees, her driveway a gash against the land's slope. Bud and I took on the chore of thinning the trees, alternating ax and shovel as we cut them down and uprooted what we could, sometimes tying a rope around a stump and pulling it out with his car. In place we planted dogwood trees around Mothie's front patio, and fruit trees, including one special apple tree grafted to grow five varieties. I don't recall it ever showing more than two or three, but that impressed us all.

Then we turned to Mothie's driveway. If there is one thing Connecticut—"the granite state"—is not short of, it is stones. We found all we needed at the foot of the hill as it rose on the forest side of Fern Valley Road, lugged those to her driveway, and built a long half-height wall against the hill, and around three sides of the parking area scooped out before her garage. That wall still stands, and our trees.

When Bud and Jill moved to Stamford our joint work continued at their new home. There Bud and I carpentered a much larger master bedroom out of two smaller rooms, and over time between our efforts and Bud's alone their grounds were transformed so that stone steps led down from their rear patio to a long, wide lot with widely spaced trees bordered by a small river. Once they moved to Stamford we established a ritual: every Sunday after church we drove into Westport, bought a box of donuts, then drove to Bud and Jill's. Mom and Mothie assured Jill they had made the donuts themselves, which awed her for years before, angered, she caught on.

Once there with the donuts handed out, Bud resumed reading the NY Times, followed by me section by section as he discarded them, at first out of interest, and then under the inspiration of Mr. Myers. Then we'd simply visit, or in the autumn Bud and I watch a Giants NFL game if on. The image of Y.A. Tittle on his knees in the rain and mud after a career-ending hit is burned into memory one such Sunday afternoon. I was in Stamford as much as I could be, and they frequently visited Weston. By 1959 there were two little Wilds, Craig and Brad, followed in 1962 by Jillian. They stayed in Stamford and Mothie in Weston after I left for college in 1960 and after Mom moved herself and Linda to California with Gar in 1963. Mothie was the last to go, she and Weston remaining a center for myself in graduate school and for Bud's family a few years more.

Thrown into this mix was my getting my license in 1958 and being allowed to drive to Staples, usually with the family's monstrous (in today's terms) Ford wagon. I drove wildly, partly encouraged by Bud's stories from his youth of outracing the police town to town, or crashing cars only to have them replaced by his father. I hurtled over twisting, hilly country roads at speeds which propelled that huge Ford into the air past a steep hill's crest before crashing down. It was teenage idiocy, and luck that nothing happened to me or another. My one crash was on Fern Valley Road as I gunned the car up the hill towards home in a snowstorm and slid off near the hill's crest into a tree that put a large V in the Ford's front.

Gar was far more understanding of a fault that wasn't his than you might expect, and took this in good kind. One element that kept us all coming back after every disappointment was that sense there was a much better man in him than he knew how to let out. Now and then that man appeared when nothing was at stake for himself and he'd surprise us by acting in good grace and understanding. Those were moments of the sun coming through a cloud—we absorbed all the brief light we could.

Sailing was added to my summer immersion in nature in Weston my last summer there. Neither Mom nor Mothie wanted to get me a boat after their experience in Westhampton trying to do so, so I took a part-time job at Food Giant in Westport to the family's surprise and worked long enough to buy a beamy, 10 foot sailing pram.

Then I quit and went sailing.

The harbor master at Compo Beach in Westport let me keep it out of the way on land in the marina. Off to Compo Beach I went on any day promising a breeze, always a question on the summer Sound, without taking sailing lessons, mastering the basics of my little craft through experience. I sailed like I drove—sailing at times in weather better sailors avoided. One particularly windy day I went out and found my light pram, sail straining, stays tight, mast bending, keeping pace with a seventeen foot Lightning.

All of this, nature, the proximity of Bud and Jill, later the sailing, compensated for the storms at home. I could be with my teen peers on a darkening evening with all the typical crosscurrents, sense that thickening of the air and almost tactile anticipation of snow, and hardly distracted by them take in those first miraculous snowflakes. Some rivalry might be underway, or a flirting: suddenly I was aware instead of our lack of significance in the larger, natural world we mostly ignore. Even in the first year in Weston when I was mercilessly teased, if I took a breather during a neighborhood touch football game in the field next to one of my friend's homes on Lyons Plains Road, I was struck instead by a shift in the breeze, the hint of a colder weather, or of leaves turning color on the edge of the field before a storm. Then it just didn't seem very important whether I played well or not, was in an argument, or teased, or not.

Once I found an old barn long abandoned not far from Lyons Plains Road. I saw by the lay of the land its fields had once been farmed before becoming part of someone's suburban spread with its trophy home. The sense of lost lives filled me, of other ways of living, of different people doing different things once certain of the 'nowness' of their lives. Things could be so different.... That added to that sense of human limitation I got beneath the Milky Way those nights I walked the Atlantic shore in Westhampton, that sense there were larger orders than mine or my family's, and the perception that without an appreciation of those our immediate lives are inflated with an importance they don't deserve.

I still visit these woods, sometimes drive by our former homes, and visited Jill in Stamford until she was 91, tugged by a sense of long-lost never replaced rootedness.

AN OLD BARN IN WESTON

stands in a field of dandelions blooming
so intensely the sky steals their hue.
A few tools rust, abandoned; the lofts sag,
barely able to support their emptiness,
and the barren stalls lose even the memory
of horse and cow or crowing barnyard fowl.
Homes fill once wheat-rich fields,
bound by law to look older than they are:
metal snakes commute down Lyons Plains Road
each morning, and each evening, home:
by day lonely women lug their wetnosed young
chore to chore or, chauffeurs by night,
drive young couples date to date
who all but couple in the backseat dark.
No matter. A trunk weathered white holds
the barn gates closed: heat warps the walls
that ice cracks in turn. If time speeded
the stained brown walls would hurry inward
under the falling roof, groaning with relief.
No one comes here now except barn mouse
and field, who was always here, and,
ghosting on wide wings as twilight falls,
great white mouse-harrowing owls.[23]

WESTON WOODS

How green the dark in Weston woods—
if you look for me here in after years
I will not be haunted, or haunting,
but imbued in a seam of bark or a rustle
of leaves or the heft of a stone from a long,
    low wall—
and if you sense my stare, turn quickly—
we will be face to face. In these woods
the years are leaves that never fall
but flutter around me so time so irreversibly
    one plus one
        runs every way down these paths, splits,
    circles,
rejoins,
    all entangled:
        the car I gun up an icy hill
    into a tree;
    a woman a girl mine who melts beneath me
as the Sound licks the shore and sighs roll
    off the swells;
    my father who slaps me after a graduation
        all-nighter;
my daughter who steps on a copperhead
    too lazy to turn and bite—she is three,
        and death sleeps:
and me, who time out of mind strains for
    sense in these woods.

Fireflies begin to light the dusk. Here
>   they are on and off at once, like ourselves,
>   at once dark
>   and blazing.[24]

REBELLION, WESTON OUTBREAK

The Lord's Prayer

Mothie taught Linda and myself simple prayers in German as children, as well as the Lord's Prayer. Raised as an Episcopalian I was duly baptized, sent to Sunday school, and taken routinely to Church in Great Neck and Manhattan. Relief from that came only in Westhampton, and even there my attraction to Alice occasionally found me beside her in the local Catholic church.

Once we moved to Weston our church became the white clapboard, spartan Episcopal Church on Lyons Plain Road a few minutes from home, presided over by an earnest young man, the Reverend John Thomas. Mom and Mothie liked him and donated materials to the church, including a movie projector Gar was startled one day to find given away. That first autumn in Weston found me attending confirmation classes with John Thomas.

At times I drew historical figures and their thoughts into our discussions. The other teens thought I was showing off. I tried to explain that past figures weren't really past to me but figures to visit as though we all lived on different floors of the same building. This put them off even more. But John Thomas looked at me speculatively, and nodded his head. He understood. I warmed to him.

I warmed to his earnestness, the whitewashed simplicity of his church, its plain pews, clear windows the light streamed through, and the simple cross over an equally simple altar. I endured his earnest sermons because he actually believed what he said. I was duly confirmed, something my father remained silent about and which obviously pleased Mom and Mothie. But neither they nor John Thomas knew of the crisis of faith I underwent the following two years. I believed I should believe but resented that 'should' as if an obligation placed on me by a parent for 'proper' behavior regardless of what I thought.

Worse, nothing stood between myself and God. He might not have the time to speak to me, but He knew what I was up to, what I thought, when I masturbated, when I lied, was angry, kind, or.... I had nowhere to hide. But when I took in a rainbow forest glowing from icy prisms which I was supposed to think was His work, I wondered. I knew the natural cause of that effect. Any event that could be explained by natural processes made me question what God had to do with, well, anything?

Perhaps He had created everything, then sat back in a tweed jacket with a pipe to watch what happened. If so, why did I need Him, now? Who did I know who ever saw a miracle contradict a scientific explanation? I intuited the miraculous is part of nature's impact and at the core of my sense of wonder and mystery. Later I found no conflict between science and poetry beyond the unpoetic nature of scientific prose. Even then I sensed great scientific leaps are made by deeply creative minds. What difference does it make if creativity turns now to hard science, now to poetry, now to erecting a religion? Each has its role in our creative response to reality: science towards the factual truth, poetry towards wonder and insight, religion towards consolation and reassurance.

With these intuitions I lost my faith.

My Churchgoing and prayers diminished until only the Lord's Prayer remained. There I stuck. Every night I lay in bed determined not to say it, and night after night failed. God might benignly puff His pipe watching His Show, ignoring me, but if I stopped offering due obeisance I was certain He'd get up and let me have it. Fear was the final bond of my faith.

One night I forced myself not to recite those words or let them slide into consciousness in my dark room.

I was cold.

I sweated.

A blow traveled through the night but never reached me.

Then it was over.

I do not pretend to know absolutely that God doesn't exist: my loss of faith was the simpler admission that I don't know that he does, and that either way *it doesn't matter* as he doesn't work individually but through those forces that shape reality. A void opened underfoot, at once a relief and frightening, a relief because I sensed the future was mine to make, frightening as I had no idea what such freedom meant. I remained haunted. But as no blow ever came I began to forget the Lord's Prayer while my sense of the majesty and wonder of the world deepened.

John Thomas wasn't happy ministering to the affluent. He chose to move to depressed, racially mixed, needy Bridgeport. I still think of him with warmth and respect.

But now I was free to break other bonds.

Another Ending, A New Beginning

Events concurrently moved forward at Young & Rubicam. Gar survived Nat Wolff's attempt to undercut him, excelled at his work and impressed everyone during the second Eisenhower Campaign. But jockeying for position was unrelenting at these agencies, and in 1958 Nat Wolff's stormy tenure ended, replaced by Gar's friend and rival Peter Levathes. Gar was angry. Despite the perfect wife and perfect cocktail and dinner parties and new scenic home and surpassingly successful activity he had hit a glass ceiling because he was Jewish.

Then he received a feeler from NBC. Robert Kintner, its president, needed a new Head of Programming. Robert Sarnoff oversaw NBC; his father, General Sarnoff, was head of the parent company, RCA, that owned the network. Had Young & Rubicam offered the position of head of television to Gar he would have stayed there even though he could see in 1958 that Hollywood and the national networks were replacing the advertising agencies as creators of TV content. But he liked the security of what he knew. Levathes' promotion provoked my father to respond favorably to NBC's feeler.

Negotiations were tense—NBC was taken aback by the safety clauses he demanded in his contract. The negotiators hesitated until Kintner stepped in.

"Give him what he wants," he said.

So after 1961 when his short, successful but tumultuous relationship ended with NBC in bitter acrimony his contract gave my father an additional five years of full salary which took him through the creation of *The Addams Family*.

His position at NBC made my father one of the three most influential men in the country as far as television and popular taste were concerned.

Under his direction NBC put on shows like *Dr. Kildare*, *Maverick* and *Bonanza*. These were great successes and restored NBC with his other innovations to the number one network again after long trailing CBS. In the background he maneuvered Johnny Carson's succession to Jack Paar at the *Tonight Show*. Perhaps his most influential act was to bring Hollywood feature films to the small screen and unite the two mediums.

This was revolutionary then, and soon imitated by CBS and ABC who had no intention of letting NBC leap further ahead of them. Despite this success he was opposed by Kintner who preferred a diet of sex and violence. Kintner's request for more of that was deliberately ignored by my father who now delighted in overcoming opposition and imposing his will. He was certain he knew better. The need to outshine his twin and become 'number one' that both Binger and Friedberg had explained to my mother, and which had been contained within familiar Y&R constraints, now came out nakedly. Kintner who held the No 1 position at NBC became a target a lifetime in the making.

So now Gar, buttressed by success, went over his head to the Sarnoffs. Robert overrode Kintner, and Gar scheduled *Saturday Night at the Movies*. Kintner seethed. Few realized the advent of feature films was the end of television's Golden Age of live, original drama.

Concurrent with this activity was an apartment overlooking Central Park made possible by an unlimited expense account. If a dress caught my father's eye in a window display at Saks Fifth Avenue he'd have the window sent home to Mom to try on. A limousine replaced the commuter train to drive him to and from his grand office which overlooked Rockefeller Plaza in the RCA building to the door in Weston or his new apartment. The Rockettes performed on a lower floor below NBC and RCA's offices, while his office looked down on the giant seasonal Christmas Tree, on iceskaters in the Plaza in the winter and in summer on umbrellas and tables as people dined in the Plaza. He was at a summit of influence.

It went to his head.

To avoid our increasingly charged life at home with an ever more difficult teenage son he stayed in New York at his new apartment as much as possible. When Mom joined him on occasion the house in Weston grew still, left to Mothie and myself, with Linda remaining safely off at the Knox School in St James with her horse. Mothie and I got along: she was always too in touch with reality to let things move to a break. I'm sure she still believed everything would work out.

Jeanne

One day in my sophomore year at Staples High School I noticed a petite girl with a brown wave of bangs over her forehead with copper highlights and a trim figure. Her blonde friend Connie was more statuesque and outgoing, but it was Jeanne I saw. Mysteriously she disappeared. When she reappeared after many months she was a pasty white. Later I learned how she had grown listless doing the multitude of chores her parents gave her. She didn't understand why her books grew so heavy: one day, mystified, she weighed them, expecting some unusual result. But as her listlessness deepened and her pallor grew her parents finally stopped threatening to take her to a doctor in the belief she was just indulging in teenage resistance, and actually did so. Mononucleosis was diagnosed. At last she was allowed to rest and recover, a lengthy process.

Her name was Jeanne Hutchings.

She was in my English class too with Victoria Higgins who was insulted when I fell asleep one midwinter day. Our paths repeatedly crossed, but though we knew each other I never called her for a date. There were others at first, the sister of a friend I practiced guitar with, for one. He and I thought we'd start a band, and became buddies driving madly over our country lanes. For a time I played well enough to write and perform a song for his sister. She sat with a bemused expression through my basic but earnest performance. We were too stunned once I was done to kiss. It was the old story, the boy at once brimming with confidence and the boy too insecure to act alternating with dizzying speed.

There was another girl among these inevitable, typical High School romances that played an altogether different role. We rode the same bus to school, and one day when I asked her out she said yes enthusiastically. I mentioned this to Mom in the natural course of events, who realized when she heard the girl's name that she was Jewish. She demanded I break off the date. I was astonished.

Aside from her justified dislike of Nanny she'd never shown any antisemitism: she was, after all, Mrs. Levy.

"How can you even think of going out with a Jewish girl after all Nanny has put me through!" she challenged me that night

She was so insistent over several days of mounting tension that I broke off the date. The next day on the bus I tried to explain to the girl this had everything to do with my mother's awful experience of her mother-in-law, and nothing to do with the girl or her family, but much as that explanation made sense within our family, it meant nothing beyond. The girl was hurt, angry, insulted. She never spoke to me again. I was ashamed. Gar was angry too when he heard, and for a rare moment we were on the same side. For the first time in the family drama I saw Mom turn against me when I didn't act perfectly attuned to her needs.

In one angry exchange shortly after this our tempers rose to such a pitch I slammed into my room and locked the door. She demanded to be let in. I refused. Incensed, she bodily battered the door down and burst into the room. After a frozen moment as we stared at each other she spun on her heel and left.

Neither of us understood how it had come to this. It would be a lifetime before I understood how my accumulating need for reality augmented with teenage urgency clashed with Gar's constant falsification of our experience and Mom and Mothie's heartfelt demand I conform to their ideality. By the summer of 1959 something even more incendiary was added to my private religious rebellion and growing family antagonisms: Jeanne. She and I began to date with an ever growing intensity.

By late fall we were lovers. We were so inexperienced.... She was late one month with her period and was distraught, and as relieved when normalcy asserted itself. But Mom and Mothie listened to our phone calls. All was exposed, including her onetime lateness. They provoked a family confrontation in Gar's study with he on his 'Throne of Pain,' except this time he tried to moderate Mom's anger. He was concerned about my rashness too, but felt Mom's rage went too far. It was another of those rare moments when the better man we sensed in him emerged as he tried to find a balanced course since it was not himself under question.

After that Jeanne was persona non grata in Weston. We carried on quietly on our own.

Her parents Roy and Joyce never knew of this crisis for Jeanne's stepmother Joyce and her father Roy were not people she confided in. She managed as much on her own as possible.

Who was Jeanne, then?

She was the daughter of Roy Hutchings and Eileen Cresswell whom he met in London before he joined the RAF at the start of WWII. The Cresswell heritage stretches back to the Norman kings, the Hutchings to English yeomanry. It is the Cresswell's internecine lawsuit in the 19th Century referred to in Dickens' *Bleak House*—when their infighting was done their aristocratic status, homes and fortune were gone, with some property left in London destroyed subsequently during the Blitz.

Roy wrote to Eileen as his "wife" during his RAF missions in the war, and Eileen signed letters as "Eileen Hutchings" although he was still married to another—his family's Welsh maid he absconded with in the late 1930s on a motorcycle he constructed. They married in Wales, but when Roy returned to London shortly thereafter, he was alone. Roy's long absences while the bombs fell in London wore on Eileen, and soon she was in the arms of another and left Jeanne behind with her Aunts, especially Aunt Violet, the woman Jeanne felt was most her mother.

When Roy returned after the war and discovered this he removed Jeanne at 4 1/2 from the only home she'd known and put her in High Trees, a boarding school in Surrey. He then went off for years to Africa. She saw no one she knew until four years later she was called into the Principal's Office. A strange, deeply tanned man sat to one side of the office. Jeanne stood before the desk, waiting as the silence dragged on. At last the Principal asked,

"Jeanne, aren't you going to say hello to your father?"

Jeanne walked over to him and held out her hand like the proper English schoolgirl she had become.

"How do you do, sir?"

Roy had been in Kenya in British East Africa in the Empire's setting glow, climaxed by becoming an engineer on the safari where *King Solomon's Mines* was filmed with Debra Kerr and Stewart Granger. There he met Joyce, a nurse: by the end of the safari and filming they were lovers. They returned to England where Joyce divorced her husband, and Roy at last divorced the Welsh maid he'd left behind in Wales. A year later they moved to the US with Jeanne and were married.

Thirty-two years passed before Jeanne saw Aunt Violet again.

By 1956 Jeanne was naturalized and Americanized but felt at any moment the rug might be pulled out from under her again, that her life with Roy and Joyce was on sufferance. Joyce went on to have two children: Jeanne's brother David developed epilepsy, and Joyce gave way to anxiety with overwrought bursts of temper almost anything could trigger which she combined with marked inflexibility. Roy was calm to a fault, and though he loved Jeanne was undemonstrative. At one point Roy's mother Ada came for a long visit from England as a prelude to staying in America with Roy and Joyce but left, in part, Jeanne later learned, because she couldn't bear to watch her son and Joyce treat Jeanne like a slave.

We had a lot to talk about. We became each other's refuge.

Every crisis deepened our relationship instead of driving us apart. We complemented each other perfectly, too: Jeanne was levelheaded, in touch with realities I had never experienced, and yet despite her traumatic background buoyant and determined to free herself. She leavened the weight of my home life, my recurrent, conflicted depressions and 'tragic sense of life.' If my background looked cosseted compared to hers, both our families had their own fraught nature that ran to extremes. I also had an instinctive assurance despite my flip insecurity, an expectation that things would work out, an inner sense of direction to—somewhere. Our families' grips loosened.

At the end of the summer of 1959 I asked Jeanne to marry me—not then, but after college, if we were still together, and still felt so intensely. Despite all those 'ifs' that was a lot to ask, but after a pause, she agreed. Into our tense lives that possible future now intruded with the approaching end of high school. Under my parents' prodding I applied to a series of Ivy League schools for which I wasn't qualified. We visited some of those colleges where I suffered through awkward interviews except at Brown where I hit it off with the admissions officer and left feeling hopeful.

That spring my parents were on a European trip when I was rejected by all. My pattern of excelling in what interested me and only getting by in what didn't had no appeal to these schools. Jeanne was accepted by all her choices and offered full one year scholarships at Wheaton, outside Providence, and Northeastern, in Boston. She chose the latter because

Northeastern in the succeeding years had a work-study program that would enable her to continue without help, unlike Wheaton. She knew her family could not help her, if otherwise supportive.

In a panic I searched for universities still open for application, and discovered Boston University was available, applied, and was accepted. When my parents returned from Europe and discovered what had happened they refused to accept Boston University. I did not hide Jeanne was going to Northeastern a few blocks away. On their own accord they applied for me at the University of Connecticut and informed me 'I' was accepted there and could attend that school in the fall, or go into the Army. Bud shook his head, and said nothing.

I declared I would go to Boston instead with Jeanne and work my way through college. My parents thought that was ridiculous given the expectations of families in our position and what they thought they knew of me and my privileged, inexperienced life. Both thought I would give in when the time came.

Shortly thereafter Jeanne and I graduated from Staples High School. There was our Graduation followed that evening by the Senior Prom, after which there were a series of parties Jeanne and I drifted through with friends: we ended up at an early breakfast in Westport. I dropped Jeanne off afterwards, and drove home. I was greeted with hysteria. Where had I been, demanded Mom? How could I stay out all night? I was surprised, having been in the company of so many others doing the same thing, but she must have thought Jeanne and I went off on our own. Gar was still home: called into the fray, angered by my defiance, he slapped me. He had never been physical before. I mocked him out the door.

Bud and Jill remained a solace though Jill was not sure I was doing the right thing. She saw Mom's side as well. But Bud I knew felt differently. He had watched the family romance sour, was convinced Gar was much in the wrong, but was not much comfort to Mom where I was concerned. Despite their closeness he harbored the belief that Daddy Wilds had favored her over himself. He saw this time I was not going to cave in, and later told me he was proud that I "stuck to my guns."

I liked Jeanne's father, Roy. He might not be demonstrative, but even more than Mothie or Bud he was in touch with reality, and accepted my relationship with Jeanne. We talked over Jeanne's and my plan to go to Boston together where I would find a job to support myself as I worked my way through school. He knew Jeanne would be in a Northeastern dormitory and I in a room elsewhere. He accepted as a matter of course that I should consult with him. He said nothing about my family, but in his world to choose to make one's own way at 18 wasn't an issue. He had done much the same in his youth, if in radically different circumstances—there was no spare money in his family. The burden of proof would be in my carrying through.

Small and large, sensible, ridiculous, long, even generationally long, and immediate events and causes had reduced myself and my family not just to mutual incomprehension, but absurdity. There was no communication between myself and my parents and as that summer wore on I went in and out my window to leave or return home wrapped in a dull and protracted sense of unreality and simultaneously in accumulating tension as September approached. An electric charge built towards an inevitable discharge like thunderclouds on a clear summer day piling on one another on the horizon, soon to spring forward and burst.

A Stolen Car

One summer morning after going out my window I picked Jeanne up to go sailing in the family Ford I was still allowed to use. My sailboat was just big enough to be fun, though once when Jeanne sat on its bow a cruiser went by without slowing, generating a large wake we dropped steeply into a moment later: Jeanne screamed as the water loomed over her. The boat bobbed up like a cork and safely crested this and the other waves in that wake....

Once back we stowed the boat away on shore, then discovered the Ford was gone. My parents had never taken it before, though we guessed Mom or Gar must have as the latest sign of their displeasure. We decided to act like normal people. We called the police.

The police contacted my parents and were irritated they had taken the car: why hadn't they told us? How were we to know? They were the unreasonable ones! They were told to pick us up....

Mom duly arrived. We got in the car in silence. She dropped Jeanne off at her home on West Parrish Road in silence. We drove home in silence.

We had run out of things to say.

A Long Walk

The day of departure loomed until one afternoon and evening I prepared to go.

I was quiet but determined that night. We moved around each other in the house without speaking. I felt like a character in a science fiction story about to step from one reality into an unknown other that shouldn't be possible but in terms of the story being lived was—for just this moment, after which that opportunity would be lost. Later that night that pending storm's first roll of thunder broke out between my mother and father. It was impossible not to hear them. I and Linda had listened to their arguments so many times in the past that this one had an all-too-familiar air that tonight was also surreal.

Gar remained adamant as Mom pled with him to give in and accept my choice of university although until this moment she had been as opposed as him. No amount of reasoning, pleading, anger and finally tearful begging moved him. He was determined, he finally admitted, not to "lose face" before me by giving in. When at last the house quieted I was sleepless as the night I had stopped reciting the Lord's Prayer.

In the morning there was little to do but have a quick breakfast and walk down Fern Valley Road to meet Jeanne at its end in the car Roy got her that summer, a '51 blue Plymouth sedan with a '53 engine. Mothie stayed home and Gar left early without seeing me. Mom waited in the kitchen, silent. I ate something but as I turned to go she broke down in an outpouring of grief that stunned me.

"Please don't go," she sobbed abruptly, restraint gone.

"Mom, I—"

"Please don't go!" she pled again and flung her arms around my neck, holding me in place as she cried brokenly on my shoulder.

"I'll persuade him to support you.... I'll make it work!" she sobbed as she held me. I was too shocked to move. Generations of grief were behind her tears, of incredulity that a hard-won, fiercely idealized view of the world had met a reality that couldn't be bent. Mothie's refusal to see the façade of her perfect, middle-class life broken by Daddy Wilds was in her grief and pleading. My mother's repeated, reluctant agreements with Mothie in her own crises in 1943 and 1947-48 not to divorce Gar were in that pleading. The painful, personal, self-compromising sacrifices exacted down the generations to maintain these lives in their appearances were in her pleading. Nevermind Gar's refusal—wasn't he in the end as committed to maintaining this life as herself? Hadn't he caved in during those great crises when he realized he might lose her, desperate to save their life together? Didn't he back down in every confrontation after she finally lost patience with his daily behavior and confronted him? Wasn't his entire modus operandi a willful rewriting of experience on the go so the awful became the admirable? She'd turn him around if only I'd stay a little longer! My leaving was a judgment against her life....

If only Daddy Wilds had lived he'd have made everything right....

I had never seen an adult dissolve into such helpless, grievous pleading and tears, let alone my mother.

"Please don't go, Lance, please stay," she sobbed on as she clung to me as once I clung to her sobbing hysterically in Great Neck crying,

"You're always going!"
as she left.

I loved her too, profoundly, despite our arguments through these years. Simultaneously there was a sense of falseness, not in her grief, but in the possibility of my shutting my eyes and pretending all would be well if only I'd do what another expected.

"Mom, I have to go," I got out, or "Jeanne's waiting," or "I'll write" or, inanely, "It will all work out for the best." Even now I feel myself pulling her arms away.

Her face dissolved in sorrow filled the kitchen behind me as I walked away. The walk down Fern Valley Road took, I thought, a very long time. All its familiar scenes felt as though they were on a screen that rolled up behind me as I passed.

Jeanne was waiting. We must have said something. I don't remember. I put my bag in the trunk, and slid in beside her. She drove off. Or did I take the wheel? I'd like to say I felt invisible chains breaking with each step I took each mile I drove towards Boston. I'd like to say I knew I was shattering a wonderful dream fatally flawed in execution. But I don't recall what I said then, or thought, or if I thought. I was in a blank, novel place.

Words took a lifetime to find their way to these pages to evoke this morning.

Of the drive to Boston I remember nothing.

DAWN IN BOSTON

Arrival and Arrival and....

On arrival in Boston Jeanne checked into her Northeastern dormitory a few blocks either way between the Boston Fens and the University on Huntington Avenue. Providentially we drove by a brownstone on Commonwealth Avenue a few blocks from the Boston Public Gardens that advertised rooms, and for $10.50 a week I found myself in a one room fourth floor walkup I provided with a hot plate and a few plates and utensils. Refrigerated food was kept in a shared refrigerator down the hall in a small communal kitchen. There was hardly time to think or feel: there was arriving, finding, settling in, all novel, all equally real and unreal.

The next morning I awoke as numb as though I suffered from food poisoning, if without the pain. My limbs were heavy as tree trunks. I felt nothing, not a challenge to explore this new city nor any aftereffects from my traumatic leave-taking. If I commanded myself, "Move!" I moved; "Sit!" I sat. When I met Jeanne after she registered for her classes at Northeastern I was an automaton driven only by her motivation. I became familiar with her dorm's common room for visitors where in that first evening she snuck me as much of a dinner as she could from her cafeteria, a pattern that endured and was later helped by her friends. I did not look for a job. I made no effort to register at Boston University for a night course. It never occurred to me to do either, or to wonder why I did neither. I did not feel anything about my behavior. I felt nothing.

Jeanne organized our free time. It was as though walking away from the life I knew left no other. I had burned out my strength in that long walk down Fern Valley Road. I didn't wonder when this would end: I just endured a passage of time, met Jeanne at her dorm, had a meal, then walked back to Commonwealth Avenue and trudged up my four flights to bed. The next morning the light awoke me, and at a snail's pace I rose, used the common bathroom, dressed, and—did nothing until it was time to meet Jeanne again. I knew what the new routine was with Jeanne, which gave a pattern to my shapeless days, but I was empty of the sense of actual time passing.

Day after day passed in this zombie fashion. I felt no stirring of emotion, no coming to terms with what I had done, not even a sense of failing to come to terms. I felt no anxiety over continuing to fail to look for work or to register for a night course at BU. Nothing mattered. Even the sense that nothing mattered, didn't matter. This went well beyond depression. That involved tension headaches from irresolvable conflicts that on occasion laid me up for days, oppressed by the feeling the world was a doomed place and I had no place in it. I had none of those feelings which, in this context, would have been an improvement!

I was dead in spirit however you understand that word. I wasn't curious about what might be happening at home which, had I thought about it, would have been days filled with anxiety and nights with arguments. It didn't occur to me to care about how my mother or father or Mothie were. I was simply here in these new and meaningless settings. They weren't even strange. That would have called for a judgment, an emotional reaction, a tingle of fear or excitement.

I was in a black hole that released no thought, feeling, or twinge of energy. I am psychologically literate, but I don't know how to analyze or describe this differently. It was not romantic. It was not contrariwise my experience of a vacuum. I was a vacuum. No doubt something went on beyond any conscious reflection or dream that might have given me an intimation of life, but my nights too were black voids I dropped into and emerged from with no recall.

I was a golem, lifeless mud shaped to look like Lance Lee, something that acted only in response to another's command. I was a blank slate on which no experience wrote itself even in the moment of its passage. I cast no shadow. Later Jeanne told me she was worried, but didn't think I'd give in and submit to my father, so just watched and waited.

Her waiting must have grown anxious as the days turned into a lifeless week. Neither her worry nor passion registered. I felt no guilt. I did not wonder at the absence of my passion. Jeanne was there. If she said "Move!" I moved, "Sit!" I sat.… I was emptiness itself. I was failing. Despair should have set in. Perhaps it did: I didn't know. Failure, shame, or the thought of a broken return home should have sparked some feeling. They did not.

I was in an astonishing state. I didn't need to 'work' at repression: I felt nothing to repress, nor did any nightmare give repression away. Whatever I was in the grip of had no grip. There was nothing to rebel against, conscious or the opposite. I hadn't fallen into an abyss: there was no 'falling.' I was an abyss. Perhaps the worst thing wasn't being unable to see a way out—there was nothing to see and no sense of loss of seeing. Such an abyss is wholly self-sufficient—it lacks nothing, as there is nothing to lack. It is not full of absence: it is quite simply absence itself. It was absolute, blind, unaware it was blind, aware only of itself as itself.

Odysseus calls himself "No One" in reply to the Cyclops asking for his name. I would have replied, "Nothing."

One morning after that week passed I woke up *here, in Boston* as certainly as before I had been nowhere. It was as though I had left my shadow in Weston and it had finally caught up and reattached itself to me. Just like that everything was fresh. I registered for English Composition at Boston University at night. I walked the short block to Newberry Street, then full of practical businesses as well as boutiques and restaurants, found an employment agency, and was sent to interview for a clerical spot at Keystone Mutual Funds across the city in the financial district.

To reach Keystone I walked down Commonwealth Avenue as though for the first time, that broad avenue in Back Bay with a wide parklike strip down its middle for the five or six blocks before Boston Public Gardens, with a center pedestrian walk lined with statues of the Boston famous. It was beautiful and stirring in the summer air. Then I crossed the Public Gardens with its absurd Swan boats, next Boston Commons, impressed by all of this in the middle of this small city, and last made my way down the narrow streets first laid in Boston's antiquity past famous stores like Filenes with its even more famous basement, to Keystone's building in the financial district. There I met Rose, who thought I'd do just fine, and found myself an employee starting the next day.

Rose's office included two girls from Boston College with whom I was soon in a friendly BU vs. BC rivalry. It helped that the previous year unheralded Boston University, which still fielded a football team, had crushed BC. An elderly lady worked there too who occasionally horrified the girls by forgetting her false teeth in the Lady's Room. The work was simply sorting financial reports into their respective piles, and delivering them to the mailroom next door. That room was filled by an impressive machine that folded the reports so their addresses showed through the envelopes clear windows into which it inserted them, then stacked them in trays ready to be sealed and taken to the Post Office.

Every morning I rose early, made myself presentable as a young man drilled in the affluent middle class knew how to, and repeated my walk across Boston to work. After work Jeanne sometimes picked me up, hazarding Boston's mad drivers, if her schedule permitted or the weather was bad. We'd drive back, have a dinner she'd sneak from the dorm cafeteria or concoct on my hot plate in my room to the dismay of the other men, young and older, on the fourth floor. Girls were not supposed to come there. We ignored them.

Boston in 1960 was the 19th Century Boston, a city of four and five story brownstones. There was no Government Center, no Prudential or Hancock Buildings: there were no Thruways to divide the city from its waterfront, no subsequent Big Dig to undo that damage. If one morning I had found the streets filled with horse drawn carts and carriages I would not have been surprised. They would have fit as well in 1960 as in 1860. A few blocks from my room was Richardson's famous Trinity Church outside which William James stood one day, unable to understand what transpired within. Facing it was the equally famous Boston Public Library, both 19th Century masterpieces.

A walk to a cinema we liked took us past the graveyard where Paul Revere sleeps. Another walk went by Faneuil Hall, where the Revolution was incubated; another went by the great relief of the doomed Colonel Shaw and the black Massachusetts 54th. A short drive to the country took us to Walden Pond for a swim, crowded unlike its splendid isolation in Thoreau's day. We canoed on the Concord River not far from where Thoreau and Emerson once lived. I was immersed at once in immediate practicality and in history, and remembered my confirmation debates with John Thomas when I explained how historical figures were my neighbors who lived on different floors in the same building as myself. In Boston this mixture of past and present is vividly apparent.

Even better the oldest, central part of Boston can be walked in less than an hour. The city sleepwalks through the often unbearable summer when one day a temperature and humidity of 99 nauseates, the next invigorates with a crisp breeze off the ocean that drops both to 71. We discovered how Boston transformed into a college city filled with youthful energy as its myriad colleges and universities came back into session. By winter if that wind off the ocean found you in the open its bitter, knife-edged coldness drove even the hardiest to seek shelter swiftly. Once, after a blizzard closed Keystone for a day, the city was an utterly unexpected still, brilliant 4 degrees that was exhilarating to walk through.

If this reads like a love letter to Boston, that's how it struck me.

My work at Keystone Mutual Funds was as close to holding a 9-5 job I ever came. I excelled. Once my paychecks arrived I rented a second floor room in my brownstone at an 'expensive' $12.50 a week that directly overlooked Commonwealth Avenue. There Jeanne came up the back stairs and down the hall to me unnoticed. Soon her visits included occasional overnights as friends covered for her at her dormitory. We were young, in love, happy as the fall leaves turned outside the window and we woke together in our narrow bed. We didn't need more, and passion, so long stolen or thwarted, flowered unhindered.

I liked Keystone and the people. I was intrigued by the business, of which I caught only a glimpse from where I was. Maybe some part of the family mythology floated in the background, of how Daddy Wilds had been a great success as a stockbroker. The monstrous machine next door intrigued me, too. I soon looked for greater challenges, and one day after work went into its room when no one was around, certain I could manage this machine too, having watched the others set it up and let it run. I ran off a large number of reports and went home thinking how pleased all would be the next morning with a leg up on the day's work.

But the next morning I heard ominous voices raised next door. The young man responsible for running that machine was receiving a severe rebuke for doing it when he shouldn't, and doing it wrong. I excused myself from Rose's room, and walked next door. They weren't happy at the interruption. But I told them I thought I was doing something useful after work and was responsible for the error, and that I would stay on my time and fix the envelopes one by one manually until all were sorted properly. There was silence. My offer was accepted. I came very late to Jeanne's dormitory that night to explain what had happened.

If Keystone was a success, so was night school. Professor Donald Born, near retirement, presided over my course because he liked the evening mix of people who were far more diverse in age and interest than those in the regular student body, even in a beginning, required course like English Composition. I didn't expect that to be of much interest, but Professor Born intrigued me, and my essays aroused his interest. As we talked over the course of the autumn he grew friendly, learned of my situation, and explored some of the options open to me at Boston University. He was part of an innovative program set up originally for veterans at the end of WWII that offered an integrated two year program that stretched from Western antiquity to the present in literature, history, philosophy, the arts including music, and science. He became my mentor. As the fall wore on he knew I would be going home for Christmas and adopted a wait and see attitude for the results of that family reunion.

The same happened at Keystone. Inevitably my situation came up in friendly talks with Rose, who soon understood my break with my family and intention to work my way through college in Boston. She and her companion next door in charge of that fateful machine talked to their superiors about me as a person of promise. They too bided their time to see the results of that upcoming Christmas visit.

Jeanne and I stayed in touch with our families over the course of the autumn, she writing normal updates, I exchanging angry letters with my father and friendlier with my mother, who as the holidays approached grew eager for me to come home for a few days, assuring me it would be pleasant. She told me my father weighed my letters in his hand to try and gauge how long a series of reproaches I had written before opening one. In each I mimicked his style and superior tone, numbering each point as he did. He must have found these infuriating.

Communication then transpired in the Dark Ages before smart phones, computers, Skype and Facetime, or free national calling plans offered as part of an internet package. There was no internet. We have lived through a sea change. Letters—snail mail—were the standard for communication, and Ma Bell, not yet broken up, was useful locally but too expensive for long distance for Jeanne and my budgets.

In our exchanges as time passed it became clear by Christmas that my choice to go to Boston, find a job, and work my way through college was validated by success, and Jeanne and I drove home together to see our families for the few days her program and Keystone permitted.

Warmth was the rule in Weston and Stamford with Mothie and Mom, Bud and Jill. There was an intimated respect from Gar. Roy was pleased I had succeeded, Bud proud. But I was disconcerted too as I realized Weston was now somewhere to visit, and parents figures to reflect on, visit, and leave behind. Home had changed into: childhood home.

Resuming the old patterns of relationship for a few days was now an all too obvious illusion. That was also only bearable for a short time. I had changed. They were the same.

Mom and Gar had come to terms with my ability to make my own way. They raised no objection to my continuing in Boston, or to Jeanne. I gave them a pair of striking copper candelabra I found in an antique store to stand on either side of the great fireplace in the Weston living room. They liked them, startled I showed a mature taste. They offered to pay for Boston University so I could attend full time. I accepted gratefully. There was no traumatic leave-taking when it was time to go. Our time together was so ordinary it was not just unprecedented, but eerie.

I let Donald Born know when we returned to Boston, and Rose and the others at Keystone. All took it in good stead, but Rose said enough I understood if things had gone differently Keystone had been prepared to promote me and work out an arrangement involving Boston University given a reciprocating commitment to Keystone from myself. I wonder at times what my life would have been like if I gone down that path instead.

I stayed at Keystone through January. Donald Born made an impassioned plea to the faculty of Boston University's Division of General Education and persuaded them to accept me full time for the spring semester.

I had walked out on a world steeped in unreality and fantasy into a new life my family expected to fail, walked away from of the conjoined Levy and Wilds dream machines shaping successive generations—and succeeded. Those myths and entanglements stretching over generations nonetheless remained part of my warp and woof that took decades to grasp and overcome. More passed before I could write about my experience with any balance, coherence, or humor. If I had followed their choices instead that autumn, no doubt in time I would have become more of my own man, but bound to our inherited unreality more deeply, blindly passing that on to my descendants. My father and mother never escaped theirs.

In another family, in different economic circumstances, my decision to work my way through a school of my choice as Jeanne was doing would have been accepted with pride and a sense of 'but, of course' with their tacit support. Yet among ourselves, with our means, locked in our myths, in our part of society, to open a door to normalcy required a traumatic break.

There was an aftermath also to my initial alternation of feeling nothing then feeling abruptly 'there' on my first arrival in Boston. For years a dream intermittently tormented me. I would become aware of an impenetrable, black presence in my room, and 'wake up.' It would still move towards me until I panted in fear—and then did wake up, unable to sleep again for hours. In time that dream had only to start and I snapped fully awake. It was many years before it faded and therapy released my repressions.

Boston was the necessary first step to learn to master rather than be mastered by the manipulations and beliefs of others, even those long past, and to come to terms with myself. Even that first sip of freedom was exhilarating.

QUANTUM DREAMS AND THE PHYSICS OF LOVE

We know so little of our minds' physics,
not even if our linear, daylit logic
is more or less true than our dreamsleep's
where near and far then and now
lie together entwined as lovers, two
bodies, one, two minds in ecstasy, none.
We say Newtonian cause and effect
is truer than quantum mysteries
where realities divide from each other
yet share at once each other's fate,
the improbability we scout in our dreams.
We wake for one, sleep for the other,
to be more than incomplete. Tell me
the heart is muscles and chambers
and bloodflow: not love's metaphor
but tissue and pulse,
that metaphor is poetry, and poetry
is not real; tell me all
that makes life desirable roots
in a forward driving time although
our minds are no steadier than scraps
of paper blown down city streets.
But then why, eyes open, do I see
my woman's lines relax as she sleeps
beside me now even as she now creeps
upstairs to my room overlooking
Commonwealth Avenue so long ago,
where soon we cannot tell ourselves apart?
Yes, I know. Who lives in such simultaneities

and stays sane? erases the straight line
between then, there; here—now;
young, then; now—old?
and does not go mad?
And yet tell me this old woman fails
to hold me then, that young woman
with all her forgone passion
fails to wrap me in her arms now!
For love's reality is stranger even than
those quanta bound together however
the void between them grows—
I know you cannot lie here now, relaxed
unless you lie there then in passion
all ages embraced at once in one's embrace.[25]

PART FOUR:
FAILURE AND METAMORPHOSES

> We seem but to linger in manhood to tell the dreams of our childhood, and they vanish out of memory ere we learn the language.
>
> Thoreau, *Journals*, 2/19/1841

> Metamorphosis:
>
> …to become transformed….
> A striking alteration in appearance, character, or circumstance.
>
> *Merriam-Webster's*, 2020

Debacle at NBC

My father knew before he arrived at NBC that he would face conflict with Robert Kintner. He knew Kintner's choice to catch up to CBS in ratings was to inject sex and violence into NBC's shows, as he had earlier at ABC. There Kintner approved Clint Walker being shown in the buff from the waist up in *Cheyenne*, then considered daring. Kintner liked *77 Sunset Strip* and *The Untouchables*, not *I Love Lucy* or *Father Knows Best*.... Contrariwise my father always fought for family values in his projects like *Dr. Kildare* and *Bonanza* at NBC, and later in its bizarre way in *The Addams Family*.

Gar narrated an early Program Board meeting at the start of his tenure at NBC in an article he wrote for *The Washington Post* in 1993.

> I came to NBC as officer in charge of network programming, and shortly after I arrived...I got specific instructions from Kintner to inject sex and violence into NBC's programs. There was nothing casual or accidental about the policy: at that meeting, the secretary of the board, Mal Breville, was ordered not to include the directive in board minutes. "We don't want that kind of stuff in our records," Kintner said.
>
> The morning that I got these instructions, I summoned to my office two former colleagues: Preston Wood and Frank Telford, with whom I'd worked at Young & Rubicam. They found Kintner's order appalling since the three of us had been conditioned by the far loftier program ideals of that advertising agency. I told them that we would find ways to ignore Kintner's directive.[26]

This adds another layer to the controversy that gathered around Gar at NBC as he challenged Kintner with such major departures like *Saturday Night at the Movies*. Perhaps that anticipated conflict lay too behind his hardball contract demands that Kintner accepted.

There may have been violence, for example, in *Bonanza*—it was a Western—but it was primarily a *'Father Knows Best in the West'* show with a heavy emphasis on family communication and values. *Dr. Kildare* centered on an idealistic young doctor, Richard Chamberlain's breakout role. In contrast Kintner put *Whispering Smith* on the air, soon a target for its sex and violence.

Rivalry for position is rife in the networks, and Kintner mistook David Levy for just another pushy executive to control or fire if things got too out of hand. He didn't know how Gar struggled for his professional existence during Nat Wolff's tenure at Y&R, of how he learned to keep a record of everything and to write minutely detailed reports of his activities. He logged every phone call at NBC, noted each call's content, sent summaries of their meetings to participants he copied to himself, and copied too every memo and letter. No one was better documented.

Senator Thomas Dodd precipitated events as he became Chairman of the Senate Subcommittee on Juvenile Delinquency in 1961. The Subcommittee was first created in 1954 to review the possible negative impact of TV on America's youth. Nothing resulted from its 1954 hearings beyond a decision to do more research after the TV executives pointed to radio which similarly had been attacked in its youthful days without there ever being proof it adversely affected society. Estes Kefauver took a turn as Chairman in 1955 with renewed testimony from social scientists, but after much smoke took no action either.

Dodd, determined to get results, held new hearings on sex and violence from June, 1961 until May, 1962. Gar relates his experience of testifying in that same article for *The Washington Post*:

> Before we appeared, I asked NBC lawyers what response we should give if asked how the decision was made to schedule *Whispering Smith*. The answer was simple: call it a group decision. Even then the net that was to protect Kintner's edict was taking form. Dodd came away from the hearings both puzzled and

frustrated. Neither he nor his key aides were able to penetrate the labyrinth of the decision-making process at NBC.[27]

Gar was congratulated on his performance at NBC, but he knew the hearings weren't over. Kintner now saw both how to escape blame for sex and violence on NBC and to deal with my father. He blamed his Head of Programming, David Levy, for the sex and violence in NBC's programming—and exiled him.

> On June 30, three weeks after I'd testified, Kintner suddenly decided that I should be reassigned to the news division and sent to India to research a project that would keep me out of the country for several months. I protested the change.... In the end, I resigned.[28]

My father had forced Kintner's hand by going over his head too often challenging his control of NBC, as well as resisting Kintner's sex and violence formula. In response to Kintner's action Gar sent detailed memos based on his painstaking documentation to Robert and General Sarnoff detailing his innocence and Kintner's guilt of fomenting sex and violence. No doubt that assured Kintner he had acted in a timely manner! Kintner was the Sarnoffs' responsibility and they supported him to contain the damage. Robert returned Gar's memo because he didn't want it in NBC's files. General Sarnoff must have disposed of his.

Someone had to take a fall.

Gar fought back in an executive session of the Senate hearings in September, 1961 with his well-documented proof it was Kintner (and by extension Robert Sarnoff who had allowed Kintner to operate) who was responsible for the network's sex and violence. Dodd now knew Kintner was to blame, but never allowed that testimony to be made public until Jack Anderson exposed him in a column many years later. Dodd did not question Kintner in 1962 in a public session about Gar's testimony.

Gar had fatally overreached. Kintner was friends with, among others, then Vice President Lyndon Baines Johnson. They had a relationship going back to earlier Texas days, and Gar later suspected that Johnson leaned on Dodd. Kintner later worked for President Johnson until Jack Anderson in a

Washington *Merry-Go-Round* column May 22, 1967 exposed Kintner's real role at NBC as the advocate of sex and violence. Three weeks later Kintner left his post in the Johnson administration. Dodd himself was eventually censured by the Senate for matters unrelated to these proceedings.

It's interesting to look at what was suppressed by Dodd. Dodd's staff concluded, according to Anderson, that:

> We think the record will show that Robert E. Kintner, the president of NBC, must bear the primary responsibility for the trend of increased sex and violence in NBC's programming.

Anderson goes on after detailing the specifics against Kintner, including Walker's buff scene in *Cheyenne* years earlier at ABC.

> The most damning witness against Kintner was David Levy who had been dismissed as NBC's program director but had been given a $50,000 annual salary subject to cancellation if he made any degrading remarks about NBC. Despite this attempt to muzzle him, Levy testified freely and frankly behind closed doors.

However,

> ...Dodd never released the transcript, thus succeeding in muzzling Levy where NBC had failed.[29]

Mom bore the brunt of Gar's obsessive drive to oust Kintner and then, that failing, to defend himself. The accumulation of materials in his self-obsessive defense was endless, as was consulting lawyers. Boxes on boxes of materiel rose in the Weston attic. When the hearings were over he was neither vindicated nor, at 49, employed.

There were no shows to rush home to review, followed by calls to the individuals in charge with a critique.

There was no one to call.

No one called him.

There was no train to ride to and from New York, where he gave up his apartment; there was no limo; there was no commute.

He was in the silence of the country, left to twiddle his thumbs, which he was incapable of doing.

No one called supportively except, to his surprise, Harry Salter, the producer of the successful, long-running *Name That Tune*. But Gar saw no future with Harry.

He had never been this isolated and inactive. It was a tremendous blow he spent the rest of his life trying to undo.

He also believed he was blackballed by Kintner. But being blackballed wasn't necessary to explain his becoming unemployable. He was now a figure of controversy on a hot button subject whom no advertising agency or network wanted to touch. He realized belatedly that if he had supinely taken Kintner's offer to be out of the country in India that he would have had renewed executive possibilities on his return, if hardly of the same scope as before.

He never held a network or advertising agency job again.

Now his nightly ritual of inspecting his bankbooks makes a better impression. They represented a wall against such traumas as, serendipitously, did his contract that extended his $50,000/year salary at NBC another five years in which to find an alternative.

The Chameleons

Chameleon:

1. ...one who changes...according to the mood...or surrounding conditions.
2. A person who is fickle or inconstant.

Webster's, 1956

First Gar fictionalized his experience at NBC in *The Chameleons* published by Dodd Mead in 1964. That book removes the need to flip through his diaries to watch again how he records as fact the way he wishes things had been. In *The Chameleons* his alter ego, Stephen Lane, is brought on board FBC (a fictional Federal Broadcasting Company, a fourth to ABC, NBC, and CBS) to head up programming by Joseph Gratton, the fictional avatar for Kintner.

Gratton measures success in TV programming by ratings and thinks the surest road to high ratings is by appealing to the lowest common denominator: sex and violence. Lane is a man of unbending honor and commitment to high program values who believes TV can be a force for good in society by exalting values like family, morality, genuine heroism, and truthfulness. They clash immediately.

There is no sense that Lane is hell-bent to replace a firstborn twin as No. 1. Instead Lane's honorability and intelligence are contrasted with Gratton's Machiavellian enjoyment of power, success, drink, and women more or less in that order. It isn't that Lane is wholly whitewashed: he is carrying on a serious affair with a young actress. Linda is tangentially present: happily, I am missing. It would have been hard to explain how so ideal a figure as Lane could have a rebellious son.

The action follows closely the pattern of the actual Senate hearings chaired by Dodd, now Senator Hillman. Although an amoral and headline hunting politician, Hillman is not about to embarrass FBC or its head, Admiral Otis instead of General Sarnoff. There are two crucial and revealing encounters in the novel.

First, Lane is friendly with the elderly Max Geller, the FBC counsel, whose health has started to fail. Max is sympathetic to Lane and aware of Lane's refusal to be tarred as the proponent of sex and violence by Gratton, who wants to use the Senate hearings to get rid of him, echoing Kintner's behavior with Dodd concerning my father. Max is also aware how well documented Lane is. He encourages Lane to send a damning memo to Otis (as my father did to the Sarnoffs) and lets Lane believe that when he testifies before Hillman's Subcommittee that he will corroborate Lane. In the event, Geller doesn't, and Lane accuses him of a stab in the back.

> "Max, you gave me your word that you would tell the truth, the truth, Max."
> "And I did! My way!"
> "There's only one way to tell the truth, Max. You chose to ignore it with your sudden silence, your sudden loss of memory, your inability to recall our conversation."

He challenges Max who has, in his eyes, no

> "sense of decency, no morality, no sense of honor, no sense of truth"[30]

The old man is crushed. Gar has invented a forum for perfectly justified moral indignation of a black and white nature. Guilt eats at Max, who is in and out of the hospital, and then asks to see Lane again. There to Lane's surprise he lets him know he, Geller, has sent a copy of all his personal notes regarding Lane to Otis. These support Lane's version of events. Geller has an inoperable condition and wants to go out on the 'right side of history.'

Lane, Geller, and Admiral Otis meet. We are ever further from my father's actual experience of being fired by Kintner, appealing futilely to the Sarnoffs, and testifying with equal futility to Dodd's Subcommittee. Instead, in the novel Otis now sees everything Lane said was right. Moreover, Lane lets him know he is returning Geller's notes to him unread in an act of moral altruism. Geller bursts out,

> "Admiral, this is your decision to make—and now, it's solely on its merits. Steve stands for something! For more than a dozen Joe Grattons! He cares about television. You mustn't let him go!"[31]

Otis is impressed with Lane, his fearlessness and honorability—and decides to let Lane know he is leaving the FBC Board and intends to make Lane its Chairman! In the future, Gratton will work for him. Lane will run the network, according to his high standards. Otis does wonder if Gratton will have an issue with this and make difficulties for Lane. No, Lane assures him, Gratton is a chameleon and will change his color to fit the circumstances.

Fantasy this may be, but in its reversal of reality it is typical of my father, and immediately prepares the ground for *The Addams Family*.

The second key encounter is an equally revealing confrontation with Lane's wife, Mary, the stand-in for my mother in *The Chameleons*. She is annoyed one evening when Lane sends Geller flowers and a get well message while he is in the hospital (just as Gar always wished his acquaintances well, even after having argued violently with them). As far as Mary is concerned, Geller let him down. She would only have thought well of Geller had he instead told the truth about Gratton to the Senate. So since Mary admires the truth so much Lane out of the blue admits he is having an affair. Why? He wants her love, not just her interest when he's down. He wants to come first. He wants to feel his needs are understood and met. What's a man to do, he implies, when they're not?

Mary doesn't buy the connection between her preference for Max Geller to have told the truth and Lane's sudden coming clean about infidelity and, I suspect, neither would most readers. She's upset enough to leave for a hotel that night. Lane goes off to see Sandra, with whom he's having the affair. She is warm and loving, unlike Mary. Lane tells her altruistically that she is just too young and he is doing her a favor by breaking off their relationship so she can find the right man. Gar in 1962 is 49, which seems to be Lane's age too: I imagine eyebrows lifting at this scruple about a younger woman among my father's contemporaries in the film and TV industries who read this book.

Climactically, as Lane and Otis seal their understanding in Max's office, Mary shows up having thought things through with tickets for a two week Caribbean cruise for herself and Lane. Otis gives them his blessing—they need a break!—and off they go.

The air of unreality that hangs over the climactic outcome as Lane becomes No. 1 pales before this handling of his relationship with Mary. But it is revealing. Gar's practice in his disputes with my mother during her flights in 1943 and 1947-48 was to turn the tables and in the first instance, make his weight an issue, and in the second, blame her for the ongoing coolness of their relationship. Here Lane has an affair because his wife doesn't meet his needs, and literally won't make him 'number one.' There is no hint in Lane of what in his behavior brought their relationship to this unhappy state: Lane is guiltless. Mary is lacking.

That some of this no doubt reveals his feelings about my mother at the time of his firing is apparent. She again contemplated divorce in 1961 but didn't carry through because, as she told me years later, "I couldn't do that to him then. It would have been like kicking someone when they were down." Mary in *The Chameleons* isn't wholly fictional.

Yes, *The Chameleons* is a work of fiction, and we skate on thin ice trying to make equivalences between fiction and reality, though the transformation my father works on his/Lane's confrontation with NBC/FBS is transparent. But the ins and outs of any intimate relationship will always be largely hidden to outsiders peering in, even as I was startled as a child to find my mother weeping on Gar's lap in Manhattan soon after we moved there in 1949.

The myths they lived by, the Golden Age Gar constantly rewrote his experience into, the perfect family into which Mom rewrote hers, are able to withstand mountains of evidence to the contrary. These validating stories of ours fill a deeper need than any momentary damage done by reality: the veil ripped open is self-healing.

By the time *The Chameleons* appeared in 1964 Mom and Gar lived in Beverly Hills where he moved in 1963 because he sensed creative development for TV was shifting to the Hollywood studios and he knew the network and advertising executive offices were closed to him now in New York. My mother lingered in Weston in 1963 to manage on her own the sale of their home and the sorting, packing, and moving of its contents to California to join him. During the course of the move she 'lost' a good many boxes of Senate testimony and related NBC papers. Gar was upset: she had had enough.

Mountainous piles of rejected items accumulated in the driveway as she cleared house. Each time she went in after depositing more items on the pile Mothie dashed down from her home, rifled through what had been thrown out, and hastily retreated with her 'finds' before my mother reappeared. When Mothie sold her home in 1967 to join Mom and Gar in Los Angeles, Jeanne and I helped her pack and clear out unwanted items. One day she followed Jeanne and I upstairs from her basement with a large artificial flower with a long green stem.

"Wouldn't you like this," she asked, as we looked at her bemused; "you can have it for 25¢!"

So ended our Weston years.

The Addams Family: An American Family

Genesis

One day in 1962 Gar walked down Fifth Avenue in New York with Donald Saltzman, a protégé of his when at NBC. Don had braved NBC security men to enter Gar's sealed office and rescue his private creative files from under the guards' noses shortly after he was fired in 1961. Something caught my father's eye as they passed a bookstore window. *Homebodies* was featured in a display of Charles Addams' works, with a group portrait of Addams' characters on its cover.

"It's a hit series!" he exclaimed.[32]

Don was puzzled, but Gar was right, and the moment stands as the genesis of *The Addams Family* series broadcast on ABC 1964-66 whose 64 episodes to this day remain the definitive 'Addams Family' show despite the large number of later attempts to revive that initial series' success. To date there have been at least 31 subsequent tries encompassing animated features, movies, a musical, a new TV series, *The Addams Family Halloween*, and video games, but it is my father's original creation filmed in black and white that still dominates cable and syndication reruns. It is the family he created from approximately 150 original Charles Addams cartoons and his own freewheeling imagination that is repeated in the subsequent imitations and variations. A complete DVD set of this original *The Addams Family* was released in 2010 by MGM. In the nearly sixty years that have passed *The Addams Family* has become an enduring part of our popular culture.

There was no family or even named characters in Charles Addams' work. He began publishing Addams family cartoons in the *New Yorker* in 1938 that were funny, mordant, subversive, and emblematic of nonconformity, their images alone carrying the implication of their confrontation with conventional society. Gar understood this, and took it further.

> Addams never conceived of them as a family. He never called them that. They were just foils for his humor…his outrageous comment on society. I knew in a situation comedy they would become America's most beloved family.…

he said to Dick Siegel who published a piece on the show in *The 13th Floor*. The piece goes on:

> Not only were they macabre figures but Levy's concept was to show them "tender and loving with a husband and wife who really have a romantic liaison and children who love them."[33]

This was written retroactively in 2016, but accurately captures Gar's creative insight into those figures he did indeed shape into the successful TV family.

Some believe Charles Addams modeled the slinky woman in them who would later be named Morticia on his first wife. That marriage ended in 1950, followed by a second from 1954-1956 to Barbara Barb, with whom both Charles Addams and my father would have a difficult time. She was "reputedly even more of a Morticia clone" as well as a practicing lawyer who "famously swindled her husband out of the TV and movie rights to his characters."[34]

Gar swiftly convinced Don Saltzman and his twin Charles to put up $1750 each to help in development costs in return for a percentage of his future royalties, one of the many elements of the dealmaking he indulged in then that would later come back to haunt him when the show became a success. He didn't need that help, but a blend of his grandiosity from NBC ('what a favor I'm doing you two') and his continuing sense of poverty from his background motivated him.

He turned to Charles Addams for permission to develop the project, and met a positive response. Addams under Gar's prodding and collaboration came up with most of the characters' names. One character and name would be wholly Gar's own, diminutive Cousin Itt with his hair to the floor, a bowler hat, and sunglasses. My father and Addams corresponded regularly and met to go over names, but then Barbara Addams interjected herself. Additional meetings ensued and with additional money her permission too was received.

The networks were not initially interested in such an offbeat comedy. The family story relates how Gar pitched the show six times to the major networks, twice to each, and was turned down each time until on the last occasion ABC responded positively. He believed this was because Kintner had put the word out against doing business with him, something he indicated in his treatment of Gratton-Kintner in *The Chameleons* whom Lane hears at one point has passed the word around not to hire him. But the record only speaks of a turndown by CBS, the development of a fifteen minute promo, and then, when news got out CBS planned to put on *The Munsters*, an enthusiastic response by ABC. Ironically, *The Munsters* typically had better ratings while *The Addams Family* received greater credit for creativity and wit.

This timeline undercuts the idea he was blackballed and inactive after 1961. He was out of NBC in 1961, done with the Congressional hearings in May, 1962, developed *The Addams Family* in 1962-63, at the same time wrote and in 1964 published *The Chameleons*, the same year he sold *The Addams Family* to ABC. Its first episode aired September 18, 1964. His phone may have stopped ringing for a time in 1961 after his immediate break with NBC, but he was soon as busy a man as ever.

Great changes were underway in his and my mother's life as this unfolded. We saw he had followed the movement of creative development to the West Coast, first living in Beverly Hills. When Mom joined him after the sale of their Weston home they bought a house on Robin Drive high in the hills next to Beverly Hills that overlooked Los Angeles. One of their new neighbors was Ricardo Montalban who enjoyed the same sweeping views. Jeanne and I visited there briefly in 1965, and there Mothie joined her in 1967. Mom and Mothie's church became All Saints Episcopal Church in Beverly Hills.

My mother left behind a lifetime of associations and friends, and far more importantly, her brother and his family. His branch of the family stayed in or near Connecticut, but hers as Linda, and I through a series of chances, settled in California. My children would hardly know Bud and Jill's, and the routine contact between Bud and 'Sis' was broken. It was a lot to ask by a man who was no longer "down," but she came. Linda and I, puzzled, watched their persistence despite their clashes.

Triumph

With ABC's purchase, development of the series' episodes moved into high gear. Filmways, an independent production company run by Al Simon, produced *The Addams Family*, and assigned Nat Perrin to oversee it. Gar became the executive producer and maintained a hands-on control over writers and plots, frequently rewriting segments to his own satisfaction, while Perrin brought an insistence on continuity, and his own background of having written for, among others, the Marx brothers. Gar knew this was a new version of *Father Knows Best* for the 1960s with a family living in a uniquely zany way. Perrin brought a sensibility of broad, farcical humor, and Charles Addams inspired the core subversive vibe, "a celebration of all things kooky, spooky, and off-the-wall, an endorsement of nonconformity."[35]

Famously, Carolyn Jones became Morticia, the subject of passionate kisses and hot, longing looks by Gomez, played by John Astin, a considerable departure from Addams' Peter Lorre lookalike for Gomez in his cartoons. TV now had its first parental couple who apparently had a sex life. Later Astin remarked:

> David told me, "This is *Father Knows Best*—with other people," Astin said. The sizzling marriage and all the other memorable aspects of the televisual family represented a considerable leap of the imagination from the source material.[36]

Ted Cassidy became the butler, Lurch, whose primary means of communication were deep, pained moans after he was summoned by a hangman's noose. Jackie Coogan took on bald Uncle Fester in his floor length black robes; Blossom Rock became Grandmama Addams, a witch; Lisa Loring and Ken Weatherwax became the children Wednesday and Pugsley.

The show made no apologies for its bizarre if loving family, making the family less ominously antisocial and more gleefully eccentric, as if unaware that their behavior is interpreted as strange to others, cheerfully inviting outsiders into their specialized world, if any of them dared to stick around long enough.[37]

They are puzzled by the horrified reactions to their own good-natured and normal behavior, since the family is under the impression that their tastes are shared by most of society. Accordingly they view "conventional" tastes with generally tolerant suspicion. Invariably, as a result of their visit to the Addamses, a visitor would be institutionalized, change professions, move out of the country, or suffer some other negative life-changing event.[38]

The first show, "The Addams Family Goes to School," gives a good introduction to *The Addams Family* world.

Sam Hilliard comes to the gothic, gloomy Addams family mansion on a mission to get their children to go to school. A disembodied hand, Thing, comes out of the mailbox to grab mail from the mailman, who wishes Hilliard good luck. The gate opens unbidden at his approach, and slams shut with a bar sliding into place behind him. He's met at the door by wan Wednesday, surprised he wants to come in. Startled, he sees Pugsley bring his pleased sister a headless doll. It's supposed to be Marie Antoinette, she explains. When Hilliard eyes a picture of a giraffe in a suit she explains he was once a friend of her father's.

Hilliard finds Morticia in the conservatory pleased at how well her poison ivy is doing, upset over her hemlock wilting, and caressed by a plant with tentacles. She doesn't deal with truancy: the law is Gomez' responsibility she tells Hilliard when he explains his presence, and rings an earsplitting gong akin to Big Ben which brings the cadaverous Lurch behind the rattled Hilliard to take him to Gomez.

That individual is in the dining room playing with a giant train set. Hilliard is alarmed as two trains speed towards each other, but Gomez assures him they won't collide and instead blows up a bridge as they enter either end, destroying the bridge and derailing the trains before they collide. Why else would an adult play with trains if not to blow them up, he explains to the puzzled Hilliard, who declines an offer to blow up another bridge.

Gomez wonders why anyone would want to have kids only to get rid of them all day when Hilliard explains his mission, and leads him to meet Grandmama, who actually deals with these issues. Grandmama and Uncle Fester are throwing knives at a life-size Lucifer image. Fester's knife whizzes past Hilliard's nose as Gomez and Hilliard open the door: Hilliard rushes off and in a brief scene with the school's Principal, Mrs. Comstock, advises her to leave the Addams kids alone.

Gomez joins Morticia in the conservatory, admires her rose bouquet as she clips off all the roses, arranging only the thorny stems, and starts kissing her arm passionately. They are both excited remembering their first night together on their honeymoon in Death Valley, spent in a bat-filled cave.

As they all settle in the living room a few days later Thing hands a letter to Wednesday who gives it to Morticia. This informs them they must enroll their children in school. They debate the worth of an education. Fester, uneducated, shows he can light bulbs in his mouth, and when Morticia intimates there are cultural reasons, he whips out his violin and plays passionately. But when challenged to do a very obscure mathematical problem he gets one digit wrong, and so going to school is justified. Morticia concludes they must have made a very favorable impression on Hilliard

They meet Mrs. Comstock in her office, who is pleased the Addamses have come as her superior, the Superintendent, can be difficult. She's sure the children will be happy, although Morticia and Gomez reply that if they wanted their children's happiness they would keep them home. They indicate Hilliard seemed unsettled, and Comstock confidentially indicates she thinks he has a booze problem. Gomez is pleased to hear that; his estimation of Hilliard goes up.

In discussing the Superintendent they soon jokingly come up with 'solutions' for his being difficult. Gomez will contact his friend DuBois in Haiti who will straighten him out with pins in a stick figure. Hilliard briefly overhears this and thinks they are talking about him. Comstock is amused, and suggests horsewhipping instead, and Gomez moves on to dipping him in boiling oil. Comstock is joking: Gomez and Morticia are not. Gomez decides he likes Mrs. Comstock.

The next afternoon as Gomez anxiously waits for the children to return from their first day at school Wednesday runs in distraught and dashes up to her room filled with vulture figures, tarantulas, and a case of headless dolls. She flings herself on her bed crying. Morticia and Gomez are shocked because Wednesday is in tears over a story in class where a dragon is killed. Who would want to kill a dragon, they wonder? They send Lurch to get Sam Hilliard.

Lurch soon returns with Hilliard in his arms, and deposits him on their best chair in the living room whose bottom falls out as Hilliard sits. A stuffed bear towers over him. Later the series uses a bear rug as a prop which growls when anyone steps on it. Hilliard is frightened as they announce they have a bone to pick with him, and further alarmed at being offered refreshments out Grandmama's steaming cauldron and a plateful of cookies shaped into lizards and frogs. Gomez invites him to eat a lizard—you can almost feel it wriggle down, he claims. Hilliard declines, and they wonder if he would like to be put to the rack because being stretched is so refreshing.

Then they launch into an attack on *Grimm's Fairy Tales* from which the dragon slaying story was taken. Hilliard is nonplussed over their description of Hansel and Gretel pushing a "lovely old woman" into the oven. Then he has an 'Aha!' moment. He thinks they are attacking violence per se instead of the violence directed against admirable figures like witches, warlocks, ogres, and dragons. He leaps from the violence in stories to how violence affects behavior like juvenile delinquency all the way to the violence of the—atomic bomb. He decides he has misunderstood the Addamses! He finds their point brilliant, and to their consternation he rushes off.

Again they gather in the living room. Heavy construction sounds are heard above: Pugsley is making Wednesday a doll house. Grandmama grows angry at Fester as they play cards because he isn't cheating. Morticia is knitting, as she had in an earlier scene when she displayed a three-armed turtleneck for a cousin. The problem with that sweater was Gomez' certainty that the cousin in question doesn't like turtlenecks. Now as she knits Morticia strokes a small dragon on the table next to her that releases smoky snorts of contentment. The phone rings, handed to them by Thing. Hilliard has talked to the Board of Education which has removed *Grimm's Fairy Tales* from the curriculum.

Gomez is pleased: they might just have saved the world he says, thinking how Hilliard linked violence to the atomic bomb.

That alarms Morticia however, who wonders if that's a good thing as the episode ends.

This initial episode shows them to be a loving couple and parents who act on their children's behalf when they have a bad experience at school. Morticia is a dedicated horticulturist; Gomez clearly not just adores but desires her. They are wholly unaware of their oddity, instead puzzled by the behavior of conventional characters, which they alter variously in positive ways. Their house is filled with oddities, but includes items like 'best chairs' for guests, and so on. They are an extended family where all get along. Even the children help one another whether with dolls or doll houses and, like any other children, have an array of pets allowed by their indulgent parents. Never mind Pugsley's is an octopus called Aristotle, or Wednesday's the tarantulas we saw in her room. The Addamses are ideal.

Audiences were and are entranced by the original *The Addams Family* whose ability to overshadow its later imitators is based on their lack of my father's unique insight into this family and the fertility of imagination it sparked.

The Real Addams Family

Everything written or quoted so far is true, and yet does not explain the inspiration for *The Addams Family*.

Gar was not a fan of the unconventional. We've seen his mind run towards *Father Knows Best* or *Dr. Kildare* or *Bonanza*. His alter ego Stephen Lane in *The Chameleons* pursues an ideal of TV close to pure public service and is as straight as they come, even altruistically ending an affair. Gar had no sympathy for the 1960s, whether the Beatniks, Beatles, student radicals, Kennedys, Martin Luther King, or Lyndon Johnson. He was a Nixon-Goldwater-Nixon man: the student riots in front of the 1968 Democratic Convention repulsed him. He did not vote Democratic after 1936. He was equally conservative in dress, unable to appear in anything but jacket and tie, and courteous in an increasingly old-fashioned way. Long hair, Afros, bra or draft-card burning, Black Power salutes, the freelove Woodstock ethic and attacks on traditional, Western oriented education equally displeased him. He was no rebel against the established order. Yet there is no doubt *The Addams Family* saw him function at a peak of creativity he did not equal again in a celebration of the abnormal and subversive that found a ready audience at the time and a permanent one thereafter.

Comedy is one of the great dramatic arts, paired with tragedy. Aristotle wrote a lost treatise on Comedy on a par with his *Poetics*. Umberto Eco places the rediscovery of that lost opus at the heart of *The Name of the Rose* where it resurfaces in a medieval monastery in which murders are being committed to keep it from seeing the light. Why? Because comedy at heart is subversive of our normal view of reality, something exemplified by *The Addams Family*.

Comedy breaks into two main streams. In the first, its storyline flirts with the tragic, whether lightly or with alarming seriousness, as on view in Branagh's film adaptation of *Much Ado About Nothing*. There Don John makes it look like the heroine, Hero, is unfaithful to her fiancé, Claudio, who publicly humiliates Hero. Crushed, she rushes away: later Claudio hears she has committed suicide. We are far from the comic at this moment, saved only by a series of nearly accidental revelations overheard by the hapless Dogberry and his comrades that malice has been afoot thanks to Don John, who is a prototype for Iago. Hero was never unfaithful. Don John is banished, and Claudio agrees as a penance to marry another, sight unseen, on whom Hero's father insists. At the altar when he lifts her veil Hero is revealed to great joy. For a moment we looked at death and the disappointment of life's hopes. That tragedy is swept away as all dance out of the cathedral in a joyous outburst of song. This strand of comedy faces the tragic only to deny it.

The second stream of comedy pursues a farcical vein whether in classic Comedia del'Arte or films like *Analyze This* where the mob boss, Paul, when advised to relieve emotional pressure by his therapist, shoots a pillow. Paul breaks down completely during a shoot-out with his enemies as he admits his childhood guilt over not doing anything to stop his father from being assassinated. He sobs away as his analyst advises him to shoot now and break down later. In frustration, the analyst picks up Paul's gun and fires in the direction of their attackers—into a refrigerator.

Characters in a farce take themselves with complete seriousness, as do Gomez and Morticia, yet everything they do is at odds with normal expectations and valuations. The denial involved here is even more sweeping than the denial of tragedy—here, tragedy is laughable, death a joke, ordinary behavior a hoot. No wonder the monks in *The Name of the Rose* find Aristotle's treatise on comedy so upsetting. From a comedic angle, they are a joke, and by implication, great as the loss is as the monastery burns down, there is a certain relief knowing that a work standing the world on its head won't be released.[39] I imagine there was a similar sense of relief in the audiences of Aristotle's time who after a day of tragic plays ended with a satyr play, at first a rollicking sexual farce.

What then do we have if we strip the comedy and farce—the denials—from *The Addams Family*?

At its center is a loving couple, but one whose tastes are plainly strange. One child is wan, another full of restless energy. The family's lives are intensely private: there are very few scenes outside the mansion in *The*

Addams Family. Its denizens are trapped within walls of their own making. They take themselves for granted—it is others who are subject to criticism and proposed extreme solutions. The parents are never wrong. Everything, ultimately, circles around a mother who has lethal tastes. Translated from poison ivy and hemlock that means: a taste for what is hurtful. The father has a jovial side, but is a man who has never fully grown up, and is under the mother's thumb.

The butler could fit into *The Walking Dead*. He is the one person in a household who sees all: and in *The Addams Family* he is half alive and anything coming out of his mouth is pained. He hasn't seen anything to be joyous about. The home's furnishings are peculiar: broken down furniture, or pieces out of proportion to the rest, as if imitating in a material way the better off, more conventional adults around them. Those who come to know these people are put off, and don't wish to share their intimacy.

We have met them before.

They have haunted these pages.

They are my father's parents, and his family life with them, transformed.

Have a look again at Disowned, earlier. There Poppy berates Charles over divorcing Erma to marry Judy: Charles is utterly wrong. He can claim nothing: he survived childhood illnesses and received his education "because your mother willed it…." He will never grow up. He hurts his mother. He allows another woman to creep into his bed dishonorably, and so on. Yet Nanny is also the woman who first tried to destroy Charles' marriage with Erma, then berated him for leaving her and, as Charles knew from his daily communions with my father, routinely denigrated my mother and Mothie. In their back and forth Charles finally accuses his father of abetting Nanny's intemperance, her morbidity, her mastery of "verbal assault and battery." There's been a hanging in the house he states, and not by him.

That grim avatar of misery, Lurch, is summoned by a hangman's noose.

Or look again at my father's letter to his mother on turning 50, this woman he could never please. "Say, this means you're fifty!" he writes. At that age she should think of all there is to enjoy—instead of, unspoken: to attack. If you stay mentally fit, he adds, a person "never cares a hoot about physical age." His peroration climaxes:

Yes on your 50th birthday you have the greatest gift of all—... and together there is a great deal of real joy and happiness to look ahead to.

The tone, as remarked, is one never elsewhere seen in my father—*except in Gomez with Morticia* in a world where all the happiness depends on the denial of a world where there was so little.

We can take this further.

Uncle Fester and Grandmama are paired in *The Addams Family* as we saw earlier. But "fester" has a somber meaning, that of grievances nursed in a continuing, aggravated fashion. Gar's grandfather Louis Levy rejected his identical twin, Abraham, for leaving his wife—and never forgave or saw him again. When you reflect on the usual closeness of identical twins, Louis' behavior is astonishing. When Poppy denounces Charles as a "cur" for remarrying, Charles and his future wife Judy were, as we saw, already divorced from their first companions—yet Poppy never spoke again to his firstborn son so favored by his mother before his death four years later.

Gar could neither give up his mother whose reproaches festered within and did much to poison his marriage, nor keep up his criticism of my mother in face of her repeated exasperated explosions, a woman, in fact, that he adored. Long after their final divorce it was her pictures he wanted on the walls of his room during his final years at the Beverly Hills Rehabilitation Center.

Not content to metamorphosize Nanny and Poppy into Morticia and Gomez, Gar repeated elements of them in Pugsley and Wednesday. On one level wan Wednesday stands in for the always dour David compared to hyperactive Pugsley/Charles. But Wednesday also delights in beheading her dolls like Morticia her roses. Pugsley aids and abets Wednesday in beheading her dolls, as Gar and Charles helped and competed with each other. But Pugsley has destructive tendencies (among other things, he invents a 'disintegrator' gun) like his father Gomez who delights in blowing up his trains. The ultimate working pair, as my cousin Bob remarked, was Nanny and Poppy: "One made the bullets, the other fired the gun."

Uncle Fester and Grandmama also repeat elements of Nanny and Poppy under their superficial differences. They are throwing knives at a figure of evil, personified as Lucifer, a good substitute for the wholly rejected Abraham by Louis Levy. The object of Nanny and Poppy's ire was always totally in the wrong. While Grandmama manages school activities in the first *The Addams Family* show we reviewed, so does Morticia activities in general with Gomez enthusiastically following along. It's well I saw Charles bring his Sunday Special to Nanny on the trip I recounted to Philadelphia after a 36 year absence, and the way she was prepared to exploit its defect (the lack of a pickle) to reject his effort—followed by Charles and my father's astonishing descent into childhood incredulity that she wouldn't even try that sandwich. How trivial, how revealing.

Uncle Fester and Grandmama are equally variants on Louis and Lena Levy. Grandmama has her cauldron, Lena her kitchen as Charles describes in his poem, "Snapshot: Louis and Lena."

> She,
> As tautly pulled together as her hair,
> Seated on the edge of the rocker.
> Squinting in the golden light,
> Tiny, stiff, alert,
> Buttoned—neck to shoe top,
> Hands on aproned knees,
> Tolerating truancy from her stove....

while Louis is idealized:

> Grandpa
> Sits at ease in the sun,
> Legs crossed,
> Benign, amused,
> His broad-brimmed straw
> Jauntily angled to shade his eyes,
> His meerschaum warm as noon,
> One hand casually clasping Grandma's shoulder....

The idealization deepens on Charles' part, as:

And in that moment's shared enchantment
I hear a far-off fiddle sing;
Happiness is an easy smile, a curling pipe,
The smell of bread and ripened pears,
A cluttered yard where chickens doze
And lilacs nod....

Grandma is taut, her hair tight, seated on the edge, squinting, alert, buttoned up, tolerating "truancy" from her stove: repressed, implicitly, and given Charles' choice of words: explosive. Grandpa, benign, amused, at ease—is hardly someone in fact festering with a lifelong rejection of an identical twin. It is all an "enchantment," which means spellbound and, more coldly, deluded. Indeed happiness is "an easy smile" for those lucky enough to have that truly characterize them, unlike Charles' permanently fixed jovial expression.

A "far-off fiddle" singing, indeed.

What's clear from even this simple example is how Charles as well as my father transmuted the lead of their experience to gold.

The Addams Family was the perfect vehicle by which my father could at last pour his long festering emotional reality into characters waiting for names and relationships to be created but metamorphosized by the magic wand of creativity into the "enchantment" of comedy frequently running to farce, with the denials of reality we saw that are essential elements of these genres. These figures are at once substitutes for those who so disappointed him, as well as embodiments of the kinds of damage he suffered at their hands. This includes dissociated elements such as the disembodied hand, Thing, or Cousin Itt, my father's unique contribution to Addams' bestiary, a figure all hair, a vacuum of personality behind sunglasses, a pure nihilism transformed into a joke.

What did Charles Addams think of all this? Linda Davis narrates a scene of a private showing for TV executives of the pilot for the series in 1964 which Addams showed up for with three lawyers—who laughed uproariously while Addams sat "stone-faced." One of his lawyers then commented: "Levy has made the Addams family more real than you have, Charlie." Addams reportedly smiled. The problem was for Addams that my father had translated his cartoons into "almost a typical suburban family. Not half as evil as my original characters...."[40]

He had placed his finger precisely on the transformation of 'evil' and family misery into comedy with all that implies, as we have seen. He could not have known my father's own history which turned Addams' cartoons into such a perfect vehicle for his transformation. Addams did ultimately come around.

> As the cartoons had done before it, the show spoke "to the monster in all children," in an age when non-conformity was beginning to be regarded as an asset, not a liability," noted a critic. "We almost had to do it," said Addams. Though "it was only a children's show," he also thought it was funny and fresh.[41]

He was wrong only in thinking the show merely one for children.

Years after *The Addams Family* on a walk in Beverly Hills Gar and I turned down a street where the city had just pruned the trees so savagely there were no leaves, just the main branches on top of the trunks, like spider legs turned to the sky. His face lit up.

"I could have used this in *The Addams Family*," he beamed. That metamorphosis of misery into comedy never lost its grip on his imagination. It is the final version of the mythic Golden Age in which he tried to live, the destructive figures of his family changed into both jokes and zany exemplars of marital and family perfection.

Of all these transformations he was unconscious, and would vociferously have denied my explanations had I understood and said any of this to him at the time. I remember in 1976 when a play of mine, *Time's Up*, was running in Los Angeles how uncertain I was about his reaction once he saw it. The play based some its action on a few of the more traumatic and flamboyant experiences we shared in Westhampton and Weston in a transparent manner. After he took in a performance I was astonished he recognized none of these experiences. But then, he rewrote experience in his mind and diaries, *The Chameleons* and *The Addams Family*, as he wanted that to be, and remembered his transformations in place of reality.

The superficially fictional nature of *The Addams Family* not only allowed him to project his real, festering family experiences freely that normally he did his best to repress, deny, or portray as the opposite of what they were, but freed his imagination as well to embroider these projections and take advantage of others' contributions, like a bear rugs that growl, disintegrator guns, and the many other oddities sundry people involved in the show contributed over time. This reversal of reality in *The Addams Family* is at the root of its continuing grip on the popular American imagination. Through its many iterations it still speaks to the "monster"(s) in all of us, its metamorphosis of unhappiness into its opposite reaching out to those with a similar need.

Denouement

Gar learned to function as an independent producer as his urge to be No. 1 made his formal connections with independent West Coast production companies like Four Stars and Filmways brief, but that career too was near its end. On March 16, 1966 H. M. Austin, the Executive VP of Filmways, made it clear to Gar that after two years *The Addams Family* would not be renewed. He wrote:

> I don't think that Tom Moore's mother could have convinced him to keep *THE ADDAMS FAMILY* on the air.[42]

Moore was the President of ABC at the time. Thereafter although Gar successfully created *The Pruitts of Southampton*, a vehicle for Phyllis Diller, 1966-1967, *The Double Life of Henry Phyffe*, 1966, and *Sarge* with George Kennedy, 1971-1972, only *The Pruitts of Southampton* lasted a year.

However, Mom finally reached the end of her endurance before *Sarge*.

And so Linda and I found ourselves waiting in the living room that surreal evening in 1968 with which we began this story waiting for our father to discover my mother had "absconded" with his bankbooks....

My mother lingered a week in Connecticut with Bud and Jill, then reappeared looking years younger. Over the course of the summer and fall she debated the terms of divorce with Gar who begged forgiveness and promised to reform with all the abject charm he could muster. She wavered, as she had always before, but insisted on a written settlement with a sizeable financial element before agreeing to continue. Over the next three years he watched helplessly as she made a determined effort to spend every cent of that money.

Once gone in 1971, she at last carried through and divorced him.

Even after that their lives life went on unchanged at Robin Drive. For another year Gar went off to his office each morning as he worked now on *Sarge*, coproduced by NBC and Harbour Productions, came home, watched shows, got on the phone, talked to associates, and was served dinner on a tray in his study by Mom or Mothie as he had been for decades in Great Neck, then Manhattan, again in Weston, and last in Los Angeles at Robin Drive.

At night he resumed his ritual with his depleted California bankbooks....

Mom resumed sleeping in the room down the hall. He gave no sign of moving.

At last Mom sold the house out from under him as she and Mothie had Mothie's Great Neck home years ago in 1949.

At the end of *Sarge* Gar was 59 and found himself living in an apartment on Wilshire Boulevard near Westwood, his file cabinets crammed into a small kitchen beside his desk, a small kitchenette table. By now I had a family, a daughter Heather born in 1963 while I was at Brandeis, having transferred from Boston University. Jeanne left Northeastern to mother her, although during my last year in graduate school at Yale's School of Drama Jeanne enrolled at Southern Connecticut State College to complete her degree. The year after I finished at Yale I taught at local universities while she finished her BS. We visited California that fateful summer, now with a second daughter, Alyssa. A series of chance events turned our visit permanent and we moved to a house in Pacific Palisades on the fringe of Los Angeles between Santa Monica and Malibu where we are still. That fall I began to teach at the University of Southern California.

Mom rebuilt a smaller home down the hill from Robin Drive in West Hollywood for herself and Mothie, using her second settlement more wisely.

Gar worked in his diminutive 'office' on Wilshire Boulevard for years but never sold another show. He turned to writing, consulting, and to developing The Producer's Guild into a force in the industry for a time.

Even as *The Addams Family* moved into popular culture and imagination, perpetuating Gar's metamorphosis of his unhappy childhood, within our contemporary family a wave generations in the making had finally broken and run up the shore and begun to sink into the sand.

ANNIVERSARY CARD

They dazzled rooms they entered,
one dark, one blond, together all
we mean by beauty. My father bragged
of his beauty queen queen of New York
models, this icon to be envied.
But even then he was unfaithful
with some singer, an affair fanned
by his mother who hated mine,
    'that shiksa.'
Phone calls were monitored, letters
steamed open, a detective hired
to undo father's lies—yet after this
I found mother in his lap in glad tears.
Were they each other's forbidden fruit?
Did they love their own beauty,
seeing themselves in each other's eyes?
Or were they just two young lovers love
lifted past their faults for love's season?
When did love stop being enough?
To think, in Venice, she returned
fatigue to ardor, or much later
reduced him to prodding pillows
    and brushes
assembled to mime herself in bed
in the separate room where she slept,
asking:
    My dear, is it you?
to find she had fled with his bankbooks.
Yet for forty years they exchanged

the same anniversary card with
a new year's greeting, a rite continued
even when he remarried. At last
she kept the card, ending even
the déjà vu love's memory had become
with a final, puzzled shrug.[43]

APPENDIX

FAMILY MATTERS IN 28 POEMS OF FAMILY AND FRIENDS

TURTLE & ELEPHANT

Three years dying....
"Oh God!" Grandmother cries
just after midnight when her mind
stumbles to a lucid moment.
She just turned 88 and remembered

to brag: now
the end.
Her iron turtle that lifts its shell
when a foot steps on its head
is in the hallway; her elephant

stands minus one ivory tusk
on her old, heavy dresser, animals
kept for luck:
they, with De Haviland China, Sheraton chairs
grouped around the white

formica-topped table, and lacquered
red chinese coffee tables
are all that's left. And Mother
faithful at her side, unlike my childhood
when Grandmother always nursed me

happy to be sick and home from school,
waiting for Mother to blow into my room, a
"Here I am!" a kiss a gift a smile
then only her fragrance left
to mix with the hot rags

fried in fat
Grandmother pressed to my chest.
Now her final breath....
Mother holds the old mouth shut
until it stays.

Three years Mother nursed like this, doing
what she couldn't,
transformed
though she wonders
when they wheel Grandmother out

and later when her ashes
join the Pacific
so what? and thinks, better a
"Here I am!" and the rest
at a swift end.

We are spared nothing. Now
the turtle's hollow closes
around her and
from the dead woman's room,
the maimed silence of the elephant.

HAWK FOREVER IN MID-DIVE

Autumn dogwood and oak clutch their yellowed
billet-doux like the old woman in her
attic, surrounded by her attar
of decay. Leave her alone with her heart's
wooden tissue. She will come downstairs soon
to escape the late heat, go out
to her covered porch and fan herself
while hawks bank overhead or stoop
on their prey, fanned like coals by the air.
She steps on old copperhead on her walk—
he gives half a twist and the barest
flash of his fangs, just as one did to
my daughter years ago. Grandmother wounded
him with stones until I took his head off
with a shovel. She was vigorous, then.
Now she edges away to her lilacs—
their flowers were spring's. Seven kinds
of apples grew from her apple tree once,
including one plain tart green one she called
"Mercy" and used for Thanksgiving.
Her feet on the patio are leaves blown
over flagstones. Aimed at her head,
beak thrust out wings angled severely
a hawk hangs frozen in mid-air,
fanned to permanent fire in her sky.

DREAMS

I move into my father as he dies—
"What a recovery!" his friends say.
Set designers for his late play
now mine show me their designs—
pastels, but for the dark passage for
dreamed knifings, rapes, innocents maimed.
Light alone determines where we are:
he's named the play: "Memory."

"How are you?" the director asks.
"I'm not myself." "David, David," he laughs,
but never spots me behind my father's eyes.
We rehearse scene after scene after…
that make a lie of our lives.
I start to cut them, cleaning up
the violence I always dreaded
he would turn towards me,

then lay the lead actress, as he would,
though she plays his hated mother he loved
after her death. I put all the truth back in
and when the play goes on my father
at 75 is finally a success.
Here I waken, my legs all knots,
imagining I hear his footsteps go past
my door through the wall into the night.

Has he found I want him dead
from pity, and so that failure
no longer diminishing him
diminishes me? Then I really waken….
Clouds flare in the night sky
until the moon lifts over the ridge
full and clear but unreadable
as a blank stare. I get up,

press my face to the screen
for the wind in the ancient privets
that half obscure the window.
Moonlight falls on my face.
Do I really think a man can remake
another, his father, with the truth?
What waking dreams flesh my father
that he moves in, secure as a fish

in a deep pool his life has worn from flint
in a light that shows him to
himself the reverse of what 'truths' I see?
I watch the night turn, wanting
nothing more of doubled vision,
shaken, naked enough, hot. At dawn
I go out to the privets and
cut them to the root, sinking

my hands in the earth, loosening
the earth until I touch the roots'
old hearts and, impartially,
urge them towards fresh shoots
until mist smokes over the near fields
and a tall shadow from the ridge falls on me
as does a father's over his son
that nothing ever quite burns away.

FATHER & SON AT 4 AM

The ground moves, or my faultlines give their slippage
    to the world
as though long shafts of lightning glow on the horizon
and cannonades of thunder shake the walls
and rising winds rush through the window
when all is still but myself....

I wonder what is mine through the aftertrembles—
this heartbeat, this sweat, this chestpain
and, confused, see my father's hands move across my chest
as they must have moved across his thirty years ago or more
when he thought he was dying

and crept from bed to write "Goodbye,"
breathing hard because of some anguish he couldn't face
    directly
but channeled into his body—
then checked his bankbooks,
ready to drop like an accountant onto a ledger.

For a moment I almost believe he's here....
We're not told when the heart stops—
nothing seems strange, then there is nothing:
so I let memory give fear shape to move in
because memory is the opening we live in

even when sourced in someone more dreaded than loved—
in father, who also smelled the slight rank rot of sweating
    flesh,
rolled fear salt and sweet on his tongue,
struggling to stay alive as the house heaved and billowed
when all was still but himself—and fell asleep, as I do....

In my dream I see the generations are an ever-opening flower
whose petals fall in a snow of lives
into a pool black past all accounting, all fear but not all
    anguish
at such wild yet leveling wealth. I waken
stiff and sore as father was, but after what dream?

To what end?
I can never tell,
only that he still counts his bankbooks at night,
talismen against all the wakes him at 4 am
but which nothing can undo.

MY HUNGER FOR MEANING

is a burned branch in clear light.
I think of going to my grandfather who remembers
the tribal rites,
but he is dead
and other men spin records in their mouths,
    "god," the "state,"
so I put my wife under that unloving burden,
I black out hunger in her body
for a time. Later
I stare at the ceiling, that old burning in me—
I look out the window where the rain becomes tears
    from the inconsolable angel
beyond radar:
cars pass on the road,
lights bright but blank as the eyes of one-time
    lovers
passing one another by accident,
and to no end.
I blur into them.[44]

SLEDDING TIME IN CARL SCHURZ PARK

The hill lays prostrate in the heat,
this barely tilted, dreaded ground
I watch myself pellmell down
in winter, age eight, hands frozen

on the sled's handles with fear and
courage, all as though filmed in old
super eight.
          Or strange boys and I play
cowboy and Indian by this deserted tree

in one of those descents to disaster
I sometimes will—frames speed by
while they tie me to the trunk and steal
my new gun, running off laughing:

I sweat shame and twist free, then
walk home like this tree has grown,
close to the ground as an old man.
In one reel Grandmother sits between

a women airing her geranium and a
man with a snake in a bag—and holds
Oscar on a string, the big box turtle
I free next week. This blooming garden

is bordered by paths that step in broad
curves to the East River Promenade—
this little plot, those few steps at war
with their vast sweep in memory,

so much less now because
I have lost childhood's greatness.
Even so I know time is more
than stony markers; it is these films

we run back and forth at once—
just now I grasp my sled's handles
and launch down the freezing slope:
the hill unspools like film unwound,

snow falls, and night reaches for me,
my face red from snowmelt, gleaming,
young, not yet trained to march
lockstep by step to my own decline.

THE GHOST

billows in full sunlight beside
the overturned chaise lounge, feet floating
over the lawn, rainsoaked rhododendron
blooms glimpsed through her dress
as purple stains. I guess

she's my young grandmother or
my mother's loose-haired loose-
clothed dream of herself on summer day
before her life settled in
come to judge me—or

my middle-aged hunger for beauty
come to taunt me with what cannot be.
I'm hungry for her to forgive me
but when I read my strangeness
in her eyes, I feel

a stone settle on my shoulders
for each compromised year and know
she is the measure of my fading.
She leaves like a photo brightening to white
I race to fill with features

of everyone I have known—and I sense
I am wrong, that she would let all of us
touch the blood of our births
to lip and tongue and again
be young, if she could. I float

over the damp grass after her like a double
exposure looking to merge with its original
until harsh with this giddiness
I pull back to the first moment
I saw her so troubled to be seen by me:

she knew then I would follow
no better angel into a second life
but locked in stubborn flesh and decay,
inevitably betray what all men do:
life, love, eternal youth.

OUR GREAT LONELINESS

Sweet Rosemary, fresh as new snow,
white skin ablush from fun as we played
on the top bunk.... Not children, not teens,
we kept our eyes on the game though I
saw the clean line of her thighs
her skirt half hid, and felt such desire
I saw myself push the game aside
and cover her with kisses,
then cover her as a man a woman,
cries of ecstasy filling my ears.
I thought she must see, and recoil,
but she played on, oblivious, or pretended
to see and feel nothing of my wild hunger....
I felt alone, and untrue, and ached.

I return to this moment often—
a silver brooch still holds her hair,
and her scent envelops me as we bend
our heads so our breathing blends,
yet never, then or later, more.... Always
I wonder at our silence, and feel
manhood and childhood begin to part
as the first mature touch of the great
loneliness a man and woman shares
brushes my heart.[45]

LATE SPRING

poems on my father:

1. WHAT A MAN GIVES

I

His heart explores its inward flaw,
his bone its wither; he is a leaf quivering
on the branch, a breath of air....

He frightened my youth,
a domineering, hostile man:
now I wonder if he will fall
as once he fainted into my arms
paying for lunch at Nate & Al's:

bills flapped in the air,
coins wheeled across the floor,

but he recovered and hurried off,
a street actor improvising for a later show
while the ambulance I called
ferried up Beverly Drive all siren,
turning each gray head....

II

Sometimes he is a house
whose rooms are grieving old women
who draw black shawls tight,
for my sister and I rarely visit here—

some love-starved child in him
made him starve those he loved in turn:
now he goes room to room,
an old child wondering where
his sundered family has gone.

He was the son less loved
by a woman so foolish
she chose between twins: early and late,
their photos show him glowering
while his twin smiles   smiles
smiles.

So he is doomed to be compressed
by love until he goes, for he fears
the more deeply love is held
the more certain love must fail.

III

Mother tired of the women
he denied to her but regaled
to me. He split himself in two,
in three, in…and thought
he was faithful to mother's part.

Now, at lunch, young waitresses
dote on him, smiling
at his flattery; they see
the shadow of a ladies man,
while he swears me to lie

so his second wife younger
than his daughter won't know
we dine in regal elegance,
lamenting "The folly of
this marriage I endure

for fear the stress of breaking
it will break me too.
I've had bad luck in women,
I've loved unwisely. I suffer
from chronic heart chronic

skin disease—some days
I'm so tired it hurts to stand.
My career gives no solace,
devoted to ephemera:
the years are stones that grow

and bear me under."

IV

When unleavened darkness rises
will he hear a song
that braids all half measures,
failures and shames
into a larger harmony?
Or dream some wild gesture,

skydiving with no parachute
to grasp death in pure defiance
expansive, released,
for choosing makes free
whatever its end?

At last put to rest
the need to be first
that gene and early accident
conspired role by role
to make him miss,

and now give all he could
or would   or should? No,
who does? He will whisper, if he can,
once there is no other choice,
or signal a final 'yes' to pull the plug,
and sink, emblematic to the end.

V

I will mourn him long and hard
and hold my sheaf of sung defiances
to slow the fading of anger and love—
only accidents of time bring

virtues to light, and not faults
to condemn a man past recall:
only pride makes a man deny
all men are of a kind.

> *My heart explores its inward flaw,*
> *my bone its wither—I am a leaf quivering*
> *on the branch, a mere breath of air....*

2. MY FATHER'S SONG

My blood is singing
behind my right eye.
I am half blind with song.
From the left
the world lurches,
me side to side.
Pains hound
across my chest after
what fox, what hare:
I feel their fear.
My right leg
declares its presence,
my right forearm aches
as though raked and torn—
suddenly I know
I am the goal
of the fleet savage feet.
Is this a stroke descending?
Or am I feeling
the mortal state
my father feels
in his barren room,
ticking after the seconds
his eyes chase
around the clock?
We are less separate,
less I/Thou than we think.
My blood is singing
his song, and his? Note

by note he scales
towards that silence
I fear one day will be
all of song I hear.

3. FATHER DEATH

Twice I had to say "Yes, that's him"
first when my father died at the home
open-mouthed between breaths,
second at Mt. Sinai where a dwarf
wheeled him in silent and bloodless
as if stunned from seeing God.
I lied identifying him we are the
       flesh's fire
not that residue there, not slag!
The dwarf leaked coldness, his face
       fine featured
but squashed, and pure white:
I had stumbled into nightmare.
How had he closed my father's mouth
that no one not me could do at the home?
Are the dead blocks of ice we hammer
       we chisel?

I watch a pretty girl as I write.
I imagine her breasts in my mouth
her milk, the rich cream of life: I need
an image to banish my father's
that rolls into view with his dwarf
when I make love, when I sit in the sun
when I examine my guilts, when I
recall our long rivalry, all unneeded.
I should have lied the truth, "No,
       that's not him:"
what would they have done? Rolled in

a series of stiffs?
"No, not him.   Not him, no.   Sorry, no!"
but as usual I conformed. "Yes," I said,
and the hearse took him off; "Yes,"
and the dwarf wheeled him out.

Later when I walk by the ocean beneath
        the Milky Way
as I have done since I was ten
to find silence and self to frame
the tensions we call living,
I fit words to the surf's rhythms, like
"Live, there is only living, each star
lives in its own milky fire; the hottest
blood burns in the coldest water:
why, father death lives in our flesh
to free us from anxious self-knowledge
when that burden grows too great—"
but I know these only gloss the unpleasant
        truth:
he must fade the way he died, by inches....

There should be more to us when we live.
There should be more to us when we die
than a bleaching like a photo under the sun—
we aren't mayflies for a season,
but he after one "I don't know if I can do this"
faded steadily into distance,   aware   helpless
        acquiescent.
                      Better to go mad.
Only now, after so many years listening
do I know what the waves really say
as they beat against my anger:
forgive   forget   forgive   forget   forgive

4. HAUNTING

A wind wheels over the meadow
and breathes through my mind
as I relax by an empty house.
Clear across the bog I see the fox's corner
where the dogs always slaver against
their chokechains. Inside, I hear
a faucet turn, water run, stop, a footstep fall.
I know it's my friend's dead daughter, Canda,
wandering where she once lived.
I freeze, changed utterly in a second, afraid
of whatever comes through
when the wall between worlds, tumbles.
The next moment I know it's not her
but my father touching unfamiliar things,
a door   a faucet   a drawer
treading a strange hallway, his breath
making a daddy longlegs tremble,
determined to find me and never let go.
I'm terrified.... Then my friend calls, *Lance!*
I breathe, myself again, but what is that—
how easily I walk with the dead,
whether ghostly or just some bodying
of guilt and loss! I worry at that
like a dog at a fox's scent: I imagine
I slip my choke chain and dash
into those shadows folded into the light,
teeth bared, snarling, sure of my prey,
then find myself stumbling among presences
just this side of known.... At a loss,

I turn a faucet: water runs through my flesh
like blood. I tread a strange hallway,
make the spider tremble in turn,
touch an arm—*Please, I'm lost, don't run,*
don't freeze so in terror at my face,
I only want to go home.
I snap to. Now I know what sound
teases just beyond the edge of hearing:
it is the sound walls make when they crumble—
and walls are always falling down.

5. BY LOVE'S DOING

      Blind in this darkness
I edge over the smallest rise, afraid
      to fall,
the ocean's weight on my shoulders;
or recoil from accordioned wrecks
as I follow the dream thread to caverns
that open and shut like mouths.

      I stop:
my father's body whitens that dark
where death is the only light—
or a window full of sky where I press my
      three year old face
shines before me, full of inexpressible longing
for a father always walking away.

      So I imagine
when the woman beside me flutters the sheets,
      hot-limbed, restless,
so long unable to wake me as I dreamed.
I am painfully sad, and think
I whitened those depths, but slid away
when I tried to touch my own death.

    I'm not sure what images are true:
we always try to give face to the inexpressible,
or discover one story disguises another,
even feel sorrows we only fear may come—
    like I may rehearse in a past loss
the death I will owe at the end.

    Only the pain is sure, and entire.

    I reach for the woman, desperate
to be pulled into flesh, love, life
    by love's doing,
away from that marrowed pain, from my childish face
pressed full of longing to the window;
    from knowing now love will leave
whatever I do to make it stay.

6. VIRGIN SPRING

Is my rage done, plowed into the meadow,
and grief let loose in the rain, the desperate drive
      to change everything
burned out by distance and sun, as much to say
time is space   heat   loam   leaf in the air?
So quickly loss doesn't matter, not really, not
after the first boil of blood, whatever trace
    stays in memory:
for what grief goes on intense now as then—
some too intense knowledge there is no
but there for the grace of God go I
      when all go that way;
some unbalanced likening of self to self lost
so we go on grieving after father death
mother death   child death   for ourselves?
For me life breaks in, fog, rain, sun, the stars
      on clear, crisp nights,
wind, love, those still here or newly come.
We are the blood pumped through the great
      heart of things,
driven in spent and expelled readied
      for new losses
like leaves that pile on the ground, decay,
      sink down, become rare
lady slippers in the woods or shoots
that crack concrete, delicate yet steady as steel.

Nothing is still, nothing stops.
Even the words that died into my loss
I could not imagine returning, return
when all seemed used, misused, and done,
gushing from my ground in a virgin spring.

7. LATE SPRING

Where has it hidden, this late spring?
Only now pheasants call like rusty gates
        forced open,
the air at last so warm and clear
Great Point Light is visible over twenty miles
        of Sound.
Heat ribbons the pines' resin through the trees,
and robins, in a fur of feathers in flight
seize the moment to mate and mate and mate.

And I, two years tending my father's dying—
peer into the marsh where ducks talk in tones
        of low strings breaking,
herding their young from shadow to shadow
as fox and coyote hunt the watery verge
and hawks swing between the day moon
        and dry, white sun,
their hunger patient, and penetrative as a
        ray of light.

Two years…. Medicines, treatments, hopes
tidal in their lift and fall, and at all times
the slide towards the fire
however we mate or pay to drug ourselves
        with the latest wonder—
why shouldn't age greet death instead as
        Friend,
have you come to end my suffering?

Tomorrow storm will again whiten the hollows
        between the groves,
whiten the leaves, whiten the sky, whiten
the air with slashes of cold, pale rain
however my heart hungers for summer
        like a fire under snow.
No wonder I yearn for purpose

as clear as coyote or fox or hawk
who set hunger on foot or give it wing,
but I am left just words for loss, for lateness,
        for the late blooming of relief,
words that matter, sure, and promise an end
but are not flesh not bone but air in my mouth
        absence in my belly,

burning in my brain.

8. SOFT WEATHERS

I lived my father's long dying
spreadeagled in the bog through a two year
        winter;
sleet-slashed, sleeked by frozen rain
I gleamed in the cold light in primary hues,

all that time unable to move,
grief layered in snowfall on fall,
then covered by floodtide for months, still
still except for the slow ooze of mud

embracing my flesh before, finally,
spring's ebb tide bared me, stunned,
        to this sun.
I sit up as the cranberry beds
lift through the ebb,

blink in the light, dazed, unsteady
        when I stand,
and wash in the stream,
then cross naked to firmer land
where the oaks are new leaved with suns,

gay streamers hanging from their boughs.
I feel grass in my toes, and smell
its hay scent where mown, taste
the musky pink vulva of lady slippers

inviting me into dim recesses—
I forgot so much, giving my senses to my
       father....
My face opens in this light,
lianas of paradise flowers entwine my arms,

rugosa roses thicket my legs. My tongue
croaks like a crow from a height,
loosens, speaks winds in a whoosh of wings,
speaks—god knows—of the forgetting
       in renewal,

of the loss of what seemed beyond loss
that turns out, in this heat-drugged air
to be something I can't even name:
speaks as though I always spoke

warm light   clear skies   soft weathers....

9. PEACE

Alpine meadow.... A brook spills over stones
to merge far below with the ocean-bound,
graygreen glacial Adige.

Near peaks shake off their covers
and yawn toothily in the sun,
gleaming like new-polished lance heads.
I burn aware with them, coughing,

sip water coldly pure as a knife in my lungs,
free at last to be ill, in myself, recover, be well,
the duties due the dying, well done....

Each to its own—death, mountain, brook,
a man alive to climb   to fall   and again work uphill
to the high place where the waters start to gather
the deep peace of the sea.

ESCAPE

Manhattan's summer evenings
steamed rings of dirt around my neck....
We found a beach flung between sea and bay,
a house hung on the dunes,

one nestled later in bayside rushes
that shook their silks in the dark like girls
      when embraced.
Light blazed from sky and sea and land
      and burned me blond,

sand in my hair, my pockets, between
      my toes:
mornings I netted blue claws, hard or soft,
and burrowing fiddlers always freed,
or heel-and-toed for clams, young flounders
      underfoot,

milky light leaning on the bay.
John and Buddy, Guy and Eddie,
Phyllis and freckled Alice,
the girl I loved each summer,

tried to teach and tame me
but I loved nature more, happiest
alone by the ocean at night,
stars, long lunar sands, waves weaving

great distances into me until I learned
to know myself the part of these grown
      self-aware.
That night sea beats in me still—
all comes, all comes, all comes

those waves drum,
words that give and take my peace
now as when despite all I felt alone
and made solitude my friend.

KIDNAPPED

Grizzled as grandfather, my kidnapper's
flesh sagged from age and vice, and I knew
he lied when he stopped me in the street
to say my parents sent him as my guide.
I hated his fetid breath, the adventure

he embodied, yet followed him inside
some tenement, anyway. I clutched
the railing with one hand, my bike
with the other. I was silent. He breathed
into my face and touched my ass, saying

what a good boy I was and did I want
to do wrong and disobey mother and father?
He grew old and insecure as I stared.
No I said abruptly.
He understood, and sighed, and let me go.

Why did I follow him? I was amazed
I had a choice and could give that man
what he never thought to force, free
to follow a dark thread in my heart
to a welcomed evil. That is like love—

a sudden presence wholly there,
a song we can't help humming
until freed by an equally blind recoil,
as when I hurried back into the light, dazed
at how easily I could go wrong.

MY BEST FRIEND

Heaven is one block from hell in New York.
My friend found my home all plush—
I found his all linoleum: we sensed
how cold the world is, and unfair.
One Christmas we rode new bikes
along the East River Promenade,

free for a weightless hour of that fate
opening doors for me closed to him:
then he crashed, the frame bent as a body
dropped seven floors. He wept
bearing it home. That summer
polio drove me from his block,

though he was untouched:
when I went to private school that fall
I left his world as surely as though
I had flown to the moon.
Did he rebel when older, go Beat and hate
the world with flowers and love,

yet when the draft notice came,
leave for Vietnam anyway?
We never escape our flaws,
though we learn the universe does not care
who we are or whether we are good
or if that knowledge frees us to live better
        than we do.

What could we say if we met again,
smiled, shook hands, searched for names?
We are old enough to know
the past and time are never equally good,
      or kind;
to prize survival higher, and the warmth
when shared that makes the world less cold.

HARD GRACE

Here is a picture: children gathered
by a Halloween bucket, dunking apples....
Even now I feel my mouth agape,
teeth sliding on the shining skin

as laughter and water mix in my throat.
Half choking, I press the apple against
the rim and bite through, smearing juice
and pulp against my palate, eating triumph.
The room is dim as memory's glow,

or the hue of sadness for the family idyll
I and my two mothers tried to uphold
against my father's lies.
Empires rise and fall,

millions die while we go on
modest, private, untouched, with time
for the slow miracle of forgiveness
to grow between my father and myself.
Sometimes great events do not outweigh

small, or measure good and evil,
but let some lives have a second chance
while so many more go down unjustly,
with no chance at all to atone.

LIVE IN THE LIE OF LOVE

Again his image haunts me,
my marbled father on his trolley
with his guardian dwarf

who shut his mouth in the cadaver palace.

He shrinks me to impotence,
lashes conscience with the guilt of survival,
and wants me to say

I am the ice sculpture lying there—

that he is my soul's all-too-human image,
my drive to death denied until now.
I won't do it. All winter

I feed the fire of my woman's flesh

to banish this haunting, but as often
sputter and fail as flare. Still, I know
only when I live in the lie of love

can I send death to death once more.

THE DEATH OF A SPARROW

Once I slung a stone in my new slingshot
and slew a sparrow. But when I looked
into his still living eye, full of knowing,
that look burned into bone.
Did I end his misery or just walk away—
even now remorse blinds memory.
Should a small death matter so?

A sparrow's death mirror the world's fate
where men rush to kill
habit-hardened, hateful, remorseless?

Is evil absolute in each act, threaded
into the texture of the day? Or relative,
tolerable-to-past-forgiveness? To whom?
Does God know? Does God care?
Does our blood's steam vanish into air
without meaning? Where is an ark
whose tablets settle these questions?

I walked away unwilling to kill again
without thought.... When I crush
swat   smash   or cook   eat

what was alive I do only what I must
How heavy my feet felt as I left that sparrow....
Every part of my body felt aware.
His death threw me into care.
Fifty years later I still see him there—
his eye full of fear stares at me
from the marrow of my heart.[46]

WILLIAM JAMES TO A FRIEND IN TRINITY CHURCH, BOSTON

"Cool your face on altar stones, let halleluias
rob your mind of thought—
however my heart yearns for more
than the death this world couples with life,
even more it hates to be deceived.
I knock on the iron door, ask the indifferent
dead to answer, and when their silence and
early morning waves of dread boil my bile
weigh varieties of faith,
but will not blur into that mind I sense watching—
passive—silent—everywhere—
some life force or, likelier, outward division
of self I greet as a stranger, not God, unless one
still to cut his teeth   stand   learn to talk.
Better to fan myself in Boston's humid air,
admit men   women   children are broken
by blows   swords   bullets   bombs;
by lies that eat the heart, like
all is well, we suffer because allowed freedom
yet God remains the way   the light   our deep relief
eternal life   unlimited power,
 void of responsibility— no:
if He is as things are, we are better off alone.
There is no excuse for just one innocent abused.

Earth   wind   fire   water and those other elements—
    flesh   blood   bone   nerve with its pent lightning:
        hunger   yearning   weakness   strength
that is never enough: rock gleaming when wet,
    water beading on the edge of singed leaves,
        a newborn's cry one floor below where others
routinely die—these are our truths
    however we tunnel in the heart after the infinite
        like miners after a rumor of gold.
God, if anything, is the life and death we live."

REVEREND JOHN THOMAS

Where are you, John Thomas,
              who left suburban ease
      to minister to the urban poor
in corrupt, dreary Bridgeport?
              I felt God, I told him before I was confirmed,
felt the burden of belief,
      felt time was a flight of stairs
              to travel up and down
to speak to the famous dead.
      The other teens laughed,

but he knew my sense of history was a quest
              for meaning and shape.
      How could he know
my father's name was absence,
              the God I felt the puritans or prophets,'
near enough to talk to but unlike theirs
      mute. I was happy
              when Thomas left us, still, in midlife,
driven by his hunger to serve.
      I imagine in another life he sculpted stone

to the same grace as a portal's saint
              in the crypt of some cathedral,
      someone I would help, smiling
among the stonechips
      in a barely lit place
where tourists never come.
      Look—chisel and hammer in hand

                    we perfect a design in stone
if only for ourselves
        in love with love's ideal,
which has no unlit places to be uncaring
                    second-rate, hurried;
        where the thing is done for its own sake,
without compromise—
            for what is given for love
is given well in all ways,
        even if the faith is a dream
        and love, God knows,
        has more betrayals
                    than the stars, numbers.

Only a poor light glows where I pause
                    beside my friend
        to brush chips and sweat from my face
as we shape ourselves,
            blow by blow.[47]

MY FATHER'S SHADE AT DELPHI AT THE WORLD'S CENTER AMID THE RUINS ABOVE THE OLIVE-SWADDLED VALLEYS

I cannot bear so much loss.
    A few stones, fewer columns,
some tiers of seats, a ruined
    arena, a thousand years of faith
gone with the temple where
    they carved, "Know Thyself"
over the entrance. That command
    still lives in my blood.
I remember the old ritual
    and let some fall from a cut
for any shade to drink
    and take body from for
an hour, but it is my father
    who surprises me here.
"Why have you neglected me?"
    he demands. "Why are you
so far from Los Angeles
    where your ashes lie?"
"All places are the same in death."
    "I loved you," I answer,
so many years of anger
    spent to let me say that:
"but you hurt us all so pointlessly
    and shrugged your guilt away."
He goes away angrily as
    the hot air warms these stones....
Below, groves of olives

    paint the valleys graygreen.
Their fruit is too bitter to eat
    unless soaked and steeped
until like the hardest memory
    we forget their native state,
and eat. I douse my head under
    what's left of the muses' spring
and shake the droplets off
    like a dog when I stand.
What is the world?
    that this place, once its center
was so forgotten we had to
    dig out it out
to find what we charge
    tourists to contemplate?
What is time?
    Just now, the water still cold
on my face as I take in the heights,
    the olive-painted valleys,
I know: *time is nothing.*
    My father, nothing
but what I make of him, then
    and now. Myself, nothing
but what I make, then and now.
    I don't need a sibyl's fumes
to give me a madness
    for others to mine for sense:
the world is empty of everything
    but this constant remaking.
Know thyself.
    It is almost more than I can bear.

                      Delphi, 2013

POKER-FACED

Was I twelve? I had just lied to father—
    mother challenged me later as we waited
at a light and the 3rd Avenue El shook
    overhead, not to say I had done wrong
but ask how I did so well. Some truth
    had to be withheld from father's unreason,
and my success, cool, calculating, adult,
    made mother think me now a full ally.
She sensed this outfacing a parent
    was my changeling moment, not some
accomplishment flung proudly at their feet
    but the daily deceits by which the family
now survived made sinew and self.
    I was cool, unflinching with her too, and
wondered what secrets might now be shared:
    surely I could cut father down farther:
this was better than our Sunday wargames
    when we fought with lead soldiers he
delighted in, but victory was unsure.
    But she turned away. I think she saw
herself mirrored, and felt how cheaply
    and with what pleasure
I flung boyhood and innocence away.[48]

HAUNTINGS IN WESTON

Fifty years—the number alone amazes—
since I lived here, the home of all
the 'where and whens'? of my youth.
Memory embraces where I left off, as though
the life lived fully elsewhere is a dream.
But those once so close are old, or gone,
the girls gone into their children's lives—
and then I was young and full of anger.

I wonder if a Cro Magnon savage
wandering from cave to cave found one
hole or another, or his wandering, *home*—
if he puzzled whether to stay each time
he stood again where once he was young
though those once so close are old, or gone,
the girls gone into their children's lives—
and then he was young and full of anger.

I am drawn to visit this place, and these
granite cliffs where I found solace
from my family's argument-riven home,
puzzled whether to stay though those
once so close are old or gone,
the girls into their children's children—
and then I was young and full of anger.
I come home only to leave again and again.[49]

THE SHOWS OF DAVID LEVY

Young & Rubicam Shows

At Y&R my father served as a writer, producer and supervisor of a very large number of shows on both radio and later on television, starting with his role(s) first as writer, director, and producer on *We The People* beginning when he was 25 in 1938. The following lists the most prominent of these, and substantiates his role as one of the 'founding fathers' of television:

We The People
The Kate Smith Hour
The Four Star Theatre
Father Knows Best
I Married Joan
Crusade In Europe
March Of Time
Arthur Godfrey's Talent Scouts
The Goodyear Television Playhouse
Twilight Zone
The Life Of Riley
The People's Choice

He also created the basic formats for television shows like:

Appointment With Adventure
Holiday Hotel
Bat Masterson

Note this summary leaves out his work reviewed in the text at the Treasury Department, 1944-1946, his continuing work after the war on bond drives for that department, and his pioneering work in broadcasting the Republican Conventions of 1948 and 1952.

Also not listed here although reviewed earlier is the work he did on the two Eisenhower campaigns of 1952 and 1956 when he was in charge of *Citizens For Eisenhower* campaign shows and a number of events on behalf of Y&R.

He also had a hand in quite a few specials on television like *The Fabulous Fifties*, which was produced by Leyland Hayward.

NBC Shows

He was only at NBC for the three tumultuous years that began in 1959 reviewed in **Debacle at NBC** (page 326). As Head of Programming at NBC he naturally oversaw the shows on NBC's schedule, which included too shows created from his own concept like *Saturday Night At The Movies*. These are the more prominent shows in which he had a significant hand:

The Dick Powell Show
Dr. Kildare
International Show Time
Hazell
Car 54
First Impressions
Bonanza
Mitch Miller
DuPont Show Of The Week
The Joey Bishop Show
Say When
Loretta Young Daytime

He either directly created or developed these:

Saturday Night At The Movies
Outlaws
The Americans
Sunday Showcase
Shirley Temple Show
The World Of...(Sophia Loren, Jimmy Doolittle, Billy Graham, etc.)

He greatly expanded *Project 20* into documentary and entertainment areas.

Among the documentaries which he spearheaded in development were:

Portrait Of Vincent Van Gogh
Cops And Robbers with Edward G. Robinson
The Real West with Gary Cooper.

Independent Shows

After leaving NBC my father functioned as noted as an independent producer in Los Angeles, where he moved in 1963 to pursue production ideas because he saw control of creative content was moving from the networks to the Hollywood TV studios. The list of shows he created as an independent producer is:

The Addams Family
The Secret Life Of Henry Phyffe
The Pruitts Of Southampton
Sarge

and

Face the Music

on which he consulted with Sandy Frank Productions.

There were no further independent productions of his own after *Sarge* with Georgy Kennedy in 1971, which ran only half a season.

NOTES AND BIBLIOGRAPHY

THE WHIRLWIND AND THE BEAUTY

1. *National Radio Magazine*, September, 1943, p. 12.

2. Wilde, Oscar. *The Importance of Being Ernest*, Penguin Classics (London, 2000), Act 2, Scene 1, p. 317.

3. "Queen of the Models," newspaper article, source unknown, with heading and date removed by Mothie, mid 1930s.

AN EARTHLY PARADISE

4. Lee, Lance. "Becoming Human." *Becoming Human*, Authors Choice Press (New York, 2001), p. 1.

5. Binger, Dr. Carl. "What I Have Learned." *The Saturday Review*, 7/25/1970, pp. 12-14, 56-57.

6. —. "The Wolf." *Becoming Human*, Authors Choice Press (New York, 2001), pp. 3-5.

7. Wordsworth, William. "The Two Part Prelude." *The Selected Poetry of William Wordsworth*, edited by Seamus Heaney, Faber & Faber (London, 2005), ls 6-15, p. 68.

8. Lee, Lance. "Cliches." *Homecomings*, Birch Brook Press (Delhi, 2015), pp. 9-10.

MANHATTAN STORIES

9. This article was found on the internet where, according to Wikipedia, it has circulated widely by fax and email, and whose authenticity is in doubt, especially as there never was a *Housekeeping Magazine* in which to publish it despite the attribution given with the article. But the article does reflect common attitudes of the day, whether written then or some years later, and accords with my memories of the attitudes towards women rife around me as I grew up and observed them in my family in the 1940s and 1950s, and with the attitudes reflected too in "The Correct Thing" etiquette photoshoots referred to in this chapter.

10. "The Correct Thing," *The New York Daily News*, in order cited, and decade:

"Manners at Home"	1940s
"Manners at the Movies"	"
"Last Name for Chauffeurs"	"
"In Automobiles"	"
"Don't Linger"	"
"Let's Go Swimming"	" (?)
"Should She Assist Him?"	"
"Visit a Bachelor's Apartment?"	"

"Selfish Youngster"	1940s
"Don't Correct Another"	"
"Don't Be Opinionated"	"
"Do You Do This"	"
"Do You Sit Gracefully"	"
"Put It Out"	*
"Hostess Leaves Tip"	"
"Guest Suggests Leaving"	"
"Protect Furniture"	1960s
"A Friend Gives the Shower"	1930s
"The Correct Wedding"	1930-1940s
"The Spring Bride"	"
"The Home Wedding"	"
"Honeymoon Start"	"
"Dress Appropriately"	1950s

MIDNIGHT IN MANHATTAN

11. Shakespeare, William. *Hamlet, The Comedies and Tragedies of Shakespeare*, Vol Two, Random House (New York, 1944), Act I, Scene 3, ls. 80-82, p. 597.

12. Freud, Sigmund. "Constructions In Analysis." *Collected Papers*, Vol 5, trans. & edited by James Strachey, Basic Books (New York, 1959), pp. 358-371.

13. Lee, Lance. "Winter." *Human/Nature*, Birch Brook Press (Delhi, 2006), pp. 106-108.

14. Milosz, Czeslaw. *Legends of Modernity*, trans. by Madeline G. Levine, Farrar Straus Giroux (New York, 2005), pp. 20-21.

15. —. *Legends of Modernity*, trans. by Madeline G. Levine, Farrar Straus Giroux (New York, 2005), p. 33.

THE WILDS MYTH

16. Winnicott, D.W. "Transitional Objects and Transitional Phenomena." *Playing and Reality*, Basic Books (New York, 1971), pp. 1-26.

17. Lee, Lance. "Grandfather Daddy Wilds." *Wrestling With The Angel*, The Smith (New York, 1990), pp. 12-13.

18. Lee, Lance. "Grandfather Daddy Wilds." *ELEMENTAL NATURES*, iUniverse (Bloomington, 2020), pp. 329-331.

SURVIVAL, WESTHAMPTON

19. —. "Escape." *Human/Nature*, Birch Brook Press (Delhi, 2006), p. 29-30.

20. —. "On the Beach." *Homecomings*, Birch Brook Press (Delhi, 2015), pp. 89-91.

REBELLION, WESTON PRELUDE

21. Kraus, Michael. *The United States To 1865*, The University of Michigan Press (Ann Arbor, 1959).

22. Dulles, Foster Rhea. *The United States Since 1865*, The University of Michigan Press (Ann Arbor, 1959).

23. —. "An Old Barn in Weston." *Becoming Human*, Author House Press (Lincoln, 2001), p. 63.

24. —. "Weston Woods." *Homecomings*, Birch Brook Press (Delhi, 2015), p. 54-55.

REBELLION, WESTON OUTBREAK

25. —. "Quantum Physics And The Nature Of Love." *ELEMENTAL NATURES*, iUniverse (Bloomington, 2020), pp. 343-4.

THE LONG DIVORCE

26. Levy, David. "Guns, Sex And Network Secrets." *The Washington Post*, August 1, 1993.

27. —. "Guns, Sex And Network Secrets." *The Washington Post*, August 1, 1993.

28. —. "Guns, Sex And Network Secrets." *The Washington Post*, August 1, 1993.

29. Anderson, Jack. "Washington Merry-Go-Round: TV Sex And Violence Attributed to Kintner." *The Madera Tribune*, Vol. 76, #6, May 22, 1967.

30. Levy, David. *The Chameleons*, Dodd Mead (New York, 1964), pp. 411-413.

31. —. *The Chameleons*, Dodd Mead (New York, 1964), p. 458.

32. Chilton, Gilmore. Culture Editor Online. *The Telegraph* (London), Dec. 9, 2014.

33. Siegel, Dick. "The Grim Truth About *THE ADDAMS FAMILY*." *13th Floor*, November 8, 2016.

34. Owen, Dan. "An Addams Family History." *Follow*, Jan. 6, 2017.

35. The Paley Center for Media, "The Addamses vs. the Munsters."

36. Smith, Tim. "John Astin is still everyone's favorite Gomez Addams." *The Baltimore Sun*, March 9, 2012.

37. —. "The Grim Truth About *THE ADDAMS FAMILY.*" *13th Floor*, November 8, 2016.

38. Wikipedia, "*The Addams Family* (1964 Series)."

39. Lee, Lance. *The Death and Life of Drama*, University of Texas Press (Austin, 2005), pp. 99-121.

40. Davis, Linda H. *CHARLES ADDAMS A Cartoonist's Life*, Turner Publishing Company (Nashville, 2006), pp. 194-195.

41. —. *CHARLES ADDAMS A Cartoonist's Life*, Turner Publishing Company (Nashville, 2006), p. 197.

42. Austin, H.M. Letter to David Levy. Executive VP, Filmways, March 16, 1966. Los Angeles, CA.

43. —. "Anniversary Card." *Human/Nature*, Birch Brook Press (Delhi, 2006), p. 35-36.

APPENDIX

44. —. *Wrestling With The Angel*, The Smith (New York, 1990), pp. 14-21, 46.

45. —. *Becoming Human*, Author House Press (Lincoln, 2001), pp. 6-7, 9-10, 12.

46. —. *Human/Nature*, Birch Brook Press (Delhi, 2006), pp. 11-34, 37, 51.

47. Lee, Lance. *Seasons of Defiance*, Birch Brook Press (Delhi, 2010), pp. 51-54.

48. —. *Homecomings*, Birch Brook Press (Delhi, 2015), pp. 72-73, 92.

49. —. *ELEMENTAL NATURES*, iUniverse (Bloomington, 2020), p. 335.

ABOUT THE AUTHOR

Lance Lee is a poet, playwright (*Time's Up and Other Plays*), novelist (*Second Chances*, and for children: *Orpheus Rising*, a Kirkus Indie Best Book 2021, and *The Tale Of Brian And The House Painter Mervyn*) and writer on drama and screenwriting (*A Poetics for Screenwriters*, and *The Death and Life of Drama*). His six previous volumes of poetry are listed under "Also by Lance Lee." His seventh, *ELEMENTAL NATURES* draws together a selection of thirty years of lyrics, sequences, and prose, with new work. His poems appear widely in America and England, between which his family is split. A past Creative Writing Fellow of the National Endowment for the Arts, his home is in Los Angeles, where he has also taught at a number of leading universities. As an environmentalist he was instrumental in forming the California State Park system in the Santa Monica Mountains.

portrait by
John Robertson

portrait by
Ron Sandford

ABOUT THE DESIGNER

Kate Cooper is a website developer, graphic designer and photographer based in London, UK. As a multi-disciplinary designer, Kate works with an extensive variety of digital media and print art forms, and has produced many wonderful collaborations for clients and industries including charities and nonprofit organizations, artists, travel, education and construction. When she is not working, Kate is an avid traveler and is happiest on the road, exploring with her camera.

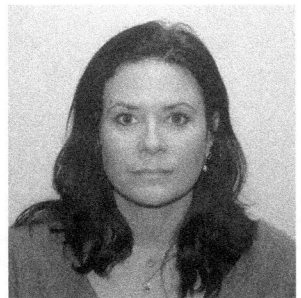

This book was formatted using Adobe InDesign, the body text set in 11pt Adobe Caslon Pro, headings in Adobe Jenson Pro, and printed by Ingram Lightning Source.

CPSIA information can be obtained
at www.ICGtesting.com
Printed in the USA
LVHW102003030123
736191LV00006B/87/J